The Larger Message:
Universalist Religious Education's Response to Theological and Cultural Challenges
1790 to 1930

The Reverend Doctor Elizabeth M. Strong

Rod — It is so good to work with you in keeping Universalist Unitarian alive! Liz Strong

The initial work of this book was presented as the 1995 Keynote Address to the New York State Convention of Universalists therefore permission was sought and given by the Convention for this publication.

Published through a very generous Grant from the New York State Convention of Universalists
And a generous Grant from the Unitarian Sunday School Society

The Larger Message:
Universalist Religious Education's Response to
Theological and Cultural Challenges
1790 to 1930

The Reverend Doctor Elizabeth M. Strong

Published by Meadville Lombard Press

Meadville Lombard Press Trade Paperback
edition published June, 2004

Cover Design by Emu Design Studio I www.emudesign.com
Interior Design by Karen Sawyer

Library of Congress Cataloging-in-Publication Data
Strong, Reverend Doctor Elizabeth M.
The Larger Message: Universalist Religious Education's
Response toTheological and Cultural Challenges 1790 to 1930
p. cm.
ISBN 0-0-9702479-6-6 Trade Paperback

Printed in the United States of America

Dedication

To my parents

Ashley Walter Strong (1901-1977)
Marie Elizabeth Miller Strong (1902-1978).

Who modeled for me how to be a Universalist

To a chosen Grandmother

Angeline V. Jones

One of the founders of the Old Stone Universalist
Church
Schuyler Lake, New York

In Memory of

The Rev. Dr. Norma G. Veridan
June 11, 1926- January 14, 2004

A proud Universalist and excellent religious educator

Contents

INTRODUCTION

Liberals can safely look back without risking their prospective vision.
David Robinson

Unitarian Universalists need to understand themselves more deeply as Unitarian Universalists. As liberal religionists in an increasingly conservative world, we must have a personal involvement with our historical and theological traditions. Within Unitarian Universalism, there is an omission of the vital religious heritage and theology of Universalism and more attention to this historical strand is needed as Unitarian Universalists move into the twenty-first century. The essence of this Universalist heritage and theology lies in the message of God as a transformative power of love given to all people which grounds us in an ethical and moral response to our individual lives and to all of humankind as participants in that love. It is the theology out of which I live my life and from which I find spiritual nurture. The theology and practice of Universalists and Unitarians from the past can ground present-day liberal religious discourse. Both sides of the story are needed to fully understand ourselves as Unitarian Universalists.

It is in our communities of faith and in our tradition where we must name for ourselves who we are as Unitarian Universalists. The naming of and reflecting upon our Unitarian Universalist heritage is, therefore, central to one's understanding of what it means to be a Unitarian Universalist. Because so many of our adult members have entered Unitarian Universalism as adults there is a continual need to name our historical ancestry before the community. In my experience this is done through the worship and religious education we do with our children, youth, and adults. It requires personal and communal interaction with our historical and theological traditions for each of us to reach a level of knowing oneself as being a Unitarian Universalist.

It is, in the terminology of Paul Tillich's circle of theological inquiry, an *a priori* knowing of our heritage that we are called to name when we engage with our faith. It is a method of inquiry based upon our past experiences. I experience it as an intuitive knowing.

I have come to realize how deeply my Universalist heritage from childhood is interwoven into what I know as an adult. I do not need to question that I am a Universalist. I understood the faith long before I knew the theology or history of Universalism. It is that depth of knowing as we engage in liberal religious discourse within Unitarian Universalism that I want Unitarian Universalists to reach in their experience and knowledge. I developed my theology from an intuitive knowing that through the years became informed by empirical study and personal experience within Universalist communities of faith.

A goal of this book is to add an account of the Universalist religious education tradition to the body of historical knowledge currently available to us. To gain a point of reference I will focus on the development of Universalist religious education thinking and practice from 1790 to 1930 using *The Murray Graded Sunday School Lessons* to understand the response of Universalism to the theological, educational and cultural movements and pressures of the time. *The Murray Graded Sunday School Lessons* will serve as the door through which I can enter this time period. The facts surrounding these lessons are not documented in our Unitarian Universalist education materials. Information about their development, organization, authors, as well as the needs these lessons fulfilled for Universalists, changes from the secular culture and field of educational theory to which they were responding, and the response to the Lessons by Universalists have not been documented.

I began the research for this book with an attempt to discover whether my experience of an excellent religious education program and my broad understanding of Universalism beyond the curriculum was universal or just a blip in my little Old Stone Church in Schuyler Lake, New York, and the commitment of the religious educators in the New York State Convention of Universalists. Was there a larger message that had been lost along the way? I knew Universalists took religious education seriously, and I wanted to know why.

I hope to make a contribution to our Unitarian Universalist ministry by demonstrating how Universalism and Universalists moved through the challenges to their theology and practices and yet maintained the integrity of their faith. For Unitarian Universalism I hope to contribute through this book a message that we have moved in our understanding of ourselves as religious and spiritual beings in the modern scientific world. The Universalist religious education story is a powerful reminder of how to remain relevant in a rapidly and vastly changing world.

Through studies of the work done by the American Sunday School Union, the influence of the Progressive Education Movement, the Higher Biblical Criticism, Darwinism and other theories of evolution, and the general cultural setting impacting the rise of the Sunday school in America, I will show how Universalist religious education developed and changed through the years from 1790 to 1930. I have sought to determine the theological, educational, cultural, and organizational issues that were prominent during those years.

I have discovered no works by Unitarian Universalist religious scholars that examine the development of the Murray Graded Sunday School Lessons. The Universalist response in religious education to the cultural, social, and secular educational changes at the turn of the twentieth century has not been examined in detail. The materials that are available seem to have a significant gap between the years 1880 and 1930. I have endeavored to determine how the changes of that era were reflected in Universalist religious education. Several sources have provided a framework for understanding educational theory and practice during the years spanning the rise of the Sunday school's development; among them the writings of Anne Boylan in *The Sunday School: The Formation of An American Institution, 1790-1880*, Edwin Wilbur Rice in *The Sunday-School Movement and the American Sunday-School Union: 1780-1917*, and Mary Boys in *Educating in Faith* have been cited in this book.[1] My task has been to organize the facts relating to Universalist religious education discourse, practice, and decisions between the years 1790 and 1930 when pivotal events occurred in the field of religious education in response to vast and rapid theological and cultural challenges.

I believe our religious educators, ministers, and lay people will benefit from historical research into this era of education discourse. Universalism met the challenges of the evolving culture head-on and remained a relevant religious expression for the twentieth century. Universalists were participants in the development of religious education curricula in evangelical Protestantism and contributed valuable scholarship in the fields of biblical criticism and theistic formulations of evolutionary theories. At the turn of the twentieth century the constitutional separation of church and state in part led to the removal of explicit biblically-based curricula from the secular schools. The churches responded with their own programs of religious instruction. The discipline of Higher Biblical Criticism within theological schools had changed the approach to teaching the Bible.

The Universalists engaged in these new approaches to biblical scholarship through theologians like Orello Cone, professor of biblical literature at St. Lawrence Theological School and president of Buchtel College during the years 1865 and 1905. They responded to the challenges of Darwin's theories of evolution through work of Marion D. Shutter, Minister of the Universalist Church in Minneapolis in his 10 lectures published in 1900 in his book *Applied Evolution.*[2] It was also a time of social challenge to theologies in the liberal churches with the rise of the Social Gospel and the Progressive Era. I will document how the Universalists responded to these challenges and changes as reflected in their religious education efforts and the development of *The Murray Graded Sunday School Lessons.*

Liberals are once again facing challenges from the religious and secular world and our educational efforts must respond to these challenges. How we responded at the end of the nineteenth century can inform our responses at the turn into the twenty-first century.

The Murray Graded Sunday School Lessons were written in 1912 as a means of teaching a more liberal theology to Universalist children. The lessons were done as a response to the progressive educational theories of the secular schools. As the progressive movement in educational theory of the time espoused a method of education grounded in graded lessons there was a movement away from *The International Uniform Lessons* used from their inception in 1872 by a large number of the Protestant churches, and by the Universalists. The Universalists decided to enter the progressive movement toward age-graded resources and write a curriculum more developmentally appropriate for their children and youth. I have documented the Universalist desire to develop a curriculum that reflected the new biblical criticism, since historically Universalists relied on biblical grounding for their beliefs in universal salvation, the nature of God, humankind, and Jesus.

This book shows that Universalists were active participants in *The International Uniform Lessons System* and were contributing members of the Lessons Committee that developed the uniform lessons and who later urged graded lessons. Through examination of *The International Uniform Lessons System* I have shown how this system was utilized by Universalists and how it later led them to develop their own curriculum. The debate over abandonment of the International Uniform Lessons and the International Graded Lessons had significant ramifications within Universalism as well as throughout most of the Protestant denominations. The International Uniform Lessons were used by nearly seventeen million children, youth, and adults in the late 1800's and to abandon them was not a move to be made without considerable thought. It was

a time within Universalism when the congregations were questioning the philosophi-
cal issues of a parochial Universalist education program of instruction for their
children rather than a broader Christian religious education program of instruction.
This discussion is still central as new curricula are being developed by the Unitarian
Universalist Association Department of Religious Education, now renamed the
Lifespan Faith Development Staff Group, with an explicit focus on our Unitarian
Universalist Principles and the lifelong process of faith development.

Because the documentation of this time in Universalist religious education history is
so sketchy, this study was needed to recover the Universalist endeavors. It was needed
to discover how denominational identity, theology, values, and world-view enhanced
the Universalism of the day. Through the "eyes" of the Murray Graded Sunday School
Lessons we gain a sense of who these Universalists were. If we do not look at this
history we fail to see the organic movement of the people, ideas, actions, discussions,
and decisions that formed the religious education we practice today.

This book engages us in a dialogue with our theological and educational heritage in an
attempt to provide a deeper understanding of who we are as liberal religious educators.
It is crucial to research Universalist religious education history and examine it
academically to further the effort to keep Universalist ideas alive within present-day
Unitarian Universalist religious education. Through a search of our theological and
educational history we will reach new depths of self-understanding which will inform
our growth and our response to the twenty-first century. It has been my goal to convey
as best I can the power of Universalism's faith, hope, and love that enabled our
ancestors to forge a then-heretical belief in a God of love and salvation for all.

INTRODUCTION

1. Anne Boylan, *The Sunday School, The Formation of an American Institution: 1790-
1880* (New Haven, Conn: Yale University Press, 1988); Mary Boys, *Educating In Faith*
(Kansas City, Sheed and Ward, 1998); Edwin Wilbur Rice, *The Sunday School Movement
1780-1917, And the American Sunday School Union, 1817-1917* (Philadelphia, Penn: The
American Sunday School Union, 1917).

2. Marion D. Shutter, *Applied Evolution* (Boston, Mass: Universalist Publishing
House, 1900).

CHAPTER ONE
Universalism Arrives In America

The story of the Universalist's Murray Graded Sunday School Lessons begins within early Universalist history. To understand the significance of the name of these lessons and the biblical and theological content we must begin before the Sunday school movement began. We begin with Universalism's development in Colonial America from a theological doctrine to a denomination. Universalism's belief in universal salvation can be traced from Origen and Clement of Alexandria in the second and third centuries of Christian history. It gained a defining spokesperson in James Relly in England in the 1700s.

> Universalism came to America through at least five channels....Samuel Gorton, who figures conspicuously in the early history of the Massachusetts, Plymouth and Rhode Island Colonies, came to Boston, from England, in March, 1636-37....[He] used to say "heaven was not a place, there was no heaven but in the hearts of good men, no hell but in the mind."....Sir Henry Vane, the younger, Governor of Massachusetts in 1636, was also a Mystic, [like Gorton] and some of his utterances read like avowals of belief in universal salvation....The second channel through which Universalism came to us was the German Baptists, sometimes called Tunkers, more often Dunkers, and as they prefer to be called, Brethren....Universalism was also brought to America by the Moravians, who came here in 1735, settling in Georgia, but removing in 1741 to Bethlehem, Pennsylvania....There was some Universalism in the Episcopal Church in America, as there also had been for many years in the same church in England....Among the Congregationalists of New England there was some Universalism prior to 1770,—the date of the arrival of John Murray in America,—and in some localities after his arrival, but wholly independent of him and his theory of redemption.[1]

The arrival of John Murray and his message of Universalism on the shores of the new world in 1770 was timely. The First Great Awakening which began in the 1730s in

New England had spread quickly throughout this new country, although it was focused primarily in New England. Revival camp meetings spread this new wave of religious fervor and created a triumph of Christian evangelicalism. The First Great Awakening lasted until the early 1760s and was a significant shaping power for the new nation's understanding of itself apart from England. The revivalist ideas of being free and independent grew into a concept of being a unique nation. It was through the convulsive outburst of piety in the First Great Awakening that American Evangelical Protestants developed the idea that they were a national reality with the ability to shape the nation's newly forming culture. Historian Mark Noll states, "The evangelicals who emerged from the Great Awakening took it upon themselves to create their own communities; at first they sought to remake the churches, but then (in the United States) they set their sights on creating a Christian nation."[2]

During the mid-1600s and early 1700s in the New World the various forms of Universalism were increasingly evident. In Pennsylvania from the 1740s through the 1790s Universalism was spread through the work of Mystic, George deBenneville (1703-1793), who had fled France to escape religious persecution for his mystical and Universalist faith. He spread his experiential Universalist faith that he had developed through many personal, mystical experiences during his lifetime, both in Europe and in America. In more than one near-death experience he came to believe that God saved all humanity through His benevolent, universal, and unconditional love. deBenneville is credited with bringing Universalism's message to the New World through his arranging for the publication of *The Everlasting Gospel* in 1753.[3] This was a work by Georg Klein-Nicoli, under the pen name of Paul Siegvolck that was previously published in England and in use by Universalist preacher and Universalism's primary spokesperson James Relly in London. This book on Universalist ideas had a great influence on many early adherents to Universalism long before any organized religious expression of it was formed in America.

In the 1750s and 1760s rural New Jersey farmer Thomas Potter had reached Universalist beliefs on his own, built a small meeting house on the shores of New Jersey, and settled down to wait for God to send him a Universalist preacher. Several Universalist historians, including Russell Miller in *The Larger Hope: The First Century of the Universalist Church in America, 1770-1870*, recounts the arrival of John Murray in the New World and his meeting with Thomas Potter. Universalism's only miracle story is that of Thomas Potter and John Murray. The "Universalist miracle" story is even told by

Elmo Arnold Robinson in his book *American Universalism* from the imaginary perspective of John Murray.

In 1770 Murray sailed from Gravesend, England aboard the brig *Hand-in-Hand,* broken-hearted and destitute because of the death of his wife and only son, a time in debtor's prison due to the debt incurred from his wife's illness, and the persecution he experienced due to his Universalist preaching. Vowing never again to preach Universalism, he sailed for the New World. Murray's ship became stranded on a sand-bar off the Cranberry Inlet of Barnegat Bay in the New World near where Thomas Potter lived in an area dubbed Good-Luck Point, New Jersey. Murray went aboard a smaller sloop with several of the crew and part of the cargo so as to lighten the stranded ship. The ship slid off the sand-bar and left, leaving Murray and a few sailors with the sloop. They were unable to get the sloop out of the bay before the wind abruptly changed again. There were no provisions on board the sloop so the crew and Murray went ashore in search of food. In John Murray's autobiography he relates his story of this meeting with Thomas Potter.

> [Potter tells Murray] "I have longed to see you, I have been expecting you
> a long time." He tells Murray of how he had built a meeting house for
> the expected preacher. "And who," it was asked, "will be your preacher?"
> I answered, "God will send me a preacher, and of a very different stamp
> from those, who have heretofore preached in my house. The preachers,
> we have heard, are perpetually contradicting themselves; but that God,
> who has put it into my heart to build this house, will send one, who shall
> deliver unto me his own truth; who shall speak of Jesus Christ, and his
> salvation."...I was astonished, immeasurably astonished at Mr. Potter's
> narrative; but yet had not the smallest idea it could ever be realized. I
> requested to know, what he could discern in my appearance, which
> could lead him to mistake me for a preacher? "What," said he, "could I
> discern, when you were in the vessel, that could induce this conclusion?
> No, sir, it is not what I saw, or see, but what I feel, which produces in my
> mind a full conviction."[4]

Potter was convinced that Murray was sent by God to preach Universalism. Murray protested, yet Potter was firm in his belief that the wind would not change until Murray preached in the meeting house. Murray stayed with Potter that night, a long agonizing night according to Murray. Potter struck a deal saying that if the wind had not changed and his sloop was still stranded in the bay by Sunday morning Murray would preach. Sunday arrived, the sloop was still stranded, and Murray, according to tradition, preached the first Universalist sermon in the New World. Murray felt unusually calm and relieved following the service. He reports "Immediately upon my return to the company, my boatmen entered the house: 'The wind is fair, sir.' Murray embarked on the sloop and sailed to New York where he began his long Universalist ministry in America. It was September of 1770 and this new faith began to spread with the preaching of John Murray, a man who Thomas Potter believed had been sent by God to the New World to preach a new message in a small meeting house.

John Murray (1741-1815) was the principle spokesperson for the Universalist theology being preached in the 1770s in New England. Murray had been introduced to Universalist ideas in England when he attended the church of Universalist preacher James Relly. Relly was a Calvinist Universalist who preached a formulation of Universal Salvation which held that in Adam all fell and in Christ all were saved.

Historian Russell Miller observes:

> Murray never abandoned completely the Calvinism in which he had been reared, nor did he ever waver in the generally accepted Christian beliefs in one great and indivisible First Cause; an omnipotent, omnipresent, and omniscient God; an overriding Divine Unity manifested in a Trinity; man as a creation of Divine Purpose, an imperfect and fallen creature after Adam; vicarious atonement through Christ; and the inspired nature of the Scriptures....On one occasion he wrote: "As I believe in Jesus Christ to be the only wise God, our Savior, I know no other God in whom to trust, or of whom to be afraid. I am a Unitarian. I believe in one God over all blessed forever, and I am persuaded that it is this one God, who is Savior of all men."[5]

Murray preached his interpretation of Scripture that all were saved in Christ as fervently as the other biblical evangelicals preached their interpretations of Scripture. Murray began his ministry following the First Great Awakening (1730-1760) and before the Second Great Awakening (1800-1830) had begun. Murray's Universalist theology provided a new vision for salvation unlike what had been heard in the First Great

Awakening theology of Jonathan Edwards, in Edwards' 1741 sermon "Sinners in the Hands of an Angry God." In this sermon Edwards preached:

> There is no Want of *Power* in god to cast wicked Men into Hell at any Moment. Mens [*sic*] Hands can't be strong when God rises up: The strongest have no Power to resist him, nor can any deliver out of his Hands.
>
> He is not only able to cast wicked Men into Hell, but he can most *easily* do it....The Wrath of God burns against them, their Damnation don't [*sic*] slumber the Pit is prepared, the Fire is made ready, the Furnace is now hot, ready to receive them, the Flames do now rage and glow. The glittering Sword is whet, and held over them, and the Pit hath opened her Mouth under them....So thus it is, that natural Men are held in the Hand of god over the Pit of Hell; they have deserved the fiery Pit, and are already sentenced to it; and God is dreadfully provoked, his Anger is as great towards them as to those that are actually suffering the Executions of the fierceness of his Wrath in Hell, and they have done nothing in the least to appease or abate that Anger, neither is God in the least bound by any Promise to hold 'em up one moment; the Devil is waiting for them, Hell is gaping for them, the Flames gather and flash about them, and would fain lay hold on them, and swallow them up; the Fire pent up in their own Hearts is struggling to break out; and they have no Interest in any Mediator, there are no Means within Reach that can be any Security to them. In short, they have no Refuge, nothing to take hold of, all that preserves them every Moment is the meer arbitrary Will, and uncovenented unobliged Forbearance of an incensed God.[6]

Murray offered a vision of salvation from a loving God, not a fear of hell from an angry God. It is no wonder Universalism's message was welcomed by those who came to hear Murray after having Edwards' words still ringing in their ears for nearly forty years.

Of the time, Universalist minister and scholar John Coleman Adams (1842-1922) writes that John Murray met an entrenched Calvinism which affirmed the five points of Calvinism:

Predestination, Particular Redemption, Total Depravity, Effectual
Calling, Final Perseverance — a tough and gloomy scheme of thought
as ever masked under the name of the gospel. To these were added, as
to a common foundation, the Trinity, the Vicarious Atonement, and
Everlasting Hell. The time was one of theological gloom and religious
pessimism....It was against this terrible scheme that the Universalist
pioneers found themselves arrayed in attack. [7]

In 1790 the Universalists created a Profession of Faith at a meeting held in Philadelphia called by Universalist clergy and prominent laymen of the day in an effort to
solidify their theology so as to face their religious compatriots with a unified front as
well as to articulate among themselves who and what they were as a unique expression
of Christianity. Benjamin Rush was one of the laymen and John Murray, one of the
clergy. John Coleman Adams, author of many Universalist publications, notes in his
book *Universalism and the Universalist Church* that in 1779 there were churches in
Oxford and Boston, Massachusetts; Philadelphia, Pennsylvania and Richmond, New
Hampshire. John Murray had formed the Independent Church of Gloucester, and Rush
attended the Universalist church in Philadelphia. Of the Universalist need to articulate
Universalism he writes:

> Wherever the heralds of the new doctrine went, they were encouraged
> and sustained in their work by those who received it with joy and
> provided for its hearing and helped its spread. They gathered in halls,
> in school-houses, in court-houses, in private dwellings, in barns,
> sometimes in the open air, to hear the proclamation of these new
> tidings of joy. They were attacked and they were slandered; they were
> threatened with violence and with the law of the land; they were made
> to suffer social ostracism and business boycott; they were treated as
> heretics and infidels; friends grew cold and enemies plotted against
> them. It was no light matter to be a Universalist in those days. [8]

Dorothy Spoerl in her Keynote address to the New York State Convention of Universalists in 1976, published in the booklet *The Universalist Heritage*, commented that this
1790 statement of faith had clear Trinitarian overtones despite the opening words, "We
believe in one God." It was a statement of faith that clearly reflected the Rellyan/
Murray Universalist theology of the 1790s. The entire Profession as printed in St.

Lawrence Theological School's Lewis B. Fisher's 1903 *A History of Universalism* follows:

> Sect. 1. OF THE HOLY SCRIPTURES.—We believe the Scriptures of the Old and New Testament to contain a revelation of the perfections and will of God, and the rule of faith and practice.
>
> Sect. 2. OF THE SUPREME BEING.—We believe in One God, infinite in all his perfections; and that those perfections are all modifications of infinite, adorable, incomprehensible and unchangeable Love.
>
> Sect. 3. OF THE MEDIATOR.—We believe that there is one mediator between God and man, the man Christ Jesus, in whom dwelleth all the fullness of the godhead bodily; who by giving himself as ransom for all had redeemed them to God by his blood; and who, by the merit of his death, and the efficacy of his Spirit, will finally restore the whole human race to happiness.
>
> Sect. 4. OF THE HOLY GHOST.—We believe in the Holy Ghost, whose office it is to make known to sinners the truth of their salvation, through the medium of the Holy Scriptures, and to reconcile the hearts of the children of men to God, and thereby dispose them to genuine holiness.
>
> Sect. 5. Of GOOD WORKS—We believe in the obligation of the moral law, as the rule of life; and we hold that the love of God manifest to man in a Redeemer, is the best means of producing obedience to that law, and promoting a holy, active, and useful life.[9]

In 1803, reflecting the influence of Hosea Ballou, which will be discussed in later chapters, a new statement of faith, known as the Winchester Profession, was also printed in Fisher's book:

> ARTICLE I.—We believe that the Holy Scriptures of the Old and New Testament contain a revelation of the character of God and of

the duty, interest and final destination of mankind.

ARTICLE II.—We believe that there is one God, whose nature is Love, revealed in one Lord Jesus Christ, by one Holy Spirit of Grace, who will finally restore the whole family of mankind to holiness and happiness.

ARTICLE III.—We believe that holiness and true happiness are inseparably connected, and that believers ought to be careful to maintain order and practise [sic] good works; for these things are good and profitable unto men.[10]

Spoerl comments, "By 1803 we believed the Bible contained 'a revelation of the character of God, and of the duty, interest and final destination of mankind.' Indeed the early arguments of Universalists for their faith were for the most part achieved by the careful perusal and quotation of biblical passages attesting to the truth of their opinions."[11] Spoerl's observations affirm that Universalist faith is grounded in the Bible and that the Bible contains a revelation of God.

By 1803 the Revolutionary War had taken place, and the nation had written its Declaration of Independence and the Constitution of the United States of America. The political principles contained in each were well established in practice. The people had been given the message that the angry God of the Calvinists would be forgiving if they repented of their sins. A sign of this forgiveness was seen in the nation's establishment and prosperity. It seemed as though God favored these people and their new nation. Optimism ran high and the people turned their attention to settling the vast westward lands. Historian William G. McLoughlin points out in his book on the Great Awakenings that by 1800, as the nation was struggling to shape itself through newly forming institutions, disagreement arose as to how to accomplish such institutional organization. What did it mean to be "American" in this unsettled society? The educated and elite were challenged in their social thinking by the ideas of the rise of the common man. There was political dissension as to which direction to look for economic growth, westward to the vast expanses of farmland or to Europe for manufacturing and mercantile trade. And in the religious world of the Second Great Awakening (1800-1830) Protestant sects were springing up as the evangelists traveled the countryside bringing new variations of the Christian message to people whose lives were changing as the new nation expanded and developed.

In the 1810s the Calvinist doctrine of depravity and predetermination came into direct conflict with the Enlightenment rationalism espoused by early Unitarian Deists Thomas Jefferson, John Locke, John Adams, John Quincy Adams, and others. The results of the Revolutionary War had validated the Deistic Enlightenment beliefs in the ability of humanity to shape its own destiny, and the War of 1812 further emboldened the optimism of this belief.

McLoughlin notes that the Calvinist God seemed to many of the time as fatalistic, the author of sin, and a cruel father to His children. The Deist faith offered the populace a benevolent God whose will was for their eternal as well as their earthly happiness and prosperity. McLoughlin further notes:

> This optimistic, self-reliant view (though Calvinists called it heretical or blasphemous) was suggested not only in the works of the French *philosophes* and English deists but also by some latitudinarian Anglicans and the new "supernatural rationalists" in New England who called themselves Unitarians and Universalists. Unitarians considered the doctrine of the trinity (a triune God) irrational and doubted that God still worked miracles. Universalists insisted that God was not so cruel as to roast innocent people forever in hell (including children who had died before conversion). Yet comparatively few Americans dared to identify themselves with these radical new positions.[12]

The spirit of the letter of the law in Calvinism was greatly weakened with the optimism in the New World, nonetheless, and a call to inspire greater Christian conversion went out from the Calvinist churches for a new awakening of religious commitment. This Second Great Awakening began the process of reshaping the spiritual core of what it meant to be American. There was a sense of independence and rugged individualism that fostered the growth of new religious expressions affirming humanity's capabilities, and God's forgiveness of repentant sinners. The Calvinist Churches became alarmed with these trends and began a concerted effort to reassert their influence.

McLoughlin quotes Clifford Geertz in defining religion that is intrinsic to understanding the impetus for the Second Great Awakening:

Religion is a system of symbols which acts to establish powerful, pervasive, and long-lasting moods and motivations in men by formulating conceptions of a general order of existence and clothing these conceptions with such an aura of factuality that the moods and motivations seem uniquely real....It is the role of the revivalist, the prophet of revitalization, to sustain the reality of the culture myths, to reinterpret them to meet the needs of social change, and to clothe them with an aura of reality that grows from his own conviction that he is a messenger of God.[13]

Therefore, the concept of manifest destiny, a belief held by the Euro-American people that they were "The Chosen Ones" in a new Covenant with God in the new Promised Land, emphasized by the revivalists, arose with the theology of the Second Great Awakening and drove the colonists westward. The revivalist camp meetings of this second awakening carried the religious fervor as a vital component of the westward expansion. In this powerful movement the Universalists found a niche that was to serve them well in the years that followed. They became evangelists of their faith with the best of them. They joined alongside the Baptists, Methodists, Presbyterians, and Congregationalists in holding camp meetings, in traveling from town to town preaching and establishing new churches. Universalists began a circuit riding evangelical movement filled with the zeal to shape the new country with its message of faith, hope, and love. They reached far and wide with their Universalist theology and its redeeming, loving God who offered Universal Salvation. The Universalists offered a powerful alternative to those preachers who spoke of an angry God, a depraved humanity, and eternal damnation of sinners in the pit fires of Hell. According to Clinton Lee Scott, by the beginning of the 1800s

Universalist circuit riding evangelists had reached communities in the Carolinas, Virginia, Georgia, Kentucky, Ohio and Indiana. By 1850 they spread their word into Alabama, Tennessee, Missouri, Illinois, Iowa, Michigan and Minnesota, and into Quebec, Canada. In the last half of the 1800s they made inroads into Kansas, Colorado and the territories of Idaho and Washington. The New England states, Pennsylvania and New York were hotbeds of Universalism before the turn of the 19th century.[14]

Universalism grew in influence in the midst of the larger Christian expansion associated with the colonial and early national periods of American history. Mary Boys writes about the movement within the dominant evangelical Protestant theology between the First and Second Great Awakening. Boys writes that the theology of the First Great Awakening began with a clear Calvinist belief in God's omnipotence that completely negated any human free will and held human nature as depraved and without hope. Jonathan Edwards, a major shaper of this first period of awakenings, began preaching a "New Light" theology that gave hope of salvation through a conversion crisis. Although Edwards's God was merciful and gracious to those who came to conversion, this God was also harsh and demanding. For Edwards, human nature was woefully fallen and depraved and deserved condemnation to everlasting Hell unless individuals obeyed God's commands and confessed their willfulness. Edwards's theology evidenced a hint of Arminianism that created a crack in the Calvinist door and gave just enough room for later evangelical Protestants to clear away the remnants of strict Calvinism. Boys notes:

> Arminianism was an early Christian controversy in the 1500s that arose with the criticism of Calvinism's doctrine of predetermination by Jacobus Arminius. It was an anti-determinism that reappeared with new meaning in the nineteenth-century American revivalism, most notably in the preaching of Charles Grandison Finney and John Wesley.[15]

Jonathan Edwards and other First Great Awakening preachers in New England's churches had suggested, and Charles Finney in revival meetings during the Second Great Awakening developed more fully, a theology that contained an "appreciation for human application of free will, denial of the depravity of children, and less harsh images of God."[16] This Arminianism began as a result of Edwards's stressing the spiritual rebirth that occurred with a crisis conversion experience. This new emphasis conveyed the suggestion that God's mercy was given when the sinner repented of his or her sins. Previously a strict Calvinist emphasis had been placed on God's omnipotence which had negated any free will on the part of a depraved humanity. The older emphasis also negated any salvific benefit of the revivals or of repentance.
Charles Grandison Finney (1792-1875) best expressed the theological changes taking place in the wider Christian world within the Second Great Awakening (1800-1830). Finney took up the modification to Calvinist theology of God's mercy while continuing to believe thoroughly in the abject depravity of human nature. For Finney, Boys notes that

the minister was called to subdue sinners, stripping them of their excuses, answering their cavils, humbling their pride, and breaking their hearts. Then the revivalist's task was to "pour in the truth, put in the probe, break up the old foundation and ...use the word of God like a fire and a hammer."[17]

Within this larger context of the 1800-1830s the Universalists began to develop an understanding of themselves as a religious group with a distinct message to bring to this new nation. Universalist theology was grounded in biblical Scripture with several formulations. Lewis B. Fisher writes that the distinct Universalist idea is that somewhere, sometime, every person will strive to know God's will and obey it. God will, in return, as attributed to lawyer, orator, and political leader Robert Ingersoll (1833-1899) speaking of Universalists, "keep the latch string out until the last child is home." Ingersoll spoke in sympathy with a faith that believed in a God who would hold out salvation for all humanity for as long as it took to accomplish universal salvation. Lewis B. Fisher states that Universalists chose that name for themselves because Universal means everyone and Universalists believed that all will be saved as they come to obey God.[18] Fisher was an 1881 graduate of St. Lawrence Theological School, professor of pastoral theology at Saint Lawrence from 1891 to 1905, president of Universalist Lombard College from 1905 to 1912 and then dean of Lombard's Ryder Divinity School when the college and divinity school moved to Chicago in 1912 to affiliate with the complex of the University of Chicago theological schools.

While Universalists were differentiating themselves in significant ways from the dominant evangelical Protestant groups, they also underwent changes and challenges from within. Hosea Ballou provided another interpretation of Universalism and made a profound impact on Universalist theology when, in 1805, he wrote *A Treatise on Atonement.* He argued that God alone was God. Jesus was a created, dependent being exalted above other men because God, as his father, so anointed him. Jesus did not die to appease an angry God or to win salvation from Hell and damnation for humanity. Ballou held that the death of Jesus on the cross was not to change God, but to change humanity. Human beings were lost and needed reconciliation to God; God did not need to be reconciled to humankind. Jesus' life and death for Ballou were messages and examples of God's infinite love sent to all humankind. In essence, God saves through His infinite and unconditional love.[19]

John Murray strongly opposed this theology as destructive to his Calvinist and trinitarian theology in which salvation by Christ was central. Lewis B. Fisher's early history of Universalism illustrates the struggle between Murray and Ballou with a story. He tells that in 1798 when John Murray was to be gone from his pulpit for ten Sundays, Hosea Ballou was invited to preach those Sundays in Murray's absence. At the end of the ten weeks Mrs. (Judith Sargent) Murray requested a member of the congregation to stand and declare that "the doctrine which has been preached here to-day is not the doctrine that is usually preached in this house." While we do not have the specific content preached during those ten weeks, it is evident that Mrs. Murray was a proponent of her husband's theology and was encouraging his congregants to hold steadfast to this theology, not Ballou's.[20]

Hosea Ballou's doctrine of the sovereignty of God held that God's power alone saved. It was an absolute power as was the sovereignty of God preached by Jonathan Edwards during the late 1700s, albeit Edwards's God was terrible in wrath and cruelty and humankind was crushed and destroyed. Both Ballou and Edwards held that humankind had no free will. Fisher observes,

> [Ballou] sometimes made it seem that man was only a puppet moved by a power not of himself, and so not responsible for what he did. Usually Ballou did not do this; but if he must sacrifice God's sovereignty or man's freedom, then he forgot man's freedom......Says Dr. [John Coleman] Adams, "His method was dignified and noble. His spirit was Christian. His practical teaching was wise and effective. He went to the people. He traversed New England and New York, preaching where a hearing could be had. He argued like Socrates. He pleaded like Paul. He was as serene as the firmament."

> So [for Fisher] Hosea Ballou laid the enduring foundation for the theology of our Church and for the theology of all those who think things through.[21]

Other voices within Universalism began to protest Ballou's sovereignty of God and humankind's lack of freedom. One such voice was Hosea Ballou 2nd the great-nephew of Hosea Ballou. Ballou 2nd was a Universalist denominational historian and editor of *The Universalist Magazine*. This magazine published the ongoing restorationist controversy debate during the years 1811 and 1832 on the nature of future punishment as it related to Hosea Ballou's belief in the sovereignty of God. Ballou 2nd was either sole editor or he collaborated with his great-uncle Hosea Ballou and Universalist Thomas Whittemore (1800-1861) who followed Ballou as minister of the Second Street Church in Boston and was instrumental in founding the Universalist Historical Society in 1834.[22]

What followed for Universalists has been termed the Restorationists Controversy; it took place between 1811 and 1832 over the issue of future punishment. Lewis B. Fisher comments, "This is the only debate that Mr. Ballou ever went into that we wish he had kept out of." This controversy threatened to split the growing denomination. The belief of no future punishment was argued fervently by Ballou on the basis that it is not death that saves the sinner as sin is finite and of this world. God's love is infinite and sovereign and therefore surpasses any worldly conditions. It also removed the salvific nature of Christ. Salvation was given by God and one could not escape salvation. Atonement was God's power alone. Because of this belief in the sovereignty of God, Ballou was dubbed by opponents, both within and without Universalist circles, as the "Death and Glory" theologian, reflecting the belief that when people died they were immediately saved by God. There was no afterlife punishment for transgressions done on earth. Sin was finite, God was infinite, and so was God's love for humankind.

The Restorationists Controversy pitted Ballou's adamant belief in no afterlife punishment against those who believed some restorative punishment must be endured for earthly sin before salvation was given by God. The controversy raged and Universalists lost creditability among the wider religious community as a result of the intense nature of the debates. Universalists were ridiculed for Ballou's intractable stand on no afterlife punishment. The length of punishment necessitated by the degree of sin was debated hotly for many years and sent conflicting messages about the faith of Universalists into the wider community. Russell Miller notes:

> In August 1831 eight ministers and several laymen met at Mendon...Massachusetts, following adjournment of the Providence Association, and formed themselves into "a religious community for the defence and promulgation of the doctrines of the Revelation in their original purity, and the promotion of their own improvement....The new group assumed the name of "Massachusetts Association of Universal Restorationists."[23]

They argued "that Regeneration — a general Judgment, Future Rewards and Punishments, to be followed by the Final Restoration of all mankind to holiness and happiness, are fundamental articles of Christian faith, and that the modern sentiments of no future accountability, connected with materialism, are unfriendly to pure religion, and subversive of the best interests of society."[24]

Even though the two factions of Universalists disagreed on what occurred at death, they held one belief in common. In the end all humankind would be in harmony with the Divine. Universal salvation was not the issue. The existence of and duration of future and restorative punishment was. The restorationist position eventually became the dominant thinking of Universalist theology.

During these same years from 1800 to the mid 1830s as part of the religious fervor of the Second Great Awakening, Universalism experienced tremendous growth out in the hinterlands of the westward expansion. Within the new territories of the United States Universalism thrived along with the growth of other popular evangelical Protestant denominations on the frontier, especially as part of the westward expansion of European Americans. Universalists preached a different message, however, about God's great mercy and love. Circuit riders and farmer preachers of all denominations, most without formal education, evangelized with the word of the Gospel. Evangelical Protestantism was, in Sydney Ahlstrom's term, "revivalized,"[25] local churches were begun and those already in existence were revitalized. The new converts and the religious fervor helped to spur the rise of denominationalism and to ensure that Christianity was the dominant religious power in the New World. The Revivalists' message of God's salvation to a repentant sinner, whether Calvinist or Universalist, and the belief in Manifest Destiny shaped the newly emerging nation and fostered the independence of the settlers in the West. Universalists, along with Methodists, unanimously opposed ideas of an educated ministry, pews, instrumental music, and the need for a congregational or stated, salaried minister. Universalism was a populist movement and its self-educated preachers traveled widely and set the world on fire with their 'good news' of universal salvation.

In western New York, called by Whitney R. Cross in his book The Burned-over District, writes of the place Universalists found themselves within the revivalist movement.

> A healthy minority opinion, propagated with forthright zeal, often serves
> to develop strength in the majority group by furnishing a definite

antithesis to be controverted. More than Catholics in western New York, did the Universalists serve as this kind of foil for the evangelists, stimulating them to ever-more-heroic efforts. Thus a thriving Universalist Church served a dual function, irritating the revivalists to action while providing a stimulus for alternative types of enthusiasm.[26]

Consequently, the going was not always easy; Universalists experienced extreme persecution through defamation of character and outright ostracism by other evangelists. Cross notes that "all evangelical sects untied...against Universalists and Unitarians." And that "the religious press constantly labeled criminals prominent in the news as Universalists, suggesting that without the fear of eternal punishment one could not remain moral." [27] Yet, through their fervent grounding of Universalist theology in Scripture and their integrity of character, the Universalists were enthusiastically accepted by the people who came to hear them. Due to the lack of a centralized denominational structure or of solid denominational missionary support behind them, they were without institutional and collegial support and were on their own traveling the countryside with their Bible and their message of a loving God and no Hell.

John Coleman Adams provides insight into the strident opposition to Universalism they faced. He writes:

> The "scheme of salvation" was a closely reasoned, logically built system, whose parts depended one upon the other, like stones in an arch. But the keystone is the vulnerable place in the arch, the strategic point, so to speak, of the structure, and the keystone of American Orthodoxy was the doctrine of everlasting punishment....If, for instance, there were no eternal hell, why should there be any need of the vicarious atonement? They [Universalists preachers] say, moreover, that to discredit this hideous doctrine would be to create an atmosphere most favorable to the reconstruction of the whole of the current theology. And it was abundantly clear that the quickest way to arouse the interest of the average man in theology was to take it up at the point where it bore the hardest upon himself and his own personal destiny....No theological question was ever debated with more eagerness and heat than that of the final salvation of all men. It was fundamental, it was pervasive, it was personal.[28]

As the Second Great Awakening progressed through the 1830s the response from the frontier slowly brought small and locally organized Universalism into the mainstream of evangelical Protestantism, and by the end of the Second Great Awakening it had grown to become the fifth largest denomination in the country. From reading Russell Miller's *The Larger Hope, The First Century of the Universalist Church in America — 1770-1870*, it can be deduced that the top four were, not in order, Baptists, Methodists, Presbyterians, and Congregationalists, or possibly Episcopalians. Ernest Cassara notes in his book *Two Centuries of Universalism: 1741-1961*, that in 1888 Universalists were claimed to be the sixth largest denomination in the United States.[29] Richard Gilbert in his 1983 New York State Convention of Universalist's Keynote Address "Soft Seats and No Hell" concurred that they were the sixth largest at that time. Gordon McKeeman, in his 1980 Keynote Address to the same Convention, "The Persistence of Universalism," stated that Universalists, by the time of the Civil War were the fifth largest denomination in the United States. Whatever place they held in rank, they were clearly formidable in number when the Second Great Awakening was over. Universalists continued their efforts to spread the 'good news' and become a significant presence within Protestant evangelical religion.[30] Russell Miller notes:

> According to the Seventh United States Census (1850), the Universalists were among the twenty-one "major sects" for which information was given. Universalists were reported to have a total of 529 churches in twenty-two states, possessing religious property valued at $1,752,316, and accommodations for 241,115 individuals.[31]

Universalism was now poised to make a significant contribution to the theological discourse in evangelical Protestantism. They had organized in defense of their faith and developed professions of that faith, joined in the evangelizing of it to the new nation, and were concerned that this faith be preserved.

ENDNOTES

1. Richard Eddy, *Universalism in America, Vol. 1, 1636-1800* (Boston, Universalist Publishing House, 3rd ed., 1891) 13, 14, 19, 35, 42, 43, 83.
2. Mark Noll, *A History of Christianity in the United States and Canada* (Grand Rapids, Mich.: William B. Eerdmans Publishing Company, 1992), 104.
3. Eddy, *Universalism in America*, 28.

4. John Murray, *The Life of Rev. John Murray* (Boston: A. Tompkins, 1844), 136-140.

5. Russell Miller, *The Larger Hope: The First Century of the Universalist Church in America: 1770-1870* (Boston: Unitarian Universalist Association, 1979), 40.

6. Jonathan Edwards, "Sinners in the Hands of an Angry God," *American Sermons: The Pilgrims to Martin Luther King, Jr.*, ed. Michael Warner, (New York: The Library of America, by Penguin Putman Inc., 1999), 348, 350, 353-354.

7. John Coleman Adams, *Universalism and the Universalist Church* (Boston: The Universalist Publishing House, The Murray Press, 1915), 25-26.

8. *Ibid.*, 22.

9. Lewis B. Fisher, D.D., *A Brief History of the Universalist Church* (Boston: Young People's Christian Union, 4th ed., rev., 1903 or 1904), 102.

10. *Ibid.*, 104.

11. Dorothy Spoerl, "We Do Not Stand, We Move," *The Universalist Heritage*, ed. Harold H. Burkart (Syracuse, NY: Quartier Group, 1993), 7.

12. William G. McLoughlin, *Revivals, Awakenings, and Reform* (Chicago: University of Chicago Press, 1978), 100.

13. *Ibid.*, 104.

14. Clinton Lee Scott, *The Universalist Church of America: A Short History* (Boston: Universalist Historical Society, 1957), 23.

15. Mary Boys, *Educating In Faith* (Kansas City, Mo., Sheed and Ward, 1989), 19.

16. *Ibid.*, 19.

17. *Ibid.*, 19-20.

18. Fisher, *A Brief History of the Universalist Church*, 10.

19. Fisher, *A Brief History of the Universalist Church*, 58-59

20. Fisher, *A Brief History of the Universalist Church*, 60.

21. Fisher, *A Brief History of the Universalist Church*, 62-63.

22. Miller, *The Larger Hope: The First Century of the Universalist Church in America*, 114-115.

23. Miller, *The Larger Hope: The First Century of the Universalist Church in America*, 119.

24. *Ibid.*, 119-120.

25. Sydney E. Ahlstrom, *A Religious History of the American People* (New Haven: Yale University Press, 1972).

26. Whitney R. Cross, *The Burned-over District: The Social and Intellectual History of Enthusiastic Religion in Western New York, 1800-1850* (New York: Harper and Row, 1950) 17,18.

27. *Ibid.*, 43, 44.

28. Adams, *Universalism and the Universalist Church*, 34, 35.

29. Ernest Cassara, *Two Centuries of Universalism: 1741-1961* (Boston: Skinner House, 1971), 39.

30. Richard S. Gilbert, "Soft Seats and No Hell," and Gordon McKeeman, "The Persistence of Universalism," in *The Universalist Heritage*, ed. Harold H. Burkart (Syracuse, NY: The Quartier Group, 1993).

31. Miller, *The Larger Hope: The First Century of the Universalist Church in America*, 164.

CHAPTER TWO

Universalism and the Rise of Formal Education: The Sunday School, The Common School, The Academy and Higher Education

As the revival movement of the Second Great Awakening expanded there emerged a growing need to educate the people in the beliefs and practices of the different denominations' faiths being preached by the revivalists. Within the Protestant educational enterprise Universalists discovered that they must speak their own voice and develop their own institutions of learning. Yet Universalist efforts were greatly influenced by the larger context that gave shape to the Sunday school, the common school, the academy, and higher education. The history of the Sunday school is one rich with Universalist activity in its earliest stages in America.

The Sunday School Comes to America

The creation and rapid growth of the Sunday school movement in Protestantism was in part an effort to utilize education for the ushering in of the Kingdom of God. Education was seen as a major activity through which to facilitate religious conversion and to socialize individuals into the religious beliefs of a particular tradition. Before 1790 religious instruction took place in the form of catechitical classes led by the local congregation's clergy on Sundays, or in the homes with family instruction usually led by the father of the household. These forms of teaching comprised a prescribed biblical question and answer lesson of memorization of the correct answers to the posed questions. The religious instruction of children in the faith of their ancestors was a high priority for the community and deeply embedded in practice in the colonial period of America. In 1791, however, a shift occurred in the organizing efforts of religious instruction and was motivated by a desire to instruct poor and marginalized children. Many of these children worked all week and evidenced no supervision as to the salvation of their souls or the socialization and civilizing of their behavior.[1]

The first Sunday schools were not part of the church. They were begun in England by

Robert Raikes in an effort to educate the poor children who worked in the pin factories of Gloucester six days of the week. In 1780 he opened a school in a private home for Sunday instruction in reading and religion for these children. The majority of people in England were not literate nor did they attend particular churches. Even the clergy of the day were barely able to read. Raikes sought to bring about reform among the people from the poverty, ignorance, and a fundamental lack of morality rampant around him. He tried working with adults but found them to be entrenched in their ways. In a moment of inspiration he got the idea of addressing the problem through the children. Because the children were not available during the week, and because there were no child labor laws to protect them from working long hours in the factories, these children were free to attend schooling only on Sunday. So, the Sunday school came into being.[2] The curriculum did not focus primarily upon religion but more on reading, grammar, and civic values and behaviors. It was the Sunday school in this form that prefigured popular education in England.

The social conditions that existed for the children of the poor and marginalized in America were similar to those in England. Many concerned leaders noticed that there was a clear deterioration in literacy, morals, and commitment to religion. It was in this climate that the American Sunday school movement began with both the Methodists and the Universalists laying claim to the first Sunday school in America. In 1790 the Methodist Conference in Charleston, South Carolina had given official recognition to Sunday schools but had failed to follow through with action.[3] Also in 1790, Dr. Benjamin Rush, an ardent Universalist in Philadelphia, Pennsylvania, was one of a group of men who came together to begin the First Day School, or Sunday School Society. The evangelical Protestants believed that education was the handmaid of religion and therefore quickly began adopting the idea of the Sunday school for America. Education was to serve religion and support the process of strengthening the churches. It was conceived as a method by which conversion at the revival meetings was deepened into conviction in the faith.

From the beginning Universalists were active in the First Day or Sunday school movement. Dr. Rush prepared a series of strongly worded resolutions on the religious instruction of children that he delivered during the 1790 Philadelphia Convention of Universalists and that were heartily adopted by that body. One such resolution as presented stated:

The Instruction of Children:—We believe it to be the duty of all
parents to instruct their children in the principles of the gospel, as the
best means to inspire them with the love of virtue, and to promote in
them good manners, and habits of industry and sobriety. As a necessary introduction to the knowledge of the gospel, we recommend the
institution of a school, or schools, to be under the direction of every
church; in which shall be taught reading, writing, arithmetic, and
psalmody. We recommend, further, that provision be made for
instructing poor children, in the said schools, gratis. As the fullest
discovery of the perfections and will of God, and of the whole duty of
man, is contained in the Bible, we wish that divine book to be read by
the youth of our churches as early and frequently as possible; and that
they should be instructed therein at stated meetings appointed for that
purpose.[4]

The Sunday or First Day schools were organized under the auspices of the ecumenical
First Day Society which was formed in 1790 to oversee the development of the schools.
The curriculum was reading and writing using the Bible as the sole source of material.
Behavior was also of primary concern, and swearing, lying, or talking in an indecent
manner were forbidden.[5]

The founders of The First Day Society were an ecumenical group described by
historian Anne Boylan as enlightened republican gentlemen. They included Episcopalians, Universalists, Friends, and at least one Catholic. They were all educationally
and socially well-bred, established in prominent careers in Philadelphia, and influenced by Enlightenment thinking to hold a faith in progress and in human rationality.
Education for these First Day Society founders included a broad cultivation, promoting good order, individually and socially, and fostering the formation of good habits
and religious practice. Their goal was for the students to become good servants and
good apprentices within the community. These men even harbored the hope that the
children would one day become good citizens and good craft masters. This faith in the
efficacy of education and in the potential for human progress provided the schools
with confidence in their ability to bring about a better society through faith, biblical
knowledge, and an educated population.[6]

By 1819 the First Day Schools were replaced by the religious schools of the evangelical

Protestant churches and the free charity schools that fostered a more secular education. These religious schools were ecumenical in their early nature, but evolved into a
separate congregational endeavor and, much later, into denomination-wide systems.

> The first distinctly Universalist Sunday School started at the Lombard
> Street Church in Philadelphia in 1816, the second was connected with
> the First Universalist Society on Hanover Street in Boston in 1817
> then under the pastorate of Rev. Paul Dean, and the third was in the
> Gloucester, Mass Independent Christian Church Universalist in 1820.
> In 1835 Boston's School Street Sunday School was organized.[7]

The lessons of the early evangelical schools had, as stated by one teacher, "the ultimate
end" of "imparting that religious knowledge, those religious impressions, and the
formation of those religious habits in the minds of children, which shall be crowned
with the salvation of their immortal souls." The result of this education, as stated by a
Sunday School Society in upstate New York, was that "Orderly lives, and minds stored
with useful knowledge, will make [children] the support and ornament of civil society;
but religion alone will give them a claim on the white robes and palms of heaven."[8]

In the 1820s a division of purposes led to the separation of the churches' Sunday
schools from those of the common public schools. The largest and most influential of
the unions that formed to take up the task of the development of the Sunday schools
was the American Sunday School Union. This broad-based association was formed in
May 1824 in Philadelphia from a merging and re-visioning of the Philadelphia Sunday
School Union and the Adult School Union, both outgrowths of the original First Day
Schools. The American Sunday School Union was a voluntary union of individuals
from different denominations, including Universalists who agreed to cooperate to
promote religious instruction through Bible study and the establishment of the
emerging Sunday school movement.

The Union's secretary, Episcopalian Frederick A. Packard and Unitarian Horace
Mann, then secretary of the Massachusetts Board of Education, were the principle
spokespersons for differing philosophical positions that helped bring about the
separation of the churches' Sunday schools and common public schools. The issue
concerned defining the word "sectarian" in the curricula presented for use in the
common schools that were under the auspices of the Massachusetts Board of Educa-

tion. When Packard proposed the book *The Child At Home,* by evangelical Christian John F. C. Abbott, Mann objected because it "would be in the highest degree offensive to the Universalists" and "would ill accord with the views of the Unitarians."[9] To Mann the book as well as publications in general of the American Sunday School Union, were considered sectarian because they taught specific orthodox Protestant doctrines that were unacceptable to liberal Protestants. Packard countered that Mann favored liberal Protestant sectarian ideas that only the Universalists and Unitarians in Massachusetts would find acceptable, ideas that he considered as antithetical to evangelicals, or even anti-evangelical. Beginning in 1824, Frederick Packard engaged in the American Sunday School Union's role, along with Horace Mann, in selecting curricula for the emerging common schools. The Massachusetts textbook law enacted in 1827, however, altered this arrangement when it determined the extent of religious content in its common school books. The effect was to limit the use of sectarian religious material in the common schools.

Without explicit Protestant evangelical resources and ideas in the common school curriculum, Packard believed that Mann's approach represented the lowest common denominator of moral Protestant education. This was untenable to the American Sunday School Union. Since the common school movement embraced Mann's leadership and philosophy, the Sunday schools were deemed of vital necessity for the teaching of a deeper Protestant moral character and the saving of souls. The leaders of the American Sunday School Union declined to form separate parochial religious schools and focused on the Sunday teaching of the Bible in accordance with their doctrinal teachings, leaving reading, writing, and arithmetic to the common schools.

While the American Sunday School Union and the subsequent Sunday school conventions were establishing the field of religious education within the evangelical Protestant Churches, which included Universalists at the time, Horace Mann was busy in Massachusetts in the 1820s and 1830s developing the common school into a universal and public education system. Mann's vision of the perfectibility of humanity and of special institutions drove his belief in the efficacy of public and universal education. He believed that once public schools were indeed universal, no evil would be able to withstand the moral influence of the schools on the lives of individual students or the organizations of the society. Universalists supported the public education system for many reasons. It enabled them to participate in common education schools without being harassed for their faith, it fostered Universalist values in democratic faith and community, and affirmed their belief in the worthiness of humankind.

The organizers of the Sunday schools were evangelicals who had experienced the Second Great Awakening and were eager to promote civility and salvation, and the Sunday school, along with their commitment to be actively involved in it provided the means to do so. Many of the Protestant voluntary associations were combined with evangelizing efforts and work on behalf of society's ills through work in temperance and urban missionary efforts to help the poor. These Protestant voluntary organizations also worked to spread their faith and a missionary emphasis was a vital part of the early Sunday schools' efforts to bring about a Christian nation. As time progressed the Sunday schools became more and more focused on the missionary work of evangelizing the faith and many of the voluntary associations became increasingly secular.

The rise by the 1830s of voluntary institutions in American society enabled Sunday schools to begin taking over the work of The First Day Schools and to maintain the growth and significance begun in the churches. As the common schools eliminated religious content from the curriculum the churches began developing Sunday schools to fill the need for religious instruction.

In the Boston area there were Sunday schools in numerous Universalist churches by the mid-1800's. A brief listing shows the success of their early efforts. All Souls Universalist Church on White Street and Church of our Father on East Broadway in South Boston, Grove Hall Universalist Church and Ashmont Parish on Bushnell and Lombard Streets in Dorchester, First Universalist Church in Roxbury on Guild Row and Dudley Streets, St. Paul's Universalist Church in Jamica Plain, Virginia Street Church in Boston, and First Universalist Society in Charlestown all reported thriving Sunday Schools.[10]

Education Becomes Important to Evangelizing: The Academy and Higher Education

The revival meetings of the Second Great Awakening were still in progress providing the converts who then needed educating in the faith. The message of the evangelical Protestant preachers in these revival meetings was, "Believe in the Lord Jesus Christ and thou shalt be saved." The single concern of the evangelists was salvation and Universalist preachers brought an alternative message, the good word of the ancient Christian heresy of universal salvation. Universalists were not considered "real"

Christians by the preachers riding the revival circuits with them in large part because of this belief in universal salvation. John Coleman Adams documents the situation faced by Universalists. He writes:

> For avowed Universalists, in the theological controversies of that
> time [1800-1830], there was no quarter given. They must wage a stout
> warfare for the faith they held, or it would gain no hearing whatever.
>
> So they took up the work and began their crusade. They assumed the
> common Protestant position, and made the Bible the ground of their
> argument and the court of their appeal. But they refused to read their
> Bible with the eyes of other people....They believed implicitly in the
> right of private judgment, and of religious liberty. In this spirit and
> this conviction they went to the people. They rallied them in churches
> when they could, in halls and court-rooms and school-houses when
> churches were denied them....There must always be a protest and
> challenge of the old thought before a lodgment can be found for the
> new....no more could the field have been prepared for the liberal faith,
> without the rude shock of the great controversy of the Larger Faith
> with the old New England theology.[11]

The denial of Universalist access to pulpits by Protestants created a felt need by the Universalists to justify their message of universal salvation in ancient Christian church history. Universalism was as ancient as Christianity itself, especially with such patristic theologians as Clement of Alexandria who taught around 190 to 196 C.E. and his student, Origen (185-253 C.E.). Universalist historian Lewis B. Fisher writes,

> One of Clement's pupils was Origen, who lived from 185 to 253 A.D.
> [*sic*] Origen is the greatest name in the early Church after Paul, and
> Origen was a Universalist. Edward Beecher says, "Two great facts
> stand out on the pages of ecclesiastical history: One that the first
> system of Christian theology was composed and issued by Origen in
> the year 230 after Christ, of which a fundamental essential element
> was the doctrine of the Universal restoration of all fallen beings to
> their original holiness, and union with god. The second is, that after
> the lapse of a little more than three centuries, in the year 544 this

doctrine was for the first time condemned and anathematized as heretical. This was done, not in a general council, but in a local council called by order of Justinian."[12]

As the Second Great Awakening advocated for education as a necessary component of its mission people began to heed the necessity of an increase in the educated populace, and it became clear that the clergy were to be among the learned. In the early 1800's many of the evangelical revivalist preachers, especially the Universalists were not accorded the validation of their calling because of their lack of a proper education. The Ordination of Universalist preachers took place during the recesses of the annual conventions and required only a letter from a previously ordained Universalist preacher or members of a local Universalist congregation. Princeton Seminary was established at Princeton College in 1812 to meet the needs of the growing call for an educated Presbyterian clergy. Andover Seminary was founded in 1808 in response to the liberalizing of Harvard by the Unitarians. This move to educate a "learned" clergy was also true from the founding of Harvard in 1638 and Yale in 1701.[13]

In the evangelical camp meetings a changing Calvinist theology was espoused and articulated along the revival circuits by Timothy Dwight, Lyman Beecher, and Nathaniel Taylor in the northeast and Charles Finney in New York and into the Midwest. Finney, like Jonathan Edwards before him, considered education to be central to his efforts and to the work of the revivalists. Schools were of highest priority and Finney served as professor and then president of Oberlin College beginning in 1835.

The Universalists also understood the importance of education for their children and for their ministers. Beginning in 1814 Universalists began to establish schools for their young people, and eventually colleges and theological schools to train its ministers. The schools available in the local communities were often operated by Christian denominations hostile to Universalist ideas which caused Universalist children to suffer ridicule and insult because of their Universalist beliefs. The children were hindered from practicing Universalism and were required to attend religious instruction of the persuasion dominant in that school. In response Hosea Ballou and others proposed in 1814 to the General Convention[14] the establishment of Nichols Academy in New Hampshire for the liberal instruction of Universalist children. As with all of the schools Universalists established, no creedal test was required and anyone sympathetic to liberal ideas was welcomed.

In 1831 the New York State Convention of Universalists, at the urging of articles in the *Evangelical Magazine and Gospel Advocate,* established the denominational Clinton Liberal Institute in Clinton, New York, which was, as Universalist historian Richard Eddy observes:

> "a literary institution designed for the instruction of youth, preparatory to the ministry of universal reconciliation." Deprecating the influence exerted on the children of Universalist parents who were educated in schools wholly under the control of the opposers of Universalism, it was argued that both means and ability were sufficient to enable Universalists to educate their children in schools where they could retain the faith taught them in their homes.[15]

On 7 November 1831 the school opened with a male department, and its female department opened on 21 November. Clinton Lee Scott notes that:

> One of the strong motives for the creation of educational institutions was the desire to prepare men and women for the Universalist ministry. Sending candidates for the liberal ministry to evangelical colleges had been found to be most undesirable. Under the influence of orthodox teachers they frequently emerged from such institutions either so conditioned to orthodoxy as to render them unfit to serve liberal congregations, or so hardened in resisting the efforts to convert them and so disgusted with sectarian teaching that they turned altogether away from the ministry. Universalists felt the need of institutions in which the pursuit of truth rather than conversion should be the object of education.[16]

The zeal of creating schools for Universalist children grew rapidly in the period between 1830 to1860. They spanned the northeast and out into the Midwest. Showing the extent of Universalist commitment to education and the extent of the geographic expanse of their efforts is a listing of a few of these schools. Western Union Seminary opened in Indiana in 1833; Waterville Liberal Institute opened in Waterville, Maine in 1835; Ohio City Institute opened in 1838 in Ohio City, Ohio; Murray Institute opened in 1839 in Gloucester, Massachusetts; Lebanon Liberal Institute opened in Lebanon, New Hampshire in 1835; Melrose Seminary opened in West Brattleboro, Vermont in

1847; and Green Mountain Perkins Academy opened in South Woodstock, Vermont in 1848. Western Liberal Institute opened in Marietta, Ohio in 1849; Orleans Liberal Institute opened in 1852 in Glover, Vermont. Jefferson Liberal Institute opened in Jefferson, Wisconsin in 1866; and Dean Academy opened in Worcester, Massachusetts in 1865. Goddard Seminary opened in 1870. The Green Mountain Perkins Academy merged with Goddard and was established in Barre, VT. Mitchell Seminary followed in 1872 in Iowa. A listing of 15 others can be found in Richard Eddy's *Universalism in America, Volume II*. Butchel College opened in Akron, Ohio in 1871.[17]

Eddy provides a history of the establishment of the theological schools for the educating of Universalist ministers. In the 1827 General Convention a committee was formed to develop a plan for the establishment of a theological seminary. Eddy reports that "an interesting discussion took place on this subject, which was discontinued without any resolution," and no further action was taken until 1835.[18] Universalist minister, editor of the Universalist magazine *The Trumpet,* and tireless opponent of the death penalty Thomas Whittemore, frustrated over the long deliberations on the creation of Universalist theological schools, commented in 1838, "The age of miracles has passed...when men were prepared for the ministry solely, by immediate communication from heaven." Russell Miller added his observation to Whittemore's that, "something more was needed than divine inspiration alone; namely, some human effort. Piety alone was insufficient; the dignity of scholarship had to be added to ministerial qualifications."[19] In 1840 another committee was appointed by the General Convention to look into the matter of establishing a theological seminary. This committee held several meetings and agreed to establish "Walnut Hill Evangelical Seminary" on property given by Mr. Charles Tufts. This was renamed in 1847 in honor of Mr. Tufts and became Tufts University where the Crane Theological School was established in 1869. In 1856 the New York State Universalist Education Society voted to establish Saint Lawrence Theological School in Canton, New York. Clinton Lee Scott remarks, "St. Lawrence University grew out of the theological school and became the first institution of higher learning in the North Country of New York State."[20] The St. Lawrence Theological School opened in 1858 with four students, including James Minton Pullman, who went on to become one of the major voices in the development of Universalist religious education. In 1861 the Rev. Otis A. Skinner, D.D., proposed the establishment of a theological department at Lombard University, which had been established in 1851 and later renamed Lombard College. In 1881 a theology department was added to Lombard and in 1890 it was named Ryder Divinity School in honor of the

Rev. William H. Ryder of Chicago, a strong financial backer of the school. Clinton
Lee Scott notes that in 1912 the divinity school was moved to Chicago and affiliated
with the Divinity School of the University of Chicago. When the Meadville Theological School (Unitarian) was moved to Chicago it was eventually merged with Ryder,
operating under Lombard College's charter and benefiting from Ryder's affiliation
with the divinity school.[21] It is noted by Richard Eddy that both Saint Lawrence and
Lombard were open to the ladies as well as to gentlemen, a bold educational position
for its day.[22]

The Universalist commitment to education as evidenced by its many academies,
colleges, and theological schools, and its Sunday schools, was a vital part of the
Universalist development as a religious body. What began as a defense against hostili-
ties from the world around them became respected institutions of learning. Their
scholarship and embracing of new theological ideas put them on firm ground when the
challenges of the next decades came from the Higher Biblical Criticism, the Progressive Education Movement, Darwin's theories of evolution, new discoveries in the field
of geology and the Modernist/Fundamentalist Controversy, to name the larger
movements affecting Protestantism.

Education Takes Center Stage

Horace Mann in 1837 had hoped to maintain the presence of nonsectarian religion in
the public schools, but sectarian squabbling made this impossible to achieve. The task
of selecting a Bible for the daily reading each day became impossible with such
religious plurality in the common schools.[23] More trouble ensued over funding of
schools established by various sects for the express purpose of teaching their specific
doctrines. This funding debate and the pressure of such religious diversity eventually
created the necessity, whereby in 1842, "the legislature decreed that in the future no
portion of the public-school funds was to be given to any school in which "any
religious sectarian doctrine or tenet should be taught, inculcated, or practiced."[24]

The American Sunday School Union headquartered in Philadelphia had developed the
'union principle,' the requirement that all Sunday schools follow lessons approved by
the Union. Resisting such centralized authority, local conventions, most of which
formed in the decades preceding the Civil War, challenged this requirement. The

conventions wanted more autonomy in the selection of curricula and in the management of the money collected in their communities.

Anne Boylan writes that with the growth of the conventions in local communities and the wide range of evangelical institutions in existence after the middle of the nineteenth century, Protestants turned their attention to evangelizing the world, and the Sunday school had a key place in their plans. In the 1860s conventions brought together publishers, missionaries, teachers, and others who were interested in an interdenominational dialogue on the issues common to them in the field of religious education. Robert Lynn comments that

> A fever of enthusiasm for the Sunday school ran high throughout
> American Protestantism during the middle and latter part of the
> nineteenth century...the Sunday school was converted into the major
> institutional form of Protestant church education... [with the result
> that]....the Sunday school was a movement on the American scale.[25]

In the wider Protestant community the question began to arise in connection with the American Sunday School Union as to whether or not any one union could speak for all evangelical Protestants in developing one, unified Protestantism. The significant issue was whether the dominant method of organization would be the "union principle" or whether each of the denominations individually through delegates would comprise the central body overseeing the world of Sunday schools. The "union principle" was the standard set by the American Sunday School Union for curriculum development and publication, and the operation of the Sunday schools. "...they were really arguing over whether the 'union principle' or denominationalism should prevail."[26]

The rise of the Sunday school conventions from the local level to city-wide to statewide organizations had been occurring since 1859, and grew into national conventions throughout the 1860s. This system fostered a new type of interdenominational cooperation. This cooperation was achieved by ignoring doctrinal and theological differences and bringing workers together on the basis of instruction in teaching technique, promoting competence in the teachers and leaders of the Sunday schools not on the content of the lessons. This emphasis enabled Universalists to remain comfortably within this evangelical Protestant circle.

The Universalists were much less organized than other denominations during the 1850s and 1860s. One factor inhibiting organization of Universalist religious education structures was the rugged individualism within the ranks of Universalist congregations and the resulting aversion to any centralized authority making decisions on what should be taught in the congregations. Universalists did, however, make efforts to provide for their own educational needs with pamphlets, catechisms, and Bible tracts. A brief history of Universalist publications shows their efforts.

The Universalists in 1862 issued stock in a publishing company and created the New England Publishing House as an incorporated entity. Dr. Alonzo A. Miner's Second (School Street) Universalist Society in Boston provided most of the funding. In 1867 the name was changed to the Universalist Publishing House. As early as 1793, however, the Universalists had been publishing periodicals, such as the 1793-1794 *Universalist Magazine* edited by the Rev. Abel Sarjent, a Universalist minister and missionary who carried the Universalist message to Maryland, Ohio, and Indiana. Of the magazine Lewis B. Fisher notes, "Its length of life did not correspond with its great name, as it expired in one brief year. However, it taught at least one of the Universals,—that of the love of God." Fisher further observed, however, that "a study of our denominational literature, while it will undoubtedly show that our work has been very largely polemical, will most emphatically disprove a somewhat common notion that we have neglected the personal religious life."[27] Fisher was referring to the defensive position Universalists often found themselves in which took up considerable printed material. An example of the anit-Universalist diatribes is the 1805 book *Universalism confounds and destroys itself* [sic], by Josiah Spaulding, pastor of a Church in Buckland. Universalists were more often than not on the defensive for their belief in universal salvation, publishing articles justifying Universalist beliefs and therefore seeming to neglect publishing materials deemed to enrich one's personal religious life. They were, however quite active in the publication of materials for the instruction of children, most prominently in the form of catechisms. A catechism was written by Judith Sergeant Stevens in 1782 that was a personal declaration of her faith.[28] Her catechism, *Some Deductions from the System Promulgated in the Page of Divine Revelations: Ranged in the Order and Form of a Catechism: Intended as an Assistant to the Christian Parent or Teacher*, is a carefully written instruction for children that reflects a Rellyan, or Calvinistic, explanation of Universalism

Richard Eddy, one of the most prominent Universalist clergymen of the 1800s wrote a two-volume history of Universalism in which he reports that at the session of the New England Convention at Oxford, Massachusetts, in September 1794, a committee was formed to "compose a short piece, simplifying a system of religion adapted to the capacity of children, to instruct them in the first rudiments of the gospel of Christ." In 1787 a twenty-four page catechism was written by Shippie Townsend of Massachusetts for the instruction of children in the churches. Of the catechism, Eddy writes: "He [Townsend] wrote it, he says, 'having been requested by some worthy friends to endeavor to put into their hands something in this way as an assistant in instructing their children.' Possibly this request may refer to the vote of the Convention. The catechism presents the Rellyan theory of Universalism."[29]

In the early 1800s children were expected to memorize New Testament passages, and, as Russell Miller notes, in 1821 Universalist children were assigned Hosea Ballou's *Child's Scriptural Catechism* to learn. The first edition of this catechism had been published in 1810 in Portsmouth, New Hampshire.[30] There were seven editions of this catechism published throughout the years between 1810 and 1837 which reflect Ballou's evolving theology as it emerged into the Ultra Universalism he espoused by the 1830's. In the 1860's the Reverend Dr. John Coleman Adams's *Universalist Catechism* was published in *The Helper*. In 1862 *The Child's Pictorial Scripture Questions Book, designed fort the Smaller Children in Sabbath Schools* by Minnie S., Davis was published by the Universalist Publishing House.

In 1865 the Rhode Island Convention "caused a catechism to be prepared which has been very widely used among us, known as the *Rhode Island Catechism*."[31] Excerpts from Ballou's 1810, 1819, and 1937 *The Child's Scriptural Catechism* versions and the *Rhode Island Catechism* of 1877 show the movement of Universalist theology during those years, and how it was conveyed to children. The *Rhode Island Catechism* reflects the Restorationist theology espoused by some of the clergy in Rhode Island dating from the Restorationist Controversy of the 1830's. The 1841 *The Christian Catechism: designed for the use of the Sabbath Schools* exhibits further development in the use of catechisms specifically within the Universalist Sabbath schools.

During the 1820s Universalist associations and state conventions began the work of forming Sunday schools but the first official encouragement from the General Convention, which was organized in 1833, did not come until 1840. By 1842 two Sunday school publications were established, *Light of Zion* and *Sabbath School Contributor* (which became the *Gospel Teacher and Sabbath School Contributor*), published in Boston; a third, the *Eastern Rose Bud*, was published in Maine. Others followed throughout the 1850s and 1860s. In the 1860s Caroline A. Soule edited *The Guiding Star*, a Sunday paper for boys and girls that was used in over half of the Universalist Sunday Schools having a circulation of 10,000. *The Sunday School Helper* was a monthly magazine published in Chicago, Boston, and New York City that provided guidance in uniform lesson planning for teachers, which Russell Miller points out, "was stoutly resisted by many."[32] *The Myrtle* was a Universalist paper for children; first published in 1851 and in wide use for over thirty years but was not discontinued altogether until 1924. In 1861 a recommendation was made that a set of graded textbooks be prepared for use in the Sunday schools, but this recommendation was not acted upon by the denomination until 1901. During this time from 1872 until 1901 the Universalist Sunday schools used *The International Uniform Lesson Plan* of the evangelical Protestant denominations. Clinton Lee Scott documents a graded series published by the Universalist Publishing House in 1901 titled *The Universalist Graded Lessons,* a Bible-centered course of study that contained extra-biblical materials as well. "A series of Manuals for adult use, edited by Revs. D. M. Hodge, F. W. Perkins and J. F. Tomlinson, based on the best known knowledge of the Bible, were a new development in addition to the International Lessons."[33] In 1912 the Universalists published *The Murray Graded Sunday School Lessons* a biblical curriculum based on the Higher Biblical Criticism, Progressive educational theories, and Darwin's theories of evolution advanced in Universalist educational and theological circles.

This listing is very brief considering that Richard Eddy listed in the bibliography to *Universalism in America: 1636-1800* 778 volumes, books, pamphlets, and periodicals published by the Universalists prior to 1870. The Sunday school publications listed were ones widely used by the Universalists and in circulation for many years.

The Hon. Henry B. Metcalf, Universalist layman, president of the General Convention of the Universalist Church of America (1891-1895), vocal temperance advocate, and successful businessman, reminiscing on the Universalist Sabbath School Union's fiftieth anniversary celebration in *The Universalist Leader* reported:

> In 1851 Universalists formed the Universalist Teachers' Union, which
> in 1856 took the name The Universalist Sabbath School Union when it
> was incorporated by a special act of the State of Massachusetts. Those

serving on the board of this Union in 1851 included Alonzo A. Miner [1814-1895] and Henry B. Metcalf [1821-1904]. The Rev. Dr. Miner, who became the second President of Tufts in 1861 was one of the Directors of the individual Sunday schools in the Union and was representing the Second school of the eleven schools in the Union. The Rev. Dr. Metcalf served as recording secretary.[34]

In 1902 when recalling the work of the Universalist Sabbath School Union's fifty years, Dr. Metcalf made these observations:

> I trust that I may be permitted to express the conviction that in the revolution that brought about these changes, [referring here to the organizing of Universalist educational institutions, the publishing house and the General Convention] the Universalist Sabbath School Union was distinctly a pioneer promoter....In the religious world, we of the Universalist Church of 1851 knew very little of tolerance or respect from any other sect of Christians, although today they have appropriated to their own use the principles for whose promulgation they condemned us, even forgetting to give us due credit....I express my conviction that no organic auxiliary to our church work has made such contribution to our Church's prosperity, as has the Universalist Sunday [*sic*] School Union....the fact remains that the key note of progress, struck by the Universalist Young People of 1851, in the organization of the Universalist Teacher's Union, has not been equalled [*sic*] in strength by any of the worthy efforts that have followed it....In 1851 the public religious work was vested organically, chiefly in the church and Sunday school.[35]

The field of religious education underwent dramatic changes in regard to the Sunday school in the time just before the Civil War and immediately following it. Jack Seymour refers to it as the move from the Sunday school to the church school. By this he means that the Sunday school moved from an institution outside the church whose focus was on religious and social redemption of children outside the individual churches to the church school which became an institution enfolded in the church and focused on the conversion and indoctrination primarily of its own children.[36]

In the mid-nineteenth century came an increased attention from the wider society on the Sunday school that was an impetus for such change within the Sunday schools. J. Paul Williams, in *The New Religious Education: A Challenge to Secular Education,* cites three reasons for this change: the rise of Protestant sects, immigration of Roman Catholics coming to America in the early stages of the Industrial Revolution, and the resulting anti-Catholic prejudice. These factors added to the eventual separation of church and state, specifically in educational matters. As noted earlier the common schools were finding it difficult to meet the religious education demands of the various religious groups. The increased rise of new religious groups within Protestantism and the rise in numbers of Catholics created an atmosphere of suspicion among the various emerging sects as they struggled to define what of religion could be included in the public educational arena. Universalism's theology of universal salvation was a specific expression of faith that was significant in this struggle to define acceptable religious teachings in the common schools, although it was not central. The result of this struggle was the Universalists' prolific expansion of their own schools. The rise of Roman Catholicism and the fragmentation of Protestantism were of more concern outside Universalism. Williams' book provides charts of the number of churches in the various denominations in the State of Massachusetts to support his claim of the dramatic increase in new religious ideas forming into organized religious sects that challenged a unified Christian message, and which became an important factor in the rise of the Sunday school. A quick glance at the chart shows Universalisms dramatic growth between 1800 and 1858 within the State of Massachusetts alone.

"The following data was taken from the United States Census of Religious Bodies for 1936, pp. 224 to 227." Williams' cites the census charts as follows:

1800 Mass. Church census		1858 Mass. Church census	
Sect	Number of Churches	Sect	Number of Churches
Congregationalists	344	Orthodox Congregationalists	490
Baptists	93	Episcopal Methodists	277
Methodists	29	Baptists	266
Episcopalians	14	Unitarians	170
Quakers	8	Universalists	135
Universalists	4	Episcopalians	65
Presbyterians	2	Roman Catholics	64

Roman Catholics	1	Christians	37
		Friends Meetings	24
		Free Will Baptists	21
		Protestant or Independent Methodists	20
		Second Adventists	15
		Wesleyan Methodist	13
		Swedenborgians	11
		Presbyterians	7
		Shakers	4
		Unclassified	12[37]

The Civil War, inclusive of the reasons that tore institutions and individuals apart before it broke out, added another dimension in the religious life of the nation. It was a crisis of self-identity that turned attention away from the religious fervor that had been generated by the Second Great Awakening. The churches were struggling with the split between North and South factions and expressions of faith within the denominations. As the war came to an end the churches began to discern what their role might be in healing themselves and the nation and re-establishing religion to a central place in the hearts, minds, and institutions of the people. They turned to the Sunday school as the place to begin.

Seymour describes this period of transition of the Sunday school to an institution within the church where the Sunday school focused on the "evangelization" and nurture of its own young. The concept of the church school as the "nursery of the church" came into play whereby it was seen as the entry point of potential new members and so the church school set about the task of nurturing future church members. The churches entered into a time of cooperative efforts in what Seymour calls 'pandenominational' evangelicalism. It was a time when Protestant denominations worked together to create a combined Christian voice to heal the brokenness of the churches, individual lives, and the nation.[38] William G. McLoughlin in his book *Revivals, Awakenings and Reform*, places the Third Great Awakening in the midst of this time period. This Awakening, as described by McLoughlin, from 1890 to 1920 sought to face the challenges of the times with a renewed Christian focus. "The prophets of the Third Awakening had to undertake an enormous rescue operation to sustain the culture. They had to redefine and relocate God, provide means of access to him, and sacralize a new world view."[39] By the early 1900's the progressive education movement began to have profound influence on the Sunday school movement beginning in 1903 with the formation of the Religious Education Association and ending with the depression in 1929.

Many Protestant Church Schools understood the need for child-centered curricula and pedagogy suited to children at different developmental stages, but in fact engaged in didactic, Bible-centered (or at least material-centered) curricula and pedagogy. Church school education was a very parochial enterprise and not yet the inclusive cultural experience espoused by progressive education.

What McLoughlin identifies as the Third Great Awakening was part of the historical context around this further development of the Sunday schools. The progressive education activity within the Third Great Awakening was seen as providing the means for the transformation of the social order. John Dewey (1859-1952) was a major leader in developing philosophical perspectives on progressive education and educational practice. Dewey's philosophy espoused his belief in humanity's ability to experience continued growth and learning. The religious quality of this experience he called "Common Faith." Dewey was greatly influential on the thinking related to education by modernist Protestant evangelicals. The clear prophets of the progressive religious education message were George Albert Coe (1862-1951) and Henry Frederick Cope (1870-1923). Coe was one of the founders of the Religious Education Association in 1903, and beginning in 1909 taught at Union Theological School while Dewey taught across the street at Columbia University in New York City. Coe struggled with his faith and historian Mary Boys writes of one such struggle that further prompted his move to an increasingly liberal theology.

[Coe's] encounter with Darwin in *The Origin of the Species* [sic] and *The Descent of Man* set off another crisis of faith, since Coe recognized the conflict between traditional religion and evolutionary theory. His subsequent resolution reveals his departure from the path taken by evangelicals: "I settled the question, as far as I was concerned, on a Sunday morning by solemnly espousing the scientific method,

including it within my religion, and resolving to follow where it
should lead." Coe himself acknowledged the critical nature of this
experience in an essay written late in his life: "I judge that the most
significant turning point in my life, religiously considered, was the
early turning away from dogmatic method to scientific method."[40]

Jack Seymour notes that Coe's work was a scientific pursuit of how religion formed
personal character and how that person then acted within the wider world to change
the social structures of the culture. Coe's central concern was to determine how
religion could shape the world. His vision of religious education was a harkening back
to the missionary components of the original Sunday school movement. Coe believed
the work of the Sunday school was broader than what took place on Sunday morning
in the churches. He wanted to reach out into the world and educate the culture. The
missionary components of the original Sunday school movement was just such a
reaching out into the community and world to educate those who were poor and
marginalized and who did not attend any church. Coe had studied in Germany like
many of the progressive and modernist theological leaders of the time. Seymour notes
that Coe

> wanted to express how Christian life could be more in tune with
> modern thought forms represented in scientific method, evolution, the
> theology of God's immanence, an 'exemplar' Christology, and a
> social interpretation of Jesus' teachings. For him, in modern Chris-
> tianity salvation occurred by education, rather than blind doctrinal
> acceptance or emotionalism. By salvation Coe meant the progressive
> transformation of the human personality to the divine will expressed
> in the social-ethical teaching of Jesus.[41]

Both Cope and Coe were advocates of the new progressive theories of education being
advanced within the progressive education movement by John Dewey and others.
Coe's contribution was to integrate liberal theology with progressive education. They
each understood education, both religious and secular, as being greater than the school
itself. It was an education of the whole child, the whole society; intellectually, spiritually, psychologically and, through the educational environment, physically. It was an
education aimed at changing the world and Universalists responded to these challenges
with what can only be described as reluctant enthusiasm. In principle these challenges

were consonant with their faith, but that old rugged individualism kept rearing its head to stave off concerted and unified efforts to bring about the changes these challenges required.

ENDNOTES

1. Anne M. Boylan, *Sunday School: The Formation of an American Institution 1790-1880* (New Haven, Conn.: Yale University Press, 1988), 6.

2. Arlo Ayers Brown, *A History of Religious Education in Recent Times* (New York: The Abingdon Press, 1923), 46, 47; George Herbert Betts, *The Curriculum of Religious Education* (Cincinnati: Abingdon Press, 1924), 66-69. And *The Encyclopedia of Sunday Schools and Religious Education,* eds. John T. McFarland and Benjamin S. Winchester, (New York: Thomas Nelson and Sons, 1915), 358-359.

3. Betts, *Curriculum of Religious Education,* 74; Brown, *History of Religious Education,* 49.

4. Richard Eddy, *Universalism in America, Volume I, 1636-1800* (Boston: Universalist Publishing House 1891), 300.

5. Boylan, *Sunday School,* 7.

6. *Ibid.,* 7, 8.

7. Henry B. Metcalf, Hon., "Early Days of the Universalist Sabbath School Union," Address in Columbus Avenue Church, Boston, 18, December, 1901, *The Universalist Leader* (Boston: Universalist Publishing House, 4 January 1902, 14.

8. *Ibid.,* 10.

9. *Ibid.,* 55.

10. P.M. Leavitt, *Souvenir Portfolio of Universalist Churches in Massachusetts* (Universalist Publishing House, 1906) 112

11. Lewis B. Fisher, *A Brief History of the Universalist Church* (Boston: Young People's Christian Union, 4th ed., rev., 1904), 17-18.

12. Eddy, *Universalism in America, Volume II, 1801-1886* (Boston: Universalist Publishing House, 1886), 416.

13. Sydney E. Ahlstrom, *A Religious History of the American People* (New Haven, Conn.: Yale University Press, 1872), 149, 295; William G. McLoughlin *Revivals, Awakenings, and Reform,* (Chicago: University of Chicago Press, 1978), 86.

14. "On September 14, 1785, a convention was held in Oxford, Massachusetts,....A Charter of Compact was adopted....The number of annual meetings held by this convention is uncertain, but in 1793 and from then on for a period of nearly one

hundred years this convention continued to meet annually. This body, usually known as the New England Convention, in 1804 changed its name to The General Convention of Universalists in the New England States and others. Again in 1833 the name was changed to the United States Convention of Universalists. It was this organization which in 1866 was chartered under the laws of the state of New York as the Universalist General Convention." Clinton Lee Scott, *The Universalist Church of America: A Short History* (Boston: Universalist Historical Society, 1957), 29.

15. John Coleman Adams, *Universalism and the Universalist Church* (Boston: Universalist Publishing House, The Murray Press, 1915), 65-66.

16. Scott, *The Universalist Church of America*, 78-79.

17. Richard Eddy, *Universalism in America, Volume II, 1801-1886,* (Boston Universalist Publishing House, 1886) 411-446.

18. *Ibid.*, Vol. II., 448.

19. Russell Miller, *The Larger Hope: The First Century of the Universalist Church in America: 1770-1870* (Boston: Unitarian Universalist Association, 1985), 421.

20 . Scott, *Universalist Church of America,* 79. See also, Eddy, *Universalism in America,* Vol. II, 469, 470.

21   Scott, *Universalist Church in America,* 82.

22   Eddy, *Universalism in America, Vol. II,* 461, 465.

23 J. Paul Williams, *The New Education and Religion: A Challenge to Secularism in Education* (New York: Association Press, 1946), 46, 47.

24. *Ibid.,* 49.

25. Robert Lynn, *Protestant Strategies in Education* (New York: Association Press, 1964), 22, 24.

26. Boylan, *Sunday School,* 79.

27. Fisher, *A Brief History of the Universalist Church,* 182, 189.

28. Bonnie Hurd Smith, *From Gloucester to Philadelphia: Thoughts from the 18th Century Letters of Judith Sargent Murray with a Biographical Introduction* (Gloucester, Mass.: Curious Traveler Press, 1998),

29. Eddy, *Universalism in America, Volume I,* 432

30. Russell Miller, *The Larger Hope, Volume I,* 276.

31. Fisher, *A Brief History of the Universalist Church,* 126, 127.

32. Miller, *The Larger Hope: The First Century of the Universalist Church,* 278.

33. Scott, *Universalist Church of America* 49.

34. Henry B. Metcalf, Hon., "Early Days of the Universalist Sabbath School Union," Address in Columbus Avenue Church, Boston, 18, December, 1901, *The*

Universalist Leader (Boston: Universalist Publishing House, 4, January, 1902), 14.

35. *Ibid.*, 14-15.

36. Jack Seymour, *From Sunday School to Church School* (New York: University Press of America, 1982), viii.

37. J. Paul Williams, *The New Education and Religion: A Challenge to Secularism in Education* (New York: Association Press, 1946), 38-40.

38. Seymour, *From Sunday School to Church School,* viii-ix.

39. William G. McLoughlin, *Revivals, Awakenings, and Reform* (Chicago: University of Chicago Press, 1978), 152.

40. Mary Boys, *Educating in Faith* (Kansas City, Mo., Sheed and Ward, 1989), 49-50.

41. Seymour, *From Sunday School to Church School*, 133.

CHAPTER THREE

Modernism Challenges Education, Religious Education, and Protestantism

Modernism, as applied to religion in the United States, is a term widely used in describing a wide range of ideas, movements, theological trends, individual thinkers, and Protestant denominations. Sydney Ahlstrom notes that it is sometimes known as liberal theology, new theology, or even progressive orthodoxy, and that biblically the Sermon on the Mount was often regarded as the central message to be preached and lived.[1] It refers to a movement in the 1880s to the 1920s in which science and religion were seen as natural parts of the world, in contrast to religion's tendency to refer to a realm transcendent to the world.

In the 1860s the advent of Modernism and the outbreak of the Civil War produced dramatic changes in religious life throughout American evangelical Protestantism. Where religion and theology had held central authority in biblical interpretation, the prevailing world view of creation, and the source of human good and evil as its consequences now new disciplines of study and the realm of ideas stretched beyond previously held boundaries. Struggles of authority on these matters emerged into a stated war between science and religion. Scientists and theologians vied for the minds of humanity with their own and opposing claims to truths.

Charles Darwin's *Origin of Species* was published in 1859, and by the 1880s and 1890s its influence was evident in books, sermons, periodicals, and tracts as a challenge to fundamental tenets of faith. The challenges came at every level: the account of creation, moral law in the idea of the survival of the fittest, and millennial beliefs with their description of nature as amoral and purposeless. The challenges created for many a crisis of faith in the 1890s and a subsequent loss of confidence in divine support of the fundamental beliefs.[2]

In Darwinian terms, human beings were merely advanced animals not made in the image of God and not destined for Heaven or Hell. In this worldview, humans were a struggling part of a neutral and natural environment that did not, as Mark Noll points out, give evidence of the existence of God in creation.[3] Darwin's assertions dispelled the logic of the "Argument from Design," a proposition that the world and creation could not be explained except by the kind of creating and sustaining God who is found in the Bible. In contrast to such a God, Englishmen Herbert Spencer and Thomas Huxley suggested that Darwin's theories of evolution provided a whole philosophy of life in which humanity progressed from a simple more primitive being and social state into a more complex one. In that construct, Christianity was placed in the simpler more primitive scope of reality and the more advanced beings had moved beyond it to a scientific and more advanced reality. John Dewey joined this cadre of thinkers and embraced it within his vision of a future made noble by science. This rise in the scientific theory of creation and evolution shook the foundations of the churches. For many Christians, the sciences engaged in blasphemy in calling the literal interpretation of the Genesis creation account into question. For others, however, the rise of science and the theory of evolution caused them to formulate new theological and intellectual ideas. Intellectual leaders in the nation's most influential universities began to support Darwin's theories. Asa Gray, a Harvard botanist, insisted that the theory of evolution was compatible with God's design of the universe. Princeton's president from 1868 to 1888, the Presbyterian James McCosh felt that traditional Christian theology and evolutionary scientific theory could be integrated into a belief in God with a belief in some form of evolution.[4]

In Universalist scholarly circles one name among many stands out as a major voice formulating new theological understandings. Dr. Orello Cone, while president of the Universalist- established Buchtel College in Akron, Ohio, published an article in the *Universalist Quarterly* in 1882 titled "Science and Religion," in which he outlined his argument that science and religion can strengthen one's belief in God, or the First Cause, through scientific research and theory. Cone believed that the new understandings of the universe only expanded the magnificence of the Creator of that universe. He was fascinated with the scientific discoveries of the relationship between energy and matter, and of the absurdity of any thought that something should come from nothing. Cone wrote:

> In the presence of the problem of the origin of things science is dumb.
> Out of the voiceless mystery of being it has won no revelation.
> ...Hence, far from coming into conflict with religion, far from
> drawing any conclusions hostile to it, science has only prepared the
> problem for the consideration of a religious philosophy, has even

contributed as much as lies in its power to establish the postulates of religion.[5]

For Cone, science helped lay a foundation for religion rather than prove that religion was false:

> The religious teacher should remember that there is much truth in the
> realm of science which no one is so well qualified to elucidate as he
> who gives all his thought to the study of physical phenomena, and that
> all truth should be welcomed by every lover of his kind. And the
> student of science should not forget that there is a realm of spirit, the
> facts and phenomena of which are as real and as much entitled to
> recognition as those with which he deals.[6]

Universalists were engaged early in the issues of modernism's struggles between science and religion as cited by Russell Miller in *The Larger Hope, The Second Century of the Universalist Church of America, 1870-1970.* The Universalists engaged in the scholarly discourse and were well disposed to being open to the intellectual currents that surrounded them. It was within this Universalist climate of rationalism, inquiry, and biblical critique that the discourse with science occurred with Orello Cone as a central intellectual figure.

Cone effectively reconciled science and religion on a theistic basis and added the support and authority of biblical criticism to his work. He was primarily an historical biblical critic but drew on source, literary, and tradition criticism as well. Cone explored the theories of evolution in connection with the creation stories in Genesis and discovered theological formulations there that demonstrated the supportive compatibility of science and religion. In a further weaving of evolutionary theory and biblical interpretation he held that the evolutionary progress of humankind was essentially the progressive revelation of the divine in the natural and human worlds. It is likely this conclusion was enriched by his study of Friedrich Schleiermacher, who also understood religion and the natural world to be one. Cone believed that for humankind to comprehend God's revelation, both revelation and humanity must evolve together. It was a human developmental process and a theological process that moved together through human and creation's history. Dr. Cone posited that science gave to religion the method of creation, not the explanation of it. For Cone, the initial divine act of creation by God was not negated by evolutionary theory that put millennia of time between that creation and the emergence of human life on earth. Of this he wrote:

> [S]cience, remaining as it does, in its own field of physical phenomena and facts, infringes neither upon the domain of religion, nor that of a theistic philosophy. For a supersensible cause being the postulate of religion, the removal of this cause through aeons of time from its effect, and the production of that effect by a process of evolution involves no denial, either of the cause, or of its efficiency.[7]

With this theological movement Universalists turned to biblical scholarship and worked to create a firm foundation upon which to build a scientific approach to biblical truths. They were ready to participate in the scientific study of the bible. Beginning in the mid 1800s German theologians put biblical texts to the scrutiny of critical analysis and placed the Bible in the realm of scientific study. This threatened the religious world at its most traditional foundation. The Universalists were firmly grounded in the Bible and so were sorely challenged by the new historical and literary criticism of Scripture. By 1899 they found it necessary to revisit their statement of faith in order to respond to these challenges. The 1803 Winchester Profession had been altered in a large number of local congregations to reflect newer theology of the modernist movement and its concern with biblical criticism, evolution, a social gospel, and progressivism. Orello Cone, while he was professor of biblical literature at St. Lawrence Theological School between 1867 and 1899 was involved in the long process of bringing about a denomination-wide change to the Universalist Winchester Profession, the statement of faith Universalists had adhered to since 1803, but with increasing dissent. Cone was a member of the committee commissioned to draft the new statement, but he confessed he had not, as he had done with earlier drafts, contributed to nor read the final draft before signing it. A severely altered statement included the original first three articles of the 1803 Winchester Profession, but added the following principles:

The conditions of fellowship shall be as follows: The acceptance of the essential principles of the Universalist faith, to wit:

1. We believe in the Universal Fatherhood of God;

2. The spiritual authority and leadership of His Son, Jesus Christ;
3. The trustworthiness of the Bible as containing a revelation from God;
4. The certainty of just retribution for sin;
5. The final harmony of all souls with God.

> The Winchester Profession is commended as containing these principles, but neither this nor any other precise form of words is required as a condition of fellowship, provided always that the principles above stated be professed. The acknowledgment of the authority of the General Convention and assent to its laws.[8]

The first sentence of the closing paragraph became known as the "liberty clause" and was evoked many times in the ensuing century of theological pluralism within Universalism. The second sentence acknowledged that authority be given to the General Convention of the Universalist Church of America in 1833.

Clinton Lee Scott writes of the liberty clause:

> For sixty-seven years, during which some churches adopted the Winchester Profession and some did not, there was no serious controversy over it. Then in 1870 it was incorporated into the organic structure of the General Convention with the "liberty clause" deleted. This was a period of organization, and of an overdue effort to bind together the loose ends of the Church. There seems to be no doubt that from 1870 to 1899, when the Five Principles were adopted at Boston, and the "liberty clause" re-instated, it was intended that the Winchester Profession be used by fellowship committees as an instrument for preserving theological regularity.[9]

Scott further comments that during the time the liberty clause was suspended the Universalist Church used its absence to dis-fellowship Minneapolis minister Herman Bisbee on the grounds he did not conform to the Winchester Profession.[10]

With its reinstatement the so-called "liberty clause" gave the rugged individualists among the Universalists the privilege and ability to state these principles in any wording they chose, but gave authority to the governing body of the General Convention of the Universalist Church of America to assert its laws. This action was done to justify calling themselves a liberal church because it affirmed the claim that they stood on principles and not on any fixed creedal statement.[11]

Dorothy Spoerl notes that "By 1899 the whole principle of interpretation and biblical criticism had entered and we came to accept the 'trustworthiness of the Bible as containing a revelation from God.'"[12] Spoerl implies that the use of the higher criticism in biblical scholarship provided a greater trustworthiness to biblical interpretation for Universalists.

Along with Orello Cone the most prominent voices speaking for the challenges of Modernism in Universalist circles were those of John Coleman Adams (1849-1922) and Marion D. Shutter (1853-1939). Universalist historian Ernest Cassara notes that Universalists, because of their use of reason in religion and their liberal heritage, chose to meet the Modernist challenges of Darwin's theories of evolution, the Higher Biblical Criticism and the Social Gospel theology head- on.[13] Universalists came through this era for the most part unscathed. Cassara further notes that Universalists engaged in debates and conversation on Darwin's theories and the new evidence in geology. John Coleman Adams, one of Universalism's prominent ministers and voices in religious education for the denomination, in his book *Universalism and the Universalist Church*, writes of the new theology emerging within Universalism:

> The trend in scientific thought, for example, has been steadily toward
> the assertion of the spiritual origin of things, of a soul at the heart of
> nature, of mind as the source or basis of matter, not matter as the basis
> of mind. In cordial response to this doctrine, Universalism affirms its
> belief in the biblical truth, "God is a Spirit." Science presents to the
> mind the unity of law, of force, of all the processes of creation.
> Universalism asserts the unity of the destiny of the moral world, the
> world, in other words, of souls and wills. So it appeals to science as
> sanctioning, at least, its faith in the united destiny of mankind. Science
> affirms a vast law or principle of progress, the steady advance of all
> life to higher levels and to greater efficiency. The Larger Faith reads
> in human history a constant, unending, upward struggle, pointing to a
> time when good shall prevail over evil, when holiness shall conquer

sin, and all things be brought into harmony with the will and purpose
of almighty God....The doctrine of evolution has reinforced the
Larger Faith at a hundred points, and still the end is not.[14]

Russell Miller notes that Adams affirmed evolutionary theories as supportive of
Universalist faith in the abilities of humankind as worthy of God's love and salvation.
When Adams wrote the introduction to the fourteenth edition of Hosea Ballou's
Treatise on Atonement in 1902 he made several points of connection between the ideas
of Ballou and those of Harvard botanist John Fiske, a well known and respected
popularizer of Darwinism.[15]

In the 1890s Marion D. Shutter, minister at the Church of the Redeemer, the largest
Universalist Church in Minneapolis, had written and delivered a series of lectures to
his congregation on topics supporting the teachings of modern science, and particu-
larly the theory of evolution. Russell Miller noted that between one thousand and
twelve hundred people attended the lectures over the course of the series. At the urging
of John Fiske, Shutter published the lectures as the book *Applied Evolution*. The book,
dedicated to Fiske, was published by the Universalist Publishing House in 1900 and
advertised widely in the *Universalist Leader*. Miller notes that Shutter "stressed the
steady evolution of religious ideas from primitive and inchoate beginnings. The
evolutionary climax was to be found, more than coincidentally, in the Universalist
conception of a God of love."[16]

The dominant Protestant creation story held that males and females were created in
the image of God, but then "fell" into sin because of the actions of Adam and Eve in
the Garden of Eden. In contrast, Shutter wrote:

> that man [*sic*] has risen and not fallen; that he did not begin perfect
> and deteriorate; but he began low and imperfect, and has been slowly
> but surely gaining in character and moral power.[17]

Jesus, then, for Shutter, is fully human and an ideal model of human moral and
spiritual evolution. He is the climax of "the religious genius of the Jewish nation...its
highest example and illustration." For Shutter, Jesus' example and teachings were a
call to do likewise. To act on a higher sense of social justice was the essence of salvation. Shutter believed that "God was not external to nature but was inside of it; man is

himself a part of nature" and that "we must find God also in him [man], predominantly in him [man]." Science and religion were compatible in Shutter's belief that the laws of gravitation and of evolution were but the manifestation of "the divine method of originating and developing the universe itself." Shutter believed that God was equated with "a system of things pervaded by unity and order...the universality of law [and] the continuity of the processes of nature." These had abolished for Shutter the old formulations of the "Argument from Design" of the more orthodox Protestants. "Science had provided a 'larger and grander teleology...an aim and plan of wider sweep and more majestic conception.'" The capstone for Shutter was the Universalist faith in a God defined by Shutter as the "Eternal Goodness." Shutter expressed a belief not only in the unity and order of the processes of nature, but also in the inherent and eternal goodness of creation. His modernist ideas of the immanence of God, evolutionary theories, Biblical Criticism and the Social Gospel provided Universalists with a strong voice in the changing times at the end of the nineteenth century.[18]

Within the wider religious world Protestants were the most profoundly affected by the challenges of Modernism. Those coming from the Higher Biblical Criticism were most difficult to meet because since the time of the Reformation Protestants had rejected as the foundation of their faith the Catholic reliance on tradition in favor of reliance on a biblical foundation. The impact of the German Higher Biblical Criticism challenged Protestant theology and biblical interpretation, and it became increasingly prominent in scholarship as the movement that came to be known as Modernism spread. Edwin Gaustad writes:

> While Protestantism suffered most in seeking or resisting accommo-
> dation to this bitterly barbed edge of modernity, neither Catholicism
> nor Judaism escaped their persisting, nagging force of a 'criticism'
> directed against that which had heretofore been immune to all
> criticism.
>
> The results of this sharply focused fight are incalculable, for the battle
> goes on. But quite early one witnessed bruising confrontation and
> sweeping condemnation. One also witnessed, however, a rebirth of
> biblical investigation, translation, and interpretation. New societies
> were born, new commentaries provided, new archaeological expedi-
> tions undertaken, and a new intensity in searching the scriptures

displayed on both sides. For liberals and conservatives alike, the question of what one did with and said about the Bible was insistent, adamant, and impossible to shake.[19]

These upheavals created the need for the Protestant denominations to clarify for themselves who and what they were as faith communities. The religious communities struggled with what was to be their response as a unique system of faith to this world of ideas surrounding them. Would they align themselves with the movements of Modernism or hold fast to the orthodoxies of their faith and traditions that had served them for centuries?

In this heady mix of ideas at the turn of the nineteenth century and into the twentieth, the modernist progressive movement's influence on philosophy, education, and democracy were making their impact through the work of John Dewey, among others. Dewey reflected on these challenges and changes when he wrote in 1934:

> The impact of astronomy not merely upon older cosmogony of religion but upon elements of creeds dealing with historic events — witness the idea of ascent to heaven - is familiar. Geological discoveries have displaced creation myths which once bulked large. Biology has revolutionized conceptions of soul and mind which once occupied a central place in religious beliefs and redemption, and immortality. Anthropology, history and literary criticism have furnished a radically different version of the historic events and personages upon which Christian religions have built. Psychology is already opening to us natural explanations of phenomena so extraordinary that once their supernatural origin was, to say, the natural explanation.
>
> The significant bearing for my purpose of all this is that new methods of inquiry and reflection have become for the educated...today the final arbiter of all questions of fact, existence, and intellectual assent. Nothing less than a revolution in the seat of intellectual authority has taken place.[20]

The Progressive Movement began in part as a response to the plight of the social conditions of the mid-to late 1800s. A large influx of East and Southern European immigrants and the increased movement into cities caused great social unrest during the late 1800s. The evangelist Dwight L. Moody's revival message [taken from poet Robert Browning] that "God's in His Heaven, all is right with the world" no longer addressed the needed hope for the new immigrants, the poor and marginalized who worked hard and stayed sober. The Protestant work ethic embedded in Calvinistic theology did not support the poor or the urban people who were out of work. Historian William G. McLoughlin states that in New York City alone, 50,000 people were out of work in 1875. New theological interpretations of the social and scientific changes were needed. At the same time, populist sentiments were increasingly calling for community transformation and better life conditions for all.[21]

The Progressive Movement embodied a radical faith that culture could be democratized so that everyone could share in the benefits of the new knowledge and advancements in the industrialization that was flooding America. Progressive ideas made their mark on philosophy, education, religion, social science, scientific inquiry and discovery, evolutionary theories, and psychology. They were woven into the modernist, liberal Protestant world through an altered understanding of revelation, human development, and education as a movement toward the common good of all.[22]

William Torrey Harris, superintendent of the St. Louis public schools from 1868 to 1880 and United States Commissioner of Education from 1889 to 1906, set out to further the vision of public education set forth by Horace Mann by incorporating insights he gained from the work of the philosopher Georg W. F. Hegel. From Hegel's rationalism and the work of Horace Mann's common public school system, Harris was to bring a rational order to public education and to recognize the context in which it occurred. Historian Lawrence Cremin writes that "Harris understood that the child is molded by family, church, civil community and state before he [or she] ever comes to school, and their influence continues unabated during his [or her] years as a student."[23] In the final analysis, Harris recommended a system of graded schools to better meet the needs of the huge influx of students with vast differences of culture, language, skills, and intelligence. Harris espoused the idea that education was life-long because he saw childhood schooling as preliminary to education for life as an adult. He advocated graded schooling to meet the differing developmental needs of the student and to enable the administration of a rational educational system. Because the school needed to meet the developmental needs of children from many different backgrounds and home environments, Harris believed it was necessary for the schools to be established on a sound rational system that provided structure for successful educating.

Religious education in the various Christian denominations was influenced by these struggles and the new visions arising for public education. Key intellectual leaders included John Dewey (1859-1952) in the broader secular educational field and George Albert Coe (1862-1951) in the field of religious education. Horace Bushnell (1802-1876) and Horace Mann (1796-1859) were forerunners from earlier decades who opened up religious education to include the nurturing of children and who organized widespread systems of common education.

The work of these men had significant impact on future Universalist religious education development. Horace Mann had provided grounding for educating the common populace to participate in democracy. He had given minority religions a freedom from indoctrination in public schools. Horace Bushnell's work on nurturing educational environments enabled Universalists to appreciate the need for child-centered curricula and to understand that faith involved, not conversion, but a child's growing within a Christian home and church environment. John Dewey's progressive, democracy-based educational theory and theology enabled Universalists to further their own concept of the child and the teacher as co-participants in the educational process in their Sunday schools. George Albert Coe brought liberal progressive education to the field of religious education and empowered Universalists to incorporate social gospel action in the curricula, child-centered pedagogy, and liberal theology in biblical curriculum. It was a social movement focused on education as the means to improve the lives of all Americans. In the mind of progressives, Cremin writes, there were at least three goals for this movement:

> To broaden the program and function of the school to include direct
> concern for health, vocation, and the quality of family and commu-
> nity life; to apply in the classroom the pedagogical principle derived
> from new scientific research in psychology and the social sciences;
> and a tailoring of instruction more and more to the different kinds of
> classes of children who were being brought within the purview of the
> school.[24]

Progressives hoped to achieve through these objectives a child-centered curriculum in the schools that met the needs of the children and their families to enable them to rise above poverty and to enjoy the benefits of the democratic society.

The Social Gospel and Liberal Theology

The Social Gospel developed within this Progressivism and Modernism in support of the working classes, and further weakened the revivalist's message that all one needed to do for salvation and a better life on earth was to buckle down and believe in God. Dwight L. Moody preached that the good times would return if only people believed in God's laws. But the good times did not return. Violence in the cities increased and the industrial revolution widened the gap between the rich and the poor, the business owners and the workers. This social condition, combined with the challenges to the "old time religion," brought about the rise of what William G. McLoughlin calls the "Third Great Awakening" in America. McLoughlin posits that for many evangelicals the coming of Darwinism, urbanism, Higher Criticism, the rise of labor unrest with its violent protests, and the dwindling numbers of self-subsistent farmers in rural America dashed the hopes and confidence in the old beliefs in God's plan for America.[25]

As the twentieth century dawned evangelical Protestant theology experienced a polarization of ideas described by historians as the "fundamentalist/modernist controversy." Modernists sought to place Christian faith within the framework of human society, a component of which led to the development of the Social Gospel movement best exemplified through its most articulate spokespersons, moderate Washington Gladden (1836-1918) and radical Walter Rauschenbusch (1861-1918). The Social Gospel was a central element of modernist theology along with intellectualism, scientific methods of inquiry and a human responsibility to act on one's faith. Darwinian theories grounded a new faith in the laws of nature and stripped it of its miraculous and transcendent core.[26]

Within Modernism's Social Gospel theology at the end of the 1800s, God's immanence was at work in human culture. Humanity was seen as responsible for its response to God's presence in working on behalf of the perfectibility of society. The insights and methods of higher criticism in biblical scholarship provided intellectual perspectives central to Modernism. Again, German scholarship provided a central influence for the whole movement. Mark Noll, in *A History of Christianity in the United States and*

Canada, notes that the teachings of church historian Adolf von Harnack influenced American scholars like A. C. [Arthur Cushman] McGiffert (1861-1933), historian of the early church and New Testament literature of Union Theological Seminary in 1917, and Shailer Matthews (1863-1941) dean of the Divinity School at the University of Chicago as they espoused their main tenets of modernism or liberal theology as the centrality of the life of Christ, a commitment to a 'scientific history' and allegiance to social ethics.[27]

Von Harnack was part of the Ritschlian School that focused the liberal movement on the centrality of Christ in Christian theology. This movement brought Schleiermacher's cultural and religious synthesis into the scientific modernist age with the distinct Christian message as embodied in the life of Christ in history. Matthews was seen by historian William R. Hutchison as the most prominent respondent to the fundamentalists' charges against liberalism during the 1920s that its theology was not true to Christian doctrine. Hutchison writes that

> the first and central response was that modernistic liberalism not only
> is Christian but also is actually closer than its rivals to the genius of
> Christianity. The second was that unless Christianity can present
> people with a liberal option, it cannot function in the modern world
> and probably cannot survive there.[28]

The modernist/fundamentalist controversy not only polarized orthodox and liberal factions within Protestantism, but created powerful struggles within local communities of faith, denominational bodies, and within individuals. The Protestant communities struggled with the theological challenges and began to articulate systematic responses to these modernist liberal or fundamentalist understandings. Within modernist liberal theology there was an optimistic view of human nature, of human perfectibility, and of the perfectibility of society as a whole.

The impact of Modernism and liberalism was pervasive in the Northeast and in the Protestant churches of Unitarians, Universalists, Methodists, Baptists, Episcopalians, Presbyterians (North), and Congregationalists. The movement, in the words of Sydney Ahlstrom, "carried forward what the Enlightenment had begun." "As their predecessors of the Enlightenment had done, liberals tried to avoid deterministic conclusions by arguments for the creative and autonomous nature of the human spirit."[29] It was a faith in the perfectibility of humankind and the social order to bring about the new Kingdom of God. William R. Hutchison, in *The Modernist Impulse in American Protestantism*, defined modernism as embodying three major aspects: "first and most notably...the conscious, intended adaptation of religious ideas to modern culture. Secondly, the idea that God is immanent in human cultural development and revealed through it, and third, that human society is moving toward realization of the Kingdom of God."[30]

Humankind was perfectible, society was redeemable, science and religion were compatible, and God was loving and empowering. By the 1920s Hutchison notes that this liberalism had spread significantly and "had become acceptable and reasonable in more than one third of the pulpits of American Protestantism and in at least one half of the educational, journalistic, social and literary or theological expressions of Protestant church life."[31]

Hutchison identifies at least two distinctive positions within liberal theology in the beginning of the 1900s, that of modernist liberals and evangelical liberals. For him the distinction was in the starting point and grounding loyalties of the two groups. "The evangelical liberal was a religious thinker who made the Christian revelation normative and then merely interpreted it in light of modern knowledge." For Hutchison, a modernist liberal was someone who made modern science his [sic] criterion and then, in a kind of afterthought, retained what he could of the Christian tradition."[32] Universalists were firmly rooted within Christianity and could be described as "evangelical liberals" during the late 1800s and early 1900s.

The counterpoint to the Modernism of the Third Great Awakening was what came to be known as fundamentalist ideas. Within the revival meetings and other religious gatherings of the Third Great Awakening (1890-1920) fundamentalism found some of its most ardent followers. Two well-known and outspoken preachers were Dwight L. Moody (1837-1899) and Billy Sunday (William Ashley Sunday, 1863-1935.) Mary Boys notes that Moody's three R's were, "Ruin by sin, Redemption by Christ, and Regeneration by the Holy Ghost." This world view was pessimistic; Moody viewed human nature as depraved and the world as wicked and wrecked. He viewed the theory of evolution as atheistic and therefore evil. Boys observes that fundamentalism

paradoxically embraced both a strong respect for intellect and a deep suspicion of it. Though much else might be said about the development of fundamentalism, this particular ambivalence toward knowing has important ramifications for the development of religious education....

Fundamentalism is best understood as a reaction to modernity, both in modernity's broad cultural manifestations and in its more specific appearance in the guise of progressive theology. Two intellectual movements in the mid-nineteenth century promulgated theories against which a "return to the fundamentals" would serve as a rallying cry. The first, new theories in geology regarding the antiquity of the earth and in biology regarding evolution, seemed to pit science against revelation, since these theories clashed with the biblical accounts of creation. The second, critical method or "higher" criticism — seemed to set in opposition a more technical, demanding way of interpreting Scripture and its plain sense. [33]

The fundamentalists got their name from a widely circulated set of twelve booklets entitled "The Fundamentals: A Testimony to the Truth," that were published between 1910 and 1915. They consisted of twelve volumes of faith defended by the evangelicals. These fundamentals, as summarized by Mark Noll, included the beliefs

> that the Bible is the inspired word of God; that Jesus Christ was God in human flesh, was born of a virgin, lived a sinless life, died on the cross for the salvation of men and women, rose from the dead, ascended into heaven, and would return at the end of the age in great glory; that sin is real, and not the product of fevered imaginations; that God's grace and not human effort is the source of salvation; and that the church is God's institution designed to build up Christians and to spread the gospel.[34]

Universalism often bore a significant portion of the brunt of the attack against liberalism by fundamentalists of the time. Universalists had embraced the higher criticism of biblical interpretation as well as the theories of evolution and findings of geology that dated the time of earth's beginnings millennia earlier than did the literal biblical interpretations of the fundamentalists. The Universalists were an easy target, and considered more blasphemous than other liberal religious groups because of their belief in universal salvation. The Universalist belief in salvation from God alone, not through Christ as Mediator, their audacity to argue that universal salvation was biblical, and their conviction that humanity was worthy of God's freely given salvation, were more than fundamentalists could tolerate. As John Coleman Adams stated, the doctrine of everlasting punishment was the keystone of American Orthodoxy, and a doctrine of universal salvation would not and could not be tolerated.[35]

The Higher Biblical Criticism

Universalists entered into the modernist discipline of the Higher Biblical Criticism as they studied the Bible in light of the challenges within Modernism. Higher Criticism became a central part of the work they did in the field of biblical interpretation used in educational materials used in their Sunday schools.

Source Criticism was the study of the sources of the material from which came the theories of the J, P, D, and E sources. The area of Form Criticism asked three questions as formulated by German theologian Hermann Gunkel (1862-1932). Werner Lemke, professor of biblical foundations at Colgate Rochester Divinity School, provides insight into utilizing Gunkel's methodology for critical biblical studies. Lemke

> proposed asking questions that discover, as Hermann Gunkel's Form Criticism would: What kind of material is this: saga, myth or legend? Why were these particular stories kept: did they serve some function in the life of the people, did it have a specific *sitz-im-leben* (setting in life) that made it important? How were these materials preserved in the ancient world, did they arise from an oral tradition?[36]

According to Lemke, Gunkel believed strongly in the existence of an oral tradition Walter Harrelson notes that Gunkel's approach to biblical form criticism was to understand the genre of the story and then it would be possible to ask the correct questions for it. For example, Gunkel stated that if Genesis is a saga then it is the story of the Hebrew people and not necessarily historically factual.

Historical criticism looked at the stages of development in the texts and the *sitz-im-leben* in which these stories took place. It studied the surrounding history and literature and religious rituals and worship practices of the people in pre-biblical and biblical times to set the context in which the Bible was written. Noth's own traditio-historical study provided an explanation of the process of the creation and development of the Bible. The tradition and historical form critic asks of a text:

> What was the character of this basic document or collection of traditions? How extensive was it? What theological outlook did it embody? What was its literary form? What function did it perform in Israelite life and worship?[37]

These forms of biblical criticism aided scholars in their study of the origins and development of the Bible. It gave theologians an understanding of the sources of the Bible's messages and provided a grounding for an interpretation relevant for the modern world. The power of the Hebrew laws, placed within the context of their time, enabled scholars to understand how these laws gave coherence to the Hebrew people as they struggled to understand their Covenant with God. By looking at the Bible through the Higher Criticism, theologians were able to better understand church doctrine and practices. Unlike the Lower Criticism which preceded it as a critique of the Bible based on Church doctrine, Higher Criticism began with the Bible, relating to doctrine and practice and thereby developing new theological understandings.

The study of Higher Criticism within Universalism was articulated by Dr. Orello Cone. Cone studied in Germany at the University of Berlin as did many of the modernist liberal scholars of the time. His first major work in the field of higher biblical criticism, *Gospel Criticism and Historical Christianity* was published in 1891. He refers to this work as Gospel-criticism, and within that approach, then, he utilizes historical, literary, and source criticism. In each of the chapters he sets the text and the canon itself into an historical perspective of place, time, culture, and individual writers. He then brings in the discipline of source criticism to evaluate the texts as to their authorship and authenticity. Cone notes in this book that "The historical treatment of the canon of the New Testament has never been regarded with favor from the dogmatic point of view, and is, indeed, of modern origin."[38] The dogmatic point of view Cone refers to is the fundamentalism that organized its refutation of the modernist impulse in the early 1900s, when liberal theology and modernism became a recognized threat to orthodox Christianity.

Utilizing the methods of scientific inquiry and Higher Biblical Criticism, Cone developed for Universalists the possibility of a theistic and scientific view of Scripture. He believed that scholarship in religion and in science did not oppose one another. He posited that science gave religion a method by which it could strengthen doctrine. For Universalism this was an opportunity to move with the evolving biblical criticism and the theory of evolution into the liberal religious mainstream and thereby remain a relevant religious movement into the twentieth century. Cone demonstrated that an intelligent understanding was possible between science and religion. His scholarship was respected in Europe because of his time of study at the University of Berlin from 1897 to 1898, because of his highly acclaimed English translation of a book by German theologian and higher criticism scholar Otto Pfleiderer, and through his own book, *Paul, the Man, the Missionary, and the Teacher*, published in 1898. His obituary noted:

> His first work in this field, *Gospel Criticism and Historical Christianity*,...was repeatedly declared by competent scholars to be the ablest work in its field that had, up to that time, appeared on this side of the Atlantic....While in London he published his chief work, *Paul, the Man, the Missionary, and the Teacher* (1898). This was pronounced by Dr. H. J. Holtzmann of Strasbourg, himself a foremost New Testament scholar, to be the ablest monograph on Paul and his teaching that had ever appeared in any language — an unusual encomium. [39]

Dr. Max Kapp of St. Lawrence wrote, I am venturing the hypothesis that Orello Cone was among the determinative pioneers who were responsible for the switch from Bible Universalism to the Universalism of the 'Higher Criticism.' Perhaps he may be called the pivotal personality in the change-over...[which] was as momentous as the change-over in Universalist Christology brought about by Hosea Ballou's *Treatise on Atonement*. [40]

The modernist theological and biblical leaders of the early twentieth century were called to develop new understandings of God and new theological formulations, while also working for new social orders. Leaders in many sections of the intellectual and civic worlds championed a theistic modernism that took evolution seriously within a progressive agenda. All of the following were influential in the development of the modernist movement in church and society: theologians and professors like Harry Emerson Fosdick at Union in New York; Orello Cone at St. Lawrence; James McCosh of Princeton; Walter Rauschenbusch of Second Baptist Church in New York City and later professor at Colgate Rochester Divinity School in Rochester, New York; Washington Gladden, a prolific author on the Social Gospel and minister of a large Congregational church in Columbus, Ohio, and Henry Ward Beecher of Plymouth Congregational Church of Brooklyn, New York; philosophers like John Dewey and George Albert Coe in New York, and William James at Harvard; scientists like Alfred North Whitehead and Asa Gray of Harvard; political scientists like Walter Lippman; humanitarians like Jane Addams; Universalists Clara Barton and Mary Livermore; and sociologists, economists and college presidents. [41]

Theistic evolutionists harmonized science and religion while progressive theologians reconciled revelation with the higher criticism of the Bible. Jesus, for these liberal Christians, or modernists, was the source of a new life of spiritual connection with God, the perfect embodiment of the human ideal. Through this belief evolved the impulse to improve the human condition in imitation of Jesus as a means of fulfilling God's promise and bringing in a social order of justice.

The movements within Modernism were to have a significant impact on the Universalists' theology and on the work done in their Sunday schools.

ENDNOTES

1. Sydney Ahlstrom, *A Religious History of the American People* (New Haven, Conn.: Yale University Press, 1972), 779.

2. Mark Noll, *A History of Christianity in America and Canada* (Grand Rapids, Mich.: William B. Eerdmans Publishing Company, 1992) 364-368.

3. Noll, *History of Christianity*, 367.

4. *Ibid.*, 371.

5. Orello Cone, "Science and Religion," *The Universalist Quarterly: General Review, New Series-Volume XIX, Article VI,* Thomas B. Thayer, D.D., ed. (Boston: Universalist Publishing House, 1882), 87-88.

6. *Ibid.*, 91-92.

7. *Ibid.*, 90.

8. John Coleman Adams, *Universalism and the Universalist Church* (Boston: The Universalist Publishing House, The Murray Press, 1915), 80, 81.

9. Clinton Lee Scott, *The Universalist Church of America: A Short History* (Boston:

The Universalist Historical Society, 1957), 41.

10. *Ibid.*, 41.

11. Lewis B. Fisher, *A Brief History of the Universalist Church for Young People*, (prepared by the Direction of the Young People's Christian Union, 1903 or 1904), 108-109.

12. Dorothy Spoerl, "We Do Not Stand We Move," *The Universalist Heritage* Harold Burkart, editor, (Syracuse, New York, The Quartier Group, 1993). 7.

13. Ernest Cassara, ed., *Universalism in America: A Documentary History of a Liberal Faith* (Boston: Skinner House, 1971). 35.

14. Adams, *Universalism*, 310.

15. Russell Miller, *The Larger Hope, The Second Century of the Universalist Church of America: 1870-1970* (Boston: Unitarian Universalist Association, 1985), 101,102.

16. *Ibid.*, 194.

17. *Ibid.*, 105.

18. Marion D. Shutter, quoted in Miller, *The Larger Hope*, 105-106.

19. Edwin S. Gaustad ed., *A Documentary History of Religion in America Since 1865* (Grand Rapids, Mich.: William B. Eerdmans Publishing Company, 1993), 310.

20. John Dewey, "A Common Faith," in Edwin S. Gaustad ed., *Documentary History*, 322.

21. William G. McLoughlin, *Revivals, Awakenings, and Reform* (Chicago: University of Chicago Press, 1978), 144.

22. Lawrence A. Cremin, *The Transformation of the Sunday School* (New York, Vintage Books Division of Random House, 1964).

23. *Ibid.*, 17.

24. *Ibid.*, viii.

25. McLoughlin, *Revivals, Awakenings, and Reform*, 142-145.

26. Ahlstrom, *A Religious History of the American People*, 769.

27. Noll, *History of Christianity*, 374.

28. William R. Hutchison, *The Modernist Impulse in American Protestantism* (Durham, N.C.:Duke University Press, 1992), 275.

29. Ahlstrom, *A Religious History of the American People*, 779.

30. Hutchison, *Modernist Impulse*, 2

31. *Ibid.*, 3.

32. *Ibid.*, 7.

33. Mary Boys, *Educating In Faith* (New York: Sheed and Ward, 1989), 24-25.

34. Knoll, *History of Christianity*, 381.

35. Adams, *Universalism and the Universalist Church*, 34, 35.

36. Werner Lemke, (class lecture on biblical foundations at Colgate Rochester Divinity School, October 7, 1980).

37. Walter Harrelson, *Interpreting the Old Testament* (New York: Holt, Rinehart and Winston, Inc., 1964).36

38. Cone, *Gospel Criticism and Historical Christianity* (New York: GP Putnam's Sons, The Knickerbocker Press, 1891), 31.

39. H.P. Forbes, *The Christian Leader* (Boston: Universalist Publishing House, 1905), 72.

40. Louis H. Pink and Rutherford E. Delmage, Eds, *Candle in the Wilderness St. Lawrence University...the First One Hundred Years* (Appleton-Century-Crofts, Inc., 1957), 39.

41. Noll, *History of Christianity.*

CHAPTER FOUR
Universalists on the Move Again

By the early 1900s Universalists had responded very well to the challenges of Progressivism and Modernism and were keeping apace with progressive changes in Protestantism, but they were never taken seriously as a legitimate expression of Protestantism by
the more orthodox evangelicals, especially by the so-called orthodox or fundamentalist
Protestants. Clinton Lee Scott notes that Universalist thinking had been moving
toward the use of reason, the reliance on scientific methods and an openness to new
truths that were characteristic of the liberalism of the time. These movements along
with the belief in universal salvation, which was considered anathema by the orthodox,
kept Universalists outside the evangelical community, but was not quite liberal
enough for admittance into the liberal community. While they had moved closer to
liberal thinking as a result of Modernism's challenges, they were not considered
liberal enough by the Unitarians, who were the main expression of liberal thought at
the time. Universalists were still attempting to remain within evangelical Protestant
circles as a liberal expression of evangelical theology. When Protestant denominations
began to develop curricula to augment or replace catechetical and rote learning, the
Universalists participated in the evangelical Protestant's efforts in religious education
materials, methodology, and teacher training.

Examples of Universalist efforts at organizing their religious education work can be
seen in the 23 September 1911 issue of the *Universalist Leader* where it was reported
that the Sunday School Association of the New York State Convention of Universalists
made a report of business and in the afternoon conducted a practical discussion and
later a round table. It did not, unfortunately, report the content, but the leader was J.
M. [John Murray] Atwood, D.D. [dean] of Canton Theological School [most likely
referring to St. Lawrence Theological School at Canton, New York].[1] In the *Leader's*
15 February 1913 issue it is reported that Mrs. Caroline C. Barney of Massachusetts
recently met with educators in Buffalo, Rochester, Syracuse, Little Falls, Troy, and
Brooklyn on topics of up-to-date Sunday school methods. Her work was under the
auspices of the New York Universalist Sunday School Association. Mrs. Barney

became the field secretary and state supervisor for the Massachusetts Universalist Sunday School Association. In that capacity she also visited Universalist churches to assist them with their religious education programs. She conducted teacher training workshops and brought curriculum suggestions with her.[2]

There were State Convention Sunday School associations or unions in the states where Universalism had grown organizationally into state conventions, but nothing that could be considered denomination-wide until the formation of the General Sunday School Association in 1913. For many years there had been a growing understanding that the religious education work within Universalism needed a central organization. There was no cohesive system for training teachers, making curriculum decisions, or supporting the church schools. Some of the State Conventions developed Sunday School Associations or Unions and sought assistance from the early efforts in Boston, as was seen with the visitations of Caroline C. Barney to New York State.

A meeting of Sunday school workers was called in July 1913 in Utica, New York, to discuss and consider ways in which interest in religious education could be revived within the denomination. From that gathering, Clinton Lee Scott recounts the emerging plans for a denominational organization for religious education and the resistance to it. In October 1913 in Chicago the Universalist General Convention gave formal approval to organize the General Sunday School Association.[3] the Rev. George E. Huntley resigned his position as professor at Saint Lawrence Theological School of St. Lawrence University to devote himself full time to the new association. He served as its executive director for sixteen years. Following him as director were Dr. A. Gertrude Earle from 1929 to 1931 and Miss Susan M. Andrews from 1931 to 1949. *The Christian Leader's* 23 October 1933 issues gives a chronology of the founding of the General Sunday School Association, Dr. (Gertrude) Earle introduced Dr. George E. Huntley in these words: "Who is so fitted to give us a glimpse of the past as the man who was our leader for sixteen years?"

> Said Dr. Huntley, referring jokingly to events of the convention, "I am a man who sometimes changes his position, so I will move to the head of the table."

> "It is a humiliating thought," he continued, "that before the G.S.S.A. was formed the ratings of the International Sunday School Association

put Universalists near the foot of the list. A General Convention (of Universalists) appointed a commission on religious education. The late Melvin S. Nash, a member of the commission, called a conference in Chicago in 1912 to see what could be done. Many suggestions were made, but one voice was raised that was prophetic. If anyone deserves to be called the founder of the General Sunday School Association it was a humble school teacher from Ohio, Marshall A. Brown. He rose on the floor of this conference in Chicago, and said that what was needed was a national organization to bring together all the forces dealing with religious education. A collection of $64.49 was taken up. When we met at Utica in 1913 with the convention of the Y.P.C.U. [Young People's Christian Union] we were all determined not to do the thing we did do. Carl A. Henry, chairman of the commission, went to Europe, but he wrote Francis A. Gibbs, who took his place, not to form a new national organization. We were called to order to kill the idea and we formed the General Sunday School Association. My candidate for president was Judge Field of Watertown, but he would not take it, so I was elected. F. Elwood Smith, who is present today, Francis Gibbs, and Mary Ballou helped draft the constitution. At the General Convention in the fall of 1913 in the list of those opposing a new organization, were almost all the trustees at the General Convention. There was living in Massachusetts then a trustee of the General Convention, Joseph L. Sweet. He went into the meeting of the trustees night after night and fought our battles. Eventually they decided that if we would leave 'finance' to them we could have our organization."[4]

Arguments for and against the establishment of the General Sunday School Association ran in *The Universalist Leader* (called *The Christian Leader* from 1879 to 1897 and again from 1926 to 1952 and *The Universalist Leader* from 1898 to 1925 and 1953 to 1961). Those against its formation advocated instead for a department of religious education of the Universalist Church and to make it a vital part of the General Convention, not a separate organization.

Universalist Sunday schools were in poor condition due to the lack of denominational organizations and support. This was reflected in, among other things, the lowest rating

of quality by the International Sunday School Association of the evangelical Protes-
tants. This rating was a source of humiliation to Huntley who had to meet with the
International Lessons Committee and acknowledge this status as being not only the
International Committee's opinion, but the Universalist reality as well.

Russell Miller recounts the frustration Huntley must have experienced:

> The Sunday school movement was [in the 1890s] disorganized and
> localized, and existed without a semblance either of uniformity or
> professionalism, using only untrained and unpaid volunteers and
> whatever teaching materials and techniques came to hand.

> In fact, Universalist Sunday schools had experienced a period of
> actual decline in numbers, size, influence and even respectability
> which lasted into the early twentieth century. The International
> Sunday School Association, in estimating the general "efficiency" of
> such organization, had placed Universalist Sunday schools below
> those of almost every Protestant denomination, low as many of them
> were....

> The idea of having a nationwide organization was first brought
> forward in definite form at a conference called by the Sunday School
> Commission which met in Chicago in 1912, with representatives from
> the Universalist Publishing House, the General Convention, and the
> theological schools. Of the some sixty individuals present, the only
> vote in favor of establishing a national Sunday school organization
> was cast by the maker of the motion.

> Not to be deterred, the proponents of the plan called a second
> conference which met in conjunction with the YPCU [Young
> People's Christian Union] in 1913, prior to the sessions of the General
> Convention.[5]

Support for this newly formed association was not uniformly forthcoming. Many did
not see its necessity, and some were concerned that the work of the General Sunday
School Association and the Young People's Christian Union would be in competition

for funds and for workers. In the 11 October 1913 issue of *The Universalist Leader,*
Brayton A. Field of Watertown, New York, wrote a plea to support the newly formed
General Sunday School Association. Field argued:

> The phenomenal progress of the Sunday school world, in which the
> Sunday school is coming to be appreciated as the most important part
> of church life, and is receiving so much merited, special attention, is
> due to the active organized life and work within the different denomi-
> nations and to the organized inter-denominational world constantly in
> progress.

> Our denomination also should be at the front in this, the most vital
> work of the church. The Sunday school is not for children alone, but
> for the people of all ages; and these ends can be attained and our
> Sunday schools brought to their proper efficiency only by working
> together in organized effort throughout the denomination to that end.

> The interests of our Sunday schools and denomination would be
> materially advanced by uniform courses of study, religious instruc-
> tion, methods, standards and teacher training, and call for united
> effort among us to organize, to attain those ends....

> The National Sunday School Association [*sic*] of our church was
> formed at Utica, New York, July last, by representative delegates of
> our denomination for that purpose and with adequate support it will
> attain that end.

> Let all who love our church support this organization and assist in
> adopting its constitution at the General Convention in Chicago.[6]

Field pleaded with Universalists at the convention to support the work done in
organizations such as the Religious Education Association and The International
Uniform Lessons System in which Universalists of the day were active participants.
He apparently was aware of the progressive education movement and hoped Universalists would support their General Sunday School Association and thereby enable the
denomination to become one of the leaders in the field of religious education develop-

ment. He asked the state conventions to work together in support of the national effort. This had not always been done due to the individualistic nature of the Universalists. Russell Miller commented in his book on the competition between the New York State Convention and the Massachusetts Convention over provision of quality programs within their respective states.[7]

Miller reports that in less than twenty years after the formation of the General Sunday School Association the decline in Universalist Sunday schools was reversed and instead showed an increase in numbers. Teacher training institutes had been established which greatly improved the quality of the schools. Miller further notes that:

> An important impulse which had resulted in the creation of the GSSA had come from chronic dissatisfaction over choice of curricular materials. The trustees of the General Convention had adopted the Bible-centered International Uniform Sunday School Lessons, widely used by Protestant churches and introduced in 1873. The lessons were published in the *Universalist Helper* (usually known simply as the *Helper*) which had been started in 1870 in Chicago by Samuel A. Briggs....Universalists by the late 1870s and early 1880s, were complaining that some of the material, reflecting orthodoxy, was not appropriate for denominational use, and called for material prepared by Universalists. Nothing was done, however, for many years to solve the problem.[8]

Clinton Lee Scott reports that the General Sunday School Association made a valuable contribution to the whole denomination, especially in the field of administration and methods of teaching that increased the quality of Universalist programs above the standards of many other Protestant denominations of the day. The General Sunday School Association operated during times of great pedagogical change and moved the Universalist curricula from Bible-centered to curriculum-centered to child-centered to experience-centered teaching during the 1920s and 1930s.[9] It made great strides in expanding the place of religious education within the local churches through enhancing the place of the child in the church, providing better space for classes, and providing for more assistance to parents for nurture in the home. The General Sunday School Association staff members increased their official visits out into the field to assist in the supervising of the local Sunday school as field visits were a major part of the GSSA's work.

As notable, however, was Scott's documentation of the Universalist religious education efforts in the area of summer institutes. Often these institutes were operated by
local Universalist women's groups, youth groups, or other agencies within the
church.[10] Each summer for one week the convention superintendent, the state Sunday
school superintendent, clergy, local Sunday school superintendents, Sunday school
teachers, and youth came together for workshops on teacher training and Sunday
school administration, to hear lectures given by ministers and field staff from GSSA
headquarters in Boston. The youth were part of these institutes and participated in
their programs and workshops while the adults were in their workshops. During meals
and free time there was interaction between youth and adults. These institutes in New
York, and throughout the country, were an important factor in the education and
leadership of the churches and were sponsored by the General Sunday School Association in cooperation with the State conventions.

Handwritten notes by Verna Carncross, a laywoman and member of the Church of the
Reconciliation (Universalist Unitarian) in Utica, New York (transcribed from *The
Evangelical Magazine and Gospel Advocate's* July 28, 1842, issue) gave the story of the
establishment of the *New York State Universalist Sunday School Society.* Carncross tells
of the organizational meeting of that society, held in 1842 in Utica. This society served
Universalists in New York State well into the next century.[11]

In 1947 Dr. Edna Bruner, president of the New York State Universalist Sunday School
Society and later, in1952-1954, director of the Department of Education for the Universalist Church of America, planned the first Summer Institute held at Oak Point. At the
17 October 1947 meeting, the Rev. John S. MacPhee, minister in Utica, New York, was
elected president. At the November 1947 meeting a summer institute commission was
named by the executive committee of the New York Convention of Universalists: for a
three-year term, the Rev. Howard B. Gilman of Little Falls, later to become superintendent of the New York State Convention and Verna Carncross; for a two- year term,
Mrs. Ruth Wallace, a laywoman from Betts Memorial Universalist Society in Syracuse,
New York; and for a one-year term, the Rev. Dr. Harold Niles, minister in Watertown,
New York. In 1947 the Sunday School Society changed its name to the New York State
Universalist Church School Association and voted to give its full-hearted support to
the Department of Education which had been authorized at the General Assembly of
the Universalist Church of America. A committee was appointed to study the organizing of a New York State Department of Education. In May of 1948 they were visited by

Margaret Winchester, field education worker from the General Sunday School Association. The meeting was held in Schuyler Lake, New York, and hosted by Mrs. Marie E. Strong, the Sunday school superintendent of the Old Stone Universalist Church in Schuyler Lake.[12]

In 1948 the General Sunday School Association was terminated by the Universalist Church of America's board of trustees in favor of establishing a department of education within the Universalist Church of America. The work of religious education was now seen as the work of the whole denomination and therefore was made a department of the central organization. The change of the names of various Sunday school and Church school associations and unions to that of religious education or Department of Education reflect the response to the progressive education concepts espoused by John Dewey and George Albert Coe, who believed that religious education was more than what took place on Sunday morning. It also reflected the idea of educating the whole congregation: children, youth, and adults. Edna Bruner was fond of referring to it as a "cradle to grave education."

As part of the more liberal attitude that had been emerging over the years between 1900 and 1930, Universalists had been making overtures for a possible alliance with the Unitarians. Clinton Lee Scott recounts the theological movement within Universalism that made such overtures tenable:

> In the 1930s controversy arose over the question of whether one who embraced humanistic convictions could honestly remain in the denomination....This controversy brought into the open a situation which for some time had disturbed many minds. There was an obvious trend in the Church toward an interpretation of Universalism which carried it beyond the historic, exclusive identification with Christianity. This tendency was disquieting to those who felt the need of preserving the inherited faith as solely within the circumference of the Christian religion. Past generations had believed that Universalism was not only Christian but that it was the original gospel of Christianity....Throughout their history Universalists consistently have defended their status as one of the Protestant denominations having, like other communions, their peculiar doctrinal distinctions....In contrast with efforts to secure and to maintain

recognition within the Protestant Christian order is the increasing
conviction that Universalism to be true to its inherent genius must
discover and embrace the values to be found in all religious
cultures....The theological differences existing within the Universalist
Church today are not mainly between reactionaries on the one had
and the progressives on the other. They are rather between those who
generally have moved beyond the Universalist position of recent
generations. Nor is the issue principally between those who hold
theistic opinions and those who are inclined to embrace Naturalistic
or Humanistic views....It is worthy to note that although Universalism in America developed from the Rellyan theology, there is
emerging a strong current of thought resembling the ideas which
characterized the religion of de Benneville and his
community....Whatever Universalism is to be, it will not be what it
has been.[13]

Gradually the Unitarian and Universalist youth and the religious educators moved
closer together and combined efforts. The Young People's Christian Union, at this
point named the Universalist Youth Fellowship (UYF), and the Young People's
Religious Union, at this point named the American Unitarian Youth (AUY), officially
joined in 1953 to form the Liberal Religious Youth (LRY).[14] The religious education
departments combined efforts in the 1940s and Universalist Churches used the New
Beacon Series developed in the 1940s under the guidance of Sophia Lyon Fahs of the
American Unitarian Association.[15]

The Council of Liberal Churches was formed by the Universalist Church of America
and the American Unitarian Association in 1953 to administer public relations,
education materials, and publications for the two denominations. Public relations and
publications did not succeed in merging, but the two departments of religious education became one Division of Education with the Rev. Ernest Kuebler, Unitarian, as the
first director.[16]

ENDNOTES

1. W. H. Skeels, Secretary, "New York State Convention of Universalists,
Rochester, New York," *Universalist Leader* (Boston: Universalist Publishing House,

September 23, 1911), 1214.

2. Universalist Leader (Boston: Universalist Publishing House, 15 February 1913), 210.

3. Clinton Lee Scott, *The Universalist Church of America: A Short History* (Boston: Universalist Historical Society, 1957), 50, 51.

4. George E. Huntley, *The Christian Leader* (Boston: Universalist Publishing House, 28 October 1933), 1363.

5. Russell Miller, *The Larger Hope: The Second Century of the Universalist Church in America: 1870-1970* (Boston: Unitarian Universalist Association, 1985), 212-213.

6. Brayton A. Field, Esq., *The Universalist Leader* (Boston: Universalist Publishing House, October 11, 1913), 1192.

7. Miller, *The Larger Hope, The Second Century.*

8. Miller, *The Larger Hope, The Second Century,* 214-215.

9. Scott, *Universalist Church of America,* 51.

10. *Ibid.,* 51.

11. Abner B. Grosch, ed., *Evangelical Magazine and Gospel Advocate* (Utica, N. Y.: 28 July 1842), 12.

12. Verna Carncross, (Handwritten notes given to this author in 1993).

13. Scott, *Universalist Church of America,* 45-46.

14. *Ibid.,* 70.

15. *Ibid.,* 55.

16. *Ibid.,* 53.

CHAPTER FIVE

The International Uniform Lessons System

Universalists participated in The International Uniform Lessons System from the 1870's to 1912. They were members of the committees developing the lessons, and were contributors to the discussions and decisions made. It is important to understand this system and how it influenced the work of Universalists in the mid-1800s.

By the 1860s in the wider religious community John H. Vincent, a Methodist minister aimed the attention of the local, state, and national evangelical Sunday School Conventions that had emerged from the American Sunday School Union in the 1850s on the training of teachers to end, in Vincent's words, "the false and injurious notion that *anybody* is competent to teach Sunday school."[1] These local conventions cooperated with the state normal schools in professionalizing the Sunday school teachers. The normal schools provided training for public school teachers, and the Sunday schools sought a comparable level of professionalism. The normal schools had begun in the 1830's through the influence of Horace Mann. In New York State many of these normal schools later became incorporated into the state's university system. New periodicals for teachers were published that differed from those of the American Sunday School Union in that they did not focus on the content of what was being taught, but on the methods and practice of teaching. This new focus on methods accented the convention's emphasis on interdenominational cooperation. The goal of each convention was to bring efficiency and professionalism to the areas where they labored in the Sunday school. This differed from the American Sunday School Union's broader goal to reform American society to its vision of a Christian America.

John H. Vincent, Methodist, Henry Clay Trumbull and Edwin W. Rice, both Congregationalists, worked for the American Sunday School Union; where they systematized Sunday school teacher training, encouraged the growing conventions, and regularized the Sunday school curriculum. Teacher training involved professionalizing the teachers, creating order in classrooms and introducing new techniques of teaching in the Sunday school. Edwin W. Rice, who was president of the First Day or Sunday

School Society and honorary editor for the American Sunday School Union, and author of *The Sunday School Movement 1780-1917 and the American Sunday-School Union 1817-1917*, had responsibility for the publications after 1875 and supervised production of lesson series and aids to teachers for Bible study. Henry Clay Trumbull was an active member of the International Uniform Lessons System and an early advocate for creating a separate series of Sunday school lessons for primary age children. John H. Vincent is credited by many authors of this era with being the inspiration for the use of the state normal school model to train Sunday school teachers. Vincent worked closely with Benjamin F. Jacobs of Chicago, in creating the International Uniform Sunday School Lessons System. These normal schools were made possible in part by the successes of the national and international Sunday-school conventions. By 1902 Vincent was a Methodist Bishop and still active in the work of the Sunday school.[2]

In the 1870's open hostility toward the American Sunday School Union focused on its organizational structure and strict doctrinal position. Organizationally, the union favored a centralized structure, whereas the conventions nurtured local systems. The doctrinal issue focused on the Union's lowest-common-denominator Protestantism and the conventions' more open, or even hands-off, policy on the rights of the specific religious beliefs held by the denominations involved in the American Sunday School Union.

The Bible was the sole resource acceptable for use in the Sunday schools by the American Sunday School Union, and from its beginnings in 1824, the method of teaching was through memorization, even in the lessons graded for the very young. In the years between 1815 and 1825, Frank Glenn Lankard notes in his doctoral dissertation, *A History of the American Sunday School Curriculum* that Sunday school pupils were expected to memorize vast numbers of Bible verses in an indiscriminate order each week. By 1835 at least three distinct groupings were publishing Sunday school materials: denominations were publishing their own materials, other materials were published by the American Sunday School Union, and private individuals published their own. All of these were in use and there was no overall plan as to how the lessons were put together by local churches. Lankard comments that the 1835 lessons' questions were wooden and mechanical in the attempt to make the pupil master the content, that they made little attempt to stimulate the imagination, and that the stories did not relate to the lives of the children. The method most widely utilized at the time was catechetical and rote. Lankard notes, "Even God was unattractive in these lessons...Too much emphasis was placed upon his justice and watchfulness of a vengeful kind. The child would hardly be led to love or communicate with, or serve God. Being good was presented as a way of escape from what would surely happen to one who pursued the wrong course." Clearly, the child was not the central consideration in the development of these lessons. It was out of this Babel period and the dissatisfaction with the material for Christian education, Lankard argues, that the stage was set for change.[3]

Lankard begins the story of the development of the International Uniform Lesson System in what he termed the "Babel" period covering the years 1815 to 1872, during which time some attempts at graded lessons for children had occurred within the rising denominationalism of that period. The infant and senior departments were most often given special attention in to the structure and content of the materials. The infant departments of the local conventions began urging separate lessons based on teacher's experiences trying to teach adult-level material to the very young. The senior, or adult, departments urged a similar separation because the basic level of lessons was too young for the adult students. The American Sunday School Union had developed the Selected Lessons for which a "Primer" for beginners and a *Child's Scripture Question Book* were published. The Union soon published a *Consecutive Questions* book for the intermediate department to help meet the requests for more graded help in the local churches. Lankard notes that while the treatment was made simpler in these books, the concepts for the most part were not. In 1845 the *Infant Teacher's Manual* was published by Daniel Wise for children in a catechetical form and included hymns carefully selected to supplement the lessons. He also published the *Child's Lesson Book* on the New Testament which was intended to follow the *Teacher's Manual*. Lankard writes that "The Massachusetts Sabbath School Society early recognized that all children could not profitably study the same lesson and in 1839 began publication of the Infant Series to meet the demand for lessons for very small children."[4]

Lankard traces the influences on the movement of the Sunday schools from the Babel period to the establishment of uniformity. The Sunday School Institute movement was preparing Sunday school teachers to become more qualified to teach competently. These institutes, created by the conventions were intended to bring Sunday school teachers similar training offered for the public school teachers. The institutes were usually held in the summer and lasted for one or two weeks. The influence of the normal schools on the public school teachers made it clear that the Sunday school teachers were woefully lacking in skills Institutes for the training of Sunday school teachers provided help in the development of lesson plans and methods of presentation, and gave the teachers the opportunity to ask for a more systematic plan of Bible study. Edwin Wilbur Rice states that "the institute was the chief agency for crystallizing the new uniform idea."[5] It was in the institutes that the concept of uniformity in Sunday school lessons was advocated and taught. Teachers embraced the concept and were in support of the uniform idea when it was proposed as the basis of curriculum a few years later.

Lankard notes that not only were the institutes an impetus for the uniform idea, but also, in the words of Henry Frederick Cope, "After the Civil War there were Sunday school giants abroad in the land."[6] These giants were Benjamin F. Jacobs, a Baptist layman from Chicago, the Rev. John Henry Vincent, then a young Methodist clergyman, and the Rev. Edward Eggleston.

Henry Frederick Cope was a cofounder of the Religious Education Association with George Albert Coe in 1903. B. F. Jacobs, as early as 1867, saw advantages to the idea of a world wide Sunday school lesson that everyone, everywhere would use. Jacobs was an astute businessman who valued order and uniformity and abhorred inefficiency and disorganization. He was a man of boundless energy, and he focused it on the development of the Uniform Lessons. Robert W. Lynn and Elliott Wright in their book *The Big Little School*, recall Jacobs in less than benevolent terms as "generalissimo Jacobs" of the "U.S. Sunday School Army," for his commanding control and power in the creation and development of the Uniform Lessons System.[7] John H. Vincent also espoused the idea of uniform lessons for all ages. In 1865 Vincent, as secretary of the Chicago Teachers' Union, began publishing a magazine, *The Sunday School Teacher's Quarterly*, in which he published a two-year course of uniform lessons, "Two Years With Jesus." When he left the position after only one year to become secretary of the Methodist Sunday School Union, he continued to write the lessons and began writing the "Berean Series" for the Methodists. The Rev. Edward Eggleston who was a Sunday school teacher and curriculum editor, took over as editor of *The Sunday School Teacher* and also began to publish his own lessons, "The National Series." Edwin Wilbur Rice noted in *The Sunday School Movement and the American Sunday School Union* that in 1869 Eggleston stated that he was in favor of one uniform lesson for the entire school with adaptations by the teachers so as to make it serviceable for all ages and capabilities. He later changed his thinking and did not favor uniformity in all grades for all ages. He stated that he saw the move to uniformity as a step backwards and that denominations would not be brought any closer together than they were at the time. He felt that the different age groups needed lessons written for their maturity level or reading comprehension abilities. Nonetheless, the personages of Vincent, Eggleston and Jacobs, and the three uniform lesson series the former two had written had a major impact on the next steps taken in the move to uniform lessons.[8]

Robert Lynn and Elliott Wright in *The Big Little School* specifically point to the efforts of these same men whom they labeled "The Illinois Band." Also named were Evangelist Dwight L. Moody and William Reynolds, a businessman from Peoria, Illinois. Moody and Reynolds, who in 1864 had been doing civilian religious work with the troops, developed a plan to become involved in the work of the Sunday schools. As support for the Uniform Lesson idea grew, two business giants, John Wanamaker, Philadelphia merchant, and H.J. Heinz of "57 Varieties" fame were added to the list. Wanamaker, like Jacobs, took delight in creating order in institutions. Jacobs and Vincent were to become the principal driving forces behind the creation and development of the Uniform Lessons System.[9] Jacobs serving as the astute businessman and Vincent as writer and visionary.

In the 1860s Jacobs, Eggleston and Vincent were impatient with the lack of effective organization on a national level within the American Sunday School Union. They set out to create a strong nationwide convention system. The Civil War had left Protestantism and the nation fragmented, and the organizations of the Sunday school were no exception. Lynn and Wright note that "The Illinois Band," like many northerners after the Civil War, were enamored with the mystical notion of "union." Jacobs had a businessman's disdain for inefficiency, coupled with a vision of unity that formed the concept of a uniform Christian education effort.

Vincent and Eggleston's lesson series became successful to the point that, as Lankard observes, Benjamin F. Jacobs took the idea of uniformity and expanded it to be

> "for the Sunday-schools of this country not only, but, blessed by God!
> We hope, for the world!" He [Jacobs] pushed it hard at the 1869
> [National Sunday School] convention, but the target date was 1872
> when he hoped delegates would adopt his scheme: A Lesson Commit-
> tee, appointed by the big convention, would draw up a list of scrip-

tural topics for Sunday schools for a seven year cycle. Each lesson would then be studied by every person, from infants to the infirm, in every Sunday school.[10]

Jacobs's plan, according to Lankard, had three definite objectives for Sunday school lessons. "They were: first, one lesson for all ages; second, one lesson for all schools throughout the world; and third, expositions of the lessons in all religious and secular papers that might be inclined to publish them." Lankard traces the steps Jacobs took to bring his idea to fruition. First, the National Sunday School Convention of the Sunday School Association [*sic*] in 1869 endorsed Jacobs's proposal to develop his uniform lessons. The convention appointed a committee to formulate plans for further action. This committee requested that the National Executive Committee convene the lesson publishers in a conference. That meeting was held in August 1871 with twenty-nine publishers present. They discovered that over thirty magazines and papers were publishing lesson notes and expositions upon almost a dozen independent series. The publishers appointed another committee to make a selection of lessons for the 1872 year as a trial project. Lutheran, Episcopal, Methodist, Baptist, and Presbyterian denominations were represented on this committee. Whether to base the lessons on doctrinal, biblical, liturgical or Christian duties was passionately discussed. Finally a compromise was reached: the lessons would be entirely biblical and the whole Bible would be covered in a cycle alternating between the Old and New Testaments. The National Sunday School Convention [*sic*] met in Indianapolis in 1872 to consider the official move to a uniform system of lessons for the Sunday school. Mr. Jacobs had come to the convention determined that his plan should be carried out. To secure such action he presented the following resolution.

> Resolved: That the convention appoint a committee to consist of five clergymen and five laymen, to select a course of Bible lessons for a series of years not exceeding seven, which shall, as far as they may decide possible, embrace a general study of the whole Bible, alternating between the Old and New Testaments semiannually or quarterly, as they shall deem best; and to publish a list of such lessons as fully as possible, and at least for the two years next ensuing, as early as the first of August, 1872; and that this convention recommend their adoption by the Sunday schools of the whole country; and that this committee have power to fill any vacancies that may occur in their number by reason of the inability of any member to serve.[11]

Vincent and Eggleston expressed opposition to the idea of such uniformity, but Vincent was eventually won over and Eggleston out voted. Eggleston's objection to the uniformity was based on his understanding of educational pedagogy that more adequately met the needs of the child or adult. Where Jacobs saw the answer to inefficiency in evangelical education and a unifying force for evangelical denominations, Eggleston saw it as stifling of sound educational theory and creativity. He had stated his belief that uniformity did not allow for individuality or innovative thinking on the part of children or adults. Jacobs's plan was approved with only ten dissenting votes Eggleston's being one of them. The International Sunday School Lesson Committee was organized at that same meeting.[12]

Jacobs' plan fostered an ecumenical unity within evangelical Protestantism that provided a common Christian language in this eventually world wide system. Individual denominations published lesson "helps" that focused on specific doctrinal tenets that maintained the vast network of the publishing houses that had sprung up over the recent decades.

Universalists participated in the Uniform Lesson System from its beginning and were very active in the publication of materials to supplement the Uniform Lessons in *The Universalist Leader* and in *The Helper*, magazines that contained materials reflective of their Universalist beliefs. Universalist participation in the Uniform Lesson Plan System stemmed in large part from their efforts to remain within the evangelical Protestant fold and the Universalist reticence to organize their own religious education efforts into a denomination-wide organization. The Rev. John Coleman Adams writes, "For a church which from the first has so heartily fostered the Sunday school the neglect to provide special organization for the work is hard to explain. Much may be laid to the spirit of independency and the fear of over-organization."[13] Miller notes that many Universalists voiced concern that the denomination could not support numerous organizations representing interest groups within the ranks. The Universalist General Sunday School Union was not formed until 1913, and even then support for its authority came slowly. With little Universalist structure to support its Sunday schools and to provide resources, it was important to the educational efforts of Universalists to align themselves with the American Sunday School Union and the Uniform Lesson Plan System.[14]

The Uniform Lesson Plan System was a highly structured and well defined program of instruction for children, youth, and adults in biblical studies. Frank Lankard provides a detailed description of the content and character of the Lessons from 1873 to 1925. This structure will later be seen in the Universalist efforts in later years as they began to develop their own curriculum.

The lessons were developed in seven-year cycles in which the majority of the Bible was to be covered. Each cycle had specific characteristics that were either lauded or sharply criticized. The Lessons Committee selected a biblical text and title for each lesson. Of note in this first seven-year Cycle (1873-1879) was the addition in the second year of the "Golden Text," a highlighted Scripture verse that was the central thought of the lesson and was to be memorized by the student. This Golden Text was printed in many local weekly newspapers as well as being part of the Sunday lesson. The placement of the Bible text varied from year to year. In the first year the Old Testament studies were interrupted with a quarter of study in the New Testament, then it was back to the Old Testament. This was changed in the second year, but in 1876 the Old and New Testament studies alternated each quarter in the year. Lankard stated that this was a pedagogical monstrosity. It was the source of the criticism that the lessons presented choppy treatment of the Bible, or that the Lessons Committee had cut apart the Bible at their own discretion. In this first cycle forty-five of the lessons were presented in the didactic method, which in Lankard's opinion made it difficult for the younger children.[15]

In the second seven-year Cycle (1880-1886), a Memory Verse was added to the title of the lesson, the lesson text and the Golden Text. Two lessons each year were left open so individual denominations could teach their specific doctrines and values. In 1882 the entire year was devoted to the study of the Gospel of Mark, giving students the benefit of a chronological and comprehensive study of it. The entire cycle was less fragmentary in that it moved back and forth between the two Testaments, but was still didactic in teaching method.

In the third seven-year Cycle (1887-1893), the Old Testament studies began with Genesis in October and continued through the story of Moses receiving the Ten Commandments. Lankard writes that more of the lessons were biographical and narrative in nature, making them more interesting to children. The study of the Gospel of Matthew in 1889 explored the gospel from start to finish, again giving children an easier time of following along. The year 1890 was devoted entirely to the Gospel of

Luke. However, several books of the Bible were never covered in any of the cycles. The fourth Cycle (1894-1900), covered a period of six years instead of seven. Noteworthy is the fact that the lessons on Jesus, which covered the entire cycle, were presented in one-year-length stories. The studies of Jesus focused on his character, and time was given to help fully develop the stories and the concepts. The Old Testament lessons presented an historical, biographical and chronological history of the Hebrews, which gave important ethical and moral lessons to the children.

The fifth six-year Cycle (1901-1906) attempted to group in a more chronological order. The sixth six-year Cycle (1907-1912) was unique in the length of time given to a portion of the Bible. The cycle was divided into only four segments of biblical arcs and provided a more comprehensive biblical study for the children. Cycle seven (1913-1917) more closely coincided with the liturgical year of the churches and improved greatly in cohesion of the development of the biblical stories. The treatment of the Bible followed the festivals of the church's liturgical year and made the children's Sunday school experiences correspond to their experiences within the whole life of the church.

The eighth eight-year Cycle, 1918 to 1925, incorporated significant changes and was issued under the new title, *Improved Uniform Lessons.* Groupings were instituted for the various departments of the school: Primary, Junior, Intermediate, Senior, Young People and Adult pupils. Also, special topics on important biblical truths, and discussions of important aspects of Christian living were added along with new memory verses and additional material to make the lessons more helpful to pupils in the different departments. Group Graded Lessons were presented in 1924.

George Herbert Betts describes Group Graded Lessons as ones in

> which the material advances by three-year steps. This series requires for each age group (primary, junior, and so on) three interchangeable units of materials, one for each year. This plan enables the smaller school to place in the same class children three years apart in ages, while at the same time giving them materials which, even if rather coarsely graded, are in some degree adapted to their use.[16]

Lankard notes that The American Sunday School Union issued lesson helps for groupings of classes, and it issued expositories, explanations, illustration, and applications designed to fit the needs of different ages. This attempt at grading was not directed toward the basic material, but rather, toward the lesson helps.[17]

Universalists used the Uniform Lessons 1901. To provide the "Universalist" message, they, like other denominations, published "helps" in the way of specific Universalist materials and interpretations. The main source of assistance for Universalist teachers using the *International Uniform Lessons* was *The Sunday School Helper*, also known as *The Universalist Helper*, or just, *The Helper*. A review and critique of four sets of *The Helper* covering one month of publications in the decades of the 1870's, 1880's, 1890's, 1900's, and 1920's follows. Volume II of *The Helper*, January 1871, begins with several articles and stories for the teacher's edification, support, or for use in the classroom. These articles are followed with lessons. The first article, "The Double Reward," by the Rev. Giles Bailey discusses the rewards of teaching Sunday school. The rewards are the consciousness of doing good and the satisfaction that comes directly to the teacher's own mind and heart:

> The successful Sunday school teacher, like the successful teacher in
> any school, is so, because he is himself a diligent student in the things
> he teaches....The teacher, then, while instructing others, is instructing
> himself....He will become better acquainted with the geography of the
> countries in which the Scriptures were written; with ancient and
> Oriental manners and customs, and with all the various facts which
> serve to explain their peculiar phraseology.[18]

The second article, God is Our Father, by the Rev. G.H. Vibbert provides the teacher with some history about the origins of the idea of God as Father. The article begins with the statement, "The truth was not entirely unknown before Christ taught it. Christianity is not the only religion to embody it. In the Hebrew Scriptures God is sometimes called Father, 'a Father of the fatherless,'....In a very ancient Hindu hymn it is said 'May our Father in Heaven be favorable to us.'" Vibbert states clearly the Universalist idea that God is love in contrast to the Hebrew image. Vibbert writes, "God is *power* in the old religion — he is *Love* under the new." He continues in the article to point out the divergence between Christian which includes Universalists, and so-called Orthodoxy: "Orthodoxy practically represents God as limiting his love to those who are obedient, and pouring endless wrath upon the disobedient....The Christian idea of the Father represents him as sending his Son after the lost and sinful *until they are found*." Vibbert is providing the teachers with

Universalist ideas of God for use with the pupils in their Sunday schools.[19]

The third article, "The Connection of the Sunday School with the Church," by J. H. F. makes the teacher aware of how important the work of the Sunday school is to the overall well-being of the church. "When it is remembered that the great purpose of the Sunday school, which should include all other purposes, is to educate the rising generation into the theory and practice of the Christian religion, it is seen that the church which exists especially and only for purely religious purposes, must naturally be the source of the deepest interest in the school." This author develops the concept of the Sunday school as the "nursery of the church" [Horace Bushnell's phrase] from which new members will come. This concept would give the teachers a deeper appreciation for the importance of the work they do and the church an appreciation for the importance of the Sunday school to the life of the whole church.

The fourth article, "Methods and Means of Sunday School Instruction," by the Sunday School Committee [of the Gloucester Convention of Universalists, most likely] at the Gloucester Convention [of Universalist Churches in Massachusetts], introduces the developing idea of uniform lessons. In explaining *The International Uniform Lessons System* the committee lists the components of the system.

> It admits of a programme [*sic*] of studies whereby teachers, scholars and parents may certainly know what subjects are to be considered at given dates, thus assisting the memory of irregular attendants. It affords peculiar facilities for preparation. Pastors, officers and teachers may help each other to the best advantage in its use....It economizes time....It affords constant opportunity for general questioning and reviews. It utilizes the pastor and superintendent, lifting them from their former respective positions of speech-maker and "time-keeper" to the important office of general teacher. It facilitates the management of the school. It saves money.[20]

The article gives a general overview of how the lessons will be implemented using the "Uniform Lessons" three Sundays a month, one Sunday for special days like Harvest Sunday, and the fifth Sunday for concerts and reviews. The Committee noted that The Uniform Lessons would be greatly enhanced by the teacher's use of *The Helper's* periodical series."[21]

A delightful short story, "Snuffy's Sum," credited to *Youth's Companion*, is presented for the teacher to read or to be told in the classroom to instill the idea of the rewards of hard work and honest living. This is followed by the article "How to Keep the Older Scholars," credited to *Sunday School Times*. It is filled with tips and suggestions as to how a teacher, minister or superintendent can do this. The pastor and the teacher are reminded of how they can work together to keep the older scholars.

> Scholars leave for the most part, not because they have a positive
> dislike to the school, but simply through indifference. They are rather
> tired of it as an old story, and as it does not seem to be a matter of
> much concern whether they continue or not, they quietly stay away.
> But let the whole body of teachers be aroused on the subject, and this
> feeling of indifference will be at once broken up.

> If we wish to retain our scholars permanently, we must have means of
> meeting the wants of growing manhood and womanhood.[22]

The "Lesson Papers" constitute the remainder of the January 1871 issue of *The Sunday School Helper.* [*sic*] The theme for the month's lessons are "The Teachings of Jesus the Christ." A brief outline of the structure of each lesson shows the Scripture used, the Golden Text, or central message to be learned, and the "Central Thought" that provides the interpretation in one sentence of the Golden Text. While the content of the Scripture and the main idea are the same, the questions have been developed to more adequately meet the needs of the different ages in the Sunday school. The questions are listed in two paragraphs. The first contains questions for the younger children and the second has questions geared for older children.

It is very interesting to note the development of these "helps" two years before the Uniform Lessons themselves were created by the National Sunday School Convention in 1872. It demonstrates that the Universalist Sunday School Committee had to be present and participating in at least some of the meetings where the Uniform Sunday School Lessons System was developed. It is likely the Universalists writers of *The Helper* were influenced by the lessons written by Edward Eggleston and John H. Vincent that preceded the formal development of the Uniform Lesson Series. As noted earlier these lessons had been used to create the first set of Uniform Lessons used in 1873. It is also of note that while the Uniform Lessons did not institute the Golden Text until 1874, it is part of this 1871 *The Helper* "Lesson Papers," giving further evidence of the Universalist's participation in the development of the Uniform Lessons. The inclusion of the Golden Text suggests the ideas for the structure of the lessons were taken by the Universalists and put into immediate use in *The Helper* before the Uniform Lessons Committee used them in the International Uniform Lessons.

A brief outline of the lessons contained in the January 1871 issue of *The Sunday School Helper* follows:

> **Note.**—The Lesson Paper is included chiefly as a guide to the pupil in studying the lesson, and an aid to the teacher in giving instruction. It should not be relied on as a question book containing all that is to be imparted, but the teacher is desired to use it as a help merely, that it may suggest thoughts for conversation. The questions for study are arranged in two paragraphs, the first containing easy questions for the small children, the second, more difficult ones for the older scholars.

> **Lesson I.**—January 1, 1871
> **Theme.** —The New Birth.
> **Scripture Lesson.**—John iii:1-11
> **Golden Text.**—For the law of the Spirit of life in Christ Jesus hath made me free from the law of sin and death. Romans viii:2.
> **Central Thought.**—The religion of Christ makes those pure in thought and desire who possess its spirit.
> **Questions for Study.** [There are paragraphs of questions that are too long for inclusion here.]

> **Lesson II.**—January 8, 1871
> **Theme.**—- Christ's Salvation
> **Scripture Lesson.**—John iii:12-21
> **Golden Text.**—In whom ye also trusted, after that ye heard the word of truth, the gospel of your salvation. Ephesians i:13.
> **Central Thought.**—Salvation is a moral and spiritual state attained through faith in Jesus Christ.
> **Questions for Study.** [not included due to length]

Lesson III.—January 15, 1871
Theme.—At Jacob's Well.
Scripture Lesson.—John iv:1-15.
Golden Text.—And Jesus said unto them, I am the bread of life: he that cometh to me shall never hunger; and he that believeth in me shall never thirst. John vi:35
Central Thought.—The truths of the gospel constitute spiritual food of which one must partake to satisfy his spiritual wants.
Questions for Study. [not included due to length]

Lesson IV.—January 22, 1871
Theme.—True Worship
Scripture Lesson.—John iv:16-26.
Golden Text.—For we are the circumcision, which worship God in the spirit, and rejoice in Christ Jesus, and have no confidence in the flesh. Philippians iii:3.
Central Thought.—God, who is a spirit, is to be worshipped in a spiritual manner, not by rite and ceremonial.
Questions for Study. [not included due to length]

Lesson V.—January 29, 1871
Theme.—The Prophet at Home.
Scripture Lesson.—Luke iv:16-29.
Golden Text.—And when the Sabbath day was come, he began to teach in the synagogues: and many, hearing him, were astonished, saying, From whence hath this man these things? And what wisdom is this which is given unto him, that even such mighty works are wrought by his hands? Mark vi:2
Central Thought.—Men of humble rank, though possessing remarkable gifts, are often not appreciated in the place of their nativity.
Questions for Study. [not included due to length][23]

Following the outline of the lessons is the section "Notes for Teachers and Bible Class Scholars." This contains background information for the teacher, including definitions of terms, historical details relevant to the lesson's Scriptural passages, and some interpretation of the passages that can be used by the teacher in answering the questions to be studied. There is no attempt to present a specific or explicit Universalist message in the teacher's notes however, the information is positive and affirming in language and concept and much in line with Universalism in general.

The January 1871 issue concludes with several pages of reports from organizations relevant to Sunday school teachers. Reports were included from the Young Men's Universalist Association of New York City, the New Hampshire Sunday School Convention, New York City Mission School Anniversary, Vermont Sunday School Convention, and other articles of activities and stories, one of which is Mr. Blake's "Walking Stick" by the Rev. Edward Eggleston.

The Sunday School Helper, Volume II, No. 13, issued January 1886, consists entirely of stories. The first is a story of William Lloyd Garrison and how he became one of the most influential and powerful abolishionist of the 1830's through the 1860's and the Civil War. The message of his determination to live and speak the truth against what he believed to be an evil is powerfully seen in his life. It gives pupils an understanding of the courage and conviction in Garrison's life and how they might develop such characteristics in their own lives. The story ends with the sentence, "It is a fitting story for the New Year, which opens out before us all, new chances and fresh resolves."[24] The second story, "A New Year's Address," is developed around the Scripture verse from Isaiah 13:16, "I will bring the blind by a way that they knew not." The story is of a little girl who is blind going on a walking trip with her father to a town four miles away. She asks him questions about where they are and where they are going, and he tells her that knowing she cannot see he will guide her and assures her she is safe. As he tells her of the milestones along the way she is comforted and more trusting of that which she cannot see. She learns from her father that God cannot be seen yet milestones are here for us to "see" with our spirit.[25] The third article, "A Few Words About Hymns," is by a Rev. J. Ruddle   His hope is for teachers to introduce singing into the classroom for the joy of singing and not for use of the lyrics for instruction.[26] Following his article are "Short Stories for the Little Ones" and "Lessons from my Bookshelf." The short stories for the youngest children have messages of caring and concern for others. The first of the two stories presents the message that it is never too late to begin again when one has not been successful or has failed to complete a task the first time. The second concerns the young people's respect and caring for the elderly and coming to appreciate them for their wisdom.[27] In the section "Lessons on the Ministry of Jesus" the teacher is given a biblical passage that is developed verse by verse to for use in discussion. Much of the development is exegetical in nature and often ends with the moral of the verse.[28]There are no questions for study or structured lessons for the teacher to follow.

The third issue of *The Sunday School Helper,* issued January 1892, is much like the 1886 *Helper* in that it contains addresses, lessons and an article by Unitarian the Rev. William Channing Gannett on the "Three Stages of the Bible." Gannett's article is written in the form of three lessons for use by the Sunday school teacher. The three stages are defined as

> the age of its writers; the second, the age of its believers or worship-
> pers; the third age of its critics and truest appreciators. The first stage
> is apt to be very long: Bibles of some nations have been a thousand
> years and more in coming into being. The second, that of its worship-
> pers, is apt to be still longer: the religions of Buddha and Confucius,
> for instance, are each nearly twenty-five hundred years old, and each
> of these rest upon a sacred book. The third stage lasts as long as the
> world continues to be interested in the book. When a Bible returns
> into literature, it may live on indefinitely: we have Bibles of religions
> that are now in ruins.[29]

A section "Moral Lessons: With Illustrations" follows in this issue of *The Helper.* The first moral lesson is "Right from Wrong." The lesson discusses voluntary and involuntary actions and motives, knowledge of right and wrong, and conscience. Illustrations of such actions, motives, and decisions are given through stories, either biblical or biographical, with Unitarian Theodore Parker being one of the illustrations of the exercise of conscience. The lessons implicitly give pupils a Universalist belief in the ability of each person to make responsible choices about what is good and bad. Biographies of those who have lived lives grounded on this belief provide the pupils with concrete connections with the ideas. These lessons are followed by the seventh lesson of the issue, "The Epistle of Paul to the Galatians." The lesson is concerned with the teachings of the law, who is subject to it and what are the interpretations of the terms used by Paul in the letter. The discussion of the pre-existence of Jesus as the son of God reflects the use of critical thinking utilizing literary and source criticism as it explores the meanings of expressions and words used by Paul, and what the source of those words and expressions were in Greek and Hebrew language and history. Lesson eight, on the history of the Church of England is a means to teach how a nation struggled for religious liberty while it sought to remain united as a nation. The concluding lesson is "New Testament Parables." It is a description of what a parable is and how it was used in the Bible. It is noted "that some of the parables were not delivered by Jesus, but belong to a later date." A series of questions are presented for the teacher to ask about the study of parables.

> 1. What was the occasion of the parable? 2. What truth was it intended to teach or enforce? 3. It will be well to bear in mind that some parables are symbolic, where a visible fact images forth a spiritual truth. 4. As to the parables of later date, perhaps the ideas some of them intended are to illustrate are no value to us.[30]

In 1905 *The Sunday School Helper* once again consists mainly of lesson development that is closely related to the Uniform Lessons. The Universalists had developed a graded series in 1901, but still relied heavily on the Uniform Lessons. The issue begins with a brief note

> that brother, Rev. A. F. Walch of St. Johnsbury, VT, has been appointed by the Sunday School Association of his state as a delegate to the Eleventh Triennial International Sunday School Association, to be held next June in Toronto, Can. [1905],...We, heretics as we have heretofore been reckoned, are now included in the broad fellowship of the International Sunday School movement. We had an appreciable Universalist delegation at the Denver Convention three years ago [1902]; we are hoping for a larger and more representative delegation at Toronto.[31]

The first article, "The Perils and Possibilities of the Church," by the Rev. Dr. Conklin, secretary and superintendent of the Universalist churches of Massachusetts, is a major address presenting the challenges, or perils, facing the Universalist Church in 1905. He cites shifting population to the cities, spiritual indifference, and destabilizing of the cities' churches. Conklin calls for a return to the aim and power of the revivals without returning to the revivals themselves. He speaks of a New Evangelism as "the old gospel of Christ reinstated and vitalized in the faith it demands, and in the new life to which it is the summons and of which it is the fountain." He defines the New Evangelism this way:

It is, to begin, this message of the Spirit of Truth, namely: that all men, without gainsaying or qualification, are God's children and heirs, — this message made so vital that no listening soul, on coming to itself, can doubt its verity.

The new Evangelism is, again, in a plain exhibit of the reality of divine retribution, unescapable by the guilty through any metaphysical device whatever; enduring so long as the sinner is dominated by his evil choices; to end by free, divine forgiveness when sinning ends and aspiration becomes in the soul a birth from above; this exhibit also made with such earnestness and relentless candor that even the self-complacent Christians will see the sin, even the moral criminality of remaining longer at ease in Zion.

The new Evangelism is again, and first, last, and always, the declaration and pressing home of the truth of God's love; the personal and unescapable and beneficent love of the Father.[32]

Conklin further discusses what he refers to as "Lyman Abbot's Real Heresy." Of this heresy Conklin contends Abbott's defining God as *Force* is considered heresy to Universalists who believe God is Love. Conklin is wanting Universalists to back away from the scientific definitions of God as First Cause or Force and return to the theism of a God of ethics and of love. Abbott held that God would strive with sinners just so long, and if they were still unrepentant, God would cease to strive and let the sinner sink, "not into purifying sulphuric flames, but into final unconsciousness." This, Conklin could not abide. For Conklin

this doctrine of absolute annihilation is more abhorrent than the affirmation of endless punishment: because we can almost conceive that even if God condemned the wicked to literal flames, he might possibly at sometime in eternity repent of his cruelty and exercise forgiving mercy; while so far as we can see, a soul obliterated, annihilated, cast into oblivion beyond recall, is a divine bereavement for which there is in all eternity no conceivable remedy or consolation. [33]

Conklin is espousing the theology of Hosea Ballou's sovereignty of God in the belief that one cannot not be saved by God. It is Conklin's hope that Abbott will come to a belief in God as Father rather than God as Force.

The Sunday school lessons for the First Quarter constitute the remainder of the February issue of *The Sunday School Helper* for 1905. Each lesson follows a set structure and covers Lesson VI, "Jesus and Jacob's Well"; Lesson VII, "The Second Miracle at Cana"; Lesson VIII, "Jesus at the Pool of Bethesda"; and Lesson IX, "The Miracle of the Loaves and Fishes." The first set of lessons are for the Intermediate Pupils and a final section, edited by Maizie Blaikie Barney, conclude *The Helper* for February 1905. The structure for the Intermediate lessons follows:

> **Introduction**: a brief explanation of the biblical story.
> **Suggestions as to Teaching**:
> **Work for the teacher**, which instructs the teacher to "Look up the Old Testament references which show the historical associations of Jacob's well."
> **Points of Contact**, which tells the teacher, "We shall find in our lesson the doctrine of an indwelling God most needed by men to day [*sic*]."
> **Some Preliminaries**. Lesson VI, "Jesus at Jacob's Well," for example, begins telling the teacher of the "Significance of this Famous Conversation Missed by the Common Interpretation." The lesson contends the well was a sacred shrine to both Jews and Samaritans and the Samaritan woman would have come to the well for spiritual reasons not merely to draw water as the common interpretation suggests.
>
> **For the Pupils**
> **Time:** the setting of the story
> **Home Reading**: suggested reading for each day of the week of passages in the Bible that reinforce the message of the main lesson.
> **Universalist Catechism**: A distinct Universalist interpretation of each lesson.
> **Golden Text**: The central biblical passage and message.
> **Preview:** A quick synopsis of the lesson for the pupil.
> **Lesson Outline**: A highlighting of the messages in the lesson and the biblical passage where the message is to be found.

Analytical Questions: Questions for the student to answer and study.
Explanatory: An explanation in detail of the outline verses for the pupils to read.
Memorable Points: What the teacher wants the pupil to remember.
Questions for Written Answers. The students are to fill in the blanks answering the questions.

For the Teacher:
"Universalist Catechism," by Rev. John Coleman Adams, D.D. This catechism provides the teacher with details of the story presented in the lesson. It is a clear Universalist development of the biblical lessons and concludes with Teaching Points for the teacher that consist of a list of the highlights of the lesson that need to be stressed. The Catechism ends with "Side-Lights" which include quotes and commentary. Some of the writers of these quotes and commentary include Lyman Abbott, Henry Ward Beecher and Marcus Dods.
"Every-Day Lesson Topics," by Rev. Henry R. Rose includes further enrichment suggestions for the teacher. Rev. Robert T. Polk contributes the section, "For the Intermediate Grade," a further description and interpretation of the lesson's biblical text and story.[34]

The Junior Department conducted [*sic*] by Maizie Blaikie Barney begins with an article by Charlotte E. Hoffman, "Ways of Dealing with Boys." It seems keeping the interest of boys was a problem even in those days. Ms. Barney notes, "The lessons must be interesting, and I found that I had to be full of the lesson." The lessons follow the topics of the Intermediate Lessons but have a much shorter development. The lessons briefly, consists of:

Golden Text: The central biblical passage and message of the lesson.
Lesson Point: A one-sentence interpretation.
Point of Contact: Instruction on how to make quick and significant contact between the pupil and the lesson.
Lesson Story: A telling of the biblical story in a junior level (ages 9 to 12) understanding.
Application: Provides an experience in the lives of the pupils relevant to the biblical story.[35]

ENDNOTES

1. Anne Boylan, *Sunday School, The Formation of an American Institution: 1790-1880* (New Haven, Conn,: Yale University Press), 87.

2. Robert W. Lynn and Elliott Wright, *The Big Little School* (New York: Harper & Row, 1971), 72.

3. Frank Glenn Lankard, *A History of the American Sunday School Curriculum*, (New York, The Abingdon Press, 1927), 198-200.

4. *Ibid.*, 194.

5. Edwin Wilbur Rice, *The Sunday School Movement 1780-1917, and the American Sunday School Union 1817-1917* (Philadelphia: The American Sunday School Union, 1917), 297.

6. Lankard, *History of the American Sunday School Union*, 204.

7. Lynn and Wright, *Big Little School*, 63.

8. Rice, *Sunday School Movement*, 297.

9. Lynn and Wright, *Big Little School*, 57.

10. *Ibid.*, 64.

11. Lankard, *History of American Sunday School Curriculum*, 234.

12. Lynn and Wright, *Big Little School,* 64, 65.

13. Iris V. Cully and Kendig Brubaker Cully, *Harper's Encyclopedia of Religious Education* (San Francisco: Harper and Row, Publishers, 1990), 1134.

14. Russell E. Miller, *The Larger Hope: The Second Century of the Universalist Church in America: 1870-1970* (Boston: Unitarian Universalist Association, 1985), 213, 214.

15. Lankard, *History of American Sunday School Union*, 238.

16. George Herbert Betts, *The Curriculum of Religious Education*, (Cincinnati, Ohio: Abingdon Press, 1924), 360, 361.

17. Lankard, *History of American Sunday School Union*, 238.

18. Samuel A. Briggs, ed., *The Sunday School Helper*, January 1871,(Chicago, The Northwestern Universalist Publishing House, 1871), 1, 10, 11.

19. *Ibid.*, 12-14.

20. *Ibid.*, 15-18.

21. *Ibid.*, 18.

22. *Ibid.*, 23.

23. Samuel A. Briggs, "The Teachings of Jesus the Christ," *The Sunday School Helper 2* (January 1871): 25-28.

24. *The Sunday School Helper*, 2, no. 13 (January 1886): 1-4.

25. *Ibid.*, 5-7.

26. *Ibid.*, 7-9.

27. *Ibid.*, 9-12.

28. *Ibid.*, 18.

29. William Channing Gannett, "The Three Stages of a Bible's Life," *The Sunday School Helper* 7, no, 1 (January, 1892): 7.

30. Frederick T. Reed, "Lessons on the New Testament Parables," *The Sunday School Helper* 8, no. 1 (January 1892): 23-24.

31. Oscar F. Safford, D.D., ed., *The Sunday School Helper* 36, no. 2, (February 1905): 1.

32. Dr. Conklin, D.D., "Perils and Possibilities of the Church," *The Sunday School Helper*, 36, no. 2 (February 1905): 3.

33. *Ibid.*, 5-6.

34. John Coleman Adams, Rev. Henry R. Rose, Rev. Robert T. Polk, Intermediate Lessons, "Universalist Catechism, Every-Day Lesson Topics, For Teachers of the Intermediate Grade," *The Sunday School Helper,* 36, no. 2 (February 1905): 7-41.

35. Maizie Blaikie Barney, The Junior Department, *The Sunday School Helper,* 36, no. 2 (February 1905): 43-48.

CHAPTER SIX

The International Uniform Lessons System Moves Toward Grading

The Uniform Lessons were not as unified in their acceptance as may be discerned from the name and the popularity they held, but they were immensely popular. John R. Sampey, professor of Old Testament Interpretation at the Southern Baptist Theological Seminary, Louisville, Kentucky and author of *The International Lesson System: The History of Its Origin and Development* noted that by 1905 more than seventeen million men, women and children were using the Uniform Lessons.[1] Even so, critics began immediately to attack the choppy presentation of biblical lessons and the inappropriateness of the lessons for the primary and beginner levels. The Uniform Lessons had been conceptualized by Benjamin F. Jacobs in a focused attempt to create efficiency in Christian education. According to Sampey, he did not listen to the advice of men like the Rev. Edward Eggleston who understood the importance of pedagogy and the needs of children. Yet the inroads from the progressive education movement and the modernist scholarship of Higher Biblical Criticism, behavioral psychology, geology, and scientific inquiry all began to exert pressure upon the organizers of the Uniform Lessons.

Lynn and Wright in their book *The Big Little School*, write:

> Then, too, the movement had to defend itself against the unwelcome intrusion of modern biblical scholarship, that disconcerting importation of textual and scientific "higher criticism" from the European continent. Within the womblike comfort of a large convention it was reassuring to hear that "Germany would not be in the grip of anti-Biblical criticism today had her children enjoyed equal privileges with ours in the curriculum of the Sabbath school."

> The Bible emerged as "the old Book," the bulwark against errors, something out of the past to be resolutely defended against the evolutionists and theological heretics. While admitting room for biblical scholarship elsewhere, the Lesson Committee reported in

1893 that "we can not have scientific study in the Sunday school. It would require a search with lighted candles to find either higher or lower critics in our ordinary Sunday-school classes." The need, the argument went on to make, was to make the Bible plain to the common people instead of introducing into lessons "the melancholy jargon" of critics.[2]

The Universalists were responding to the work of Dr. Orello Cone, at this time Richardson Professor of Biblical Theology at Saint Lawrence (1900-1905). Cone had engaged in biblical study from 1897 to 1898 in Europe, partly at the University of Berlin, focusing on the new theology of the Higher Biblical Criticism. He utilized the knowledge he gained while there in teaching the young men and women at St. Lawrence Theological School who became Universalist ministers. The Rev. Dr. James M. Pullman, a graduate of St. Lawrence in the first class of 1861, was a colleague of Cone, as was the Rev. Dr. John Coleman Adams, both prominent figures in the publication of materials for religious education. Adams edited *The Helper,* and Pullman wrote accompanying expositions of biblical texts to supplement the Uniform Lessons.[3]

One such exposition, written by James M. Pullman and Frank Oliver Hall between 1929 and 1931, is an example of those written for Universalists using the Uniform Lessons. The authors employ a question and answer catechetical format and provide biblical texts to support and illustrate the given answers. The following example is entitled "Bible Universalism":

Q. What is the fundamental principle upon which all teachings of Universalism are based?

A. The Universal Fatherhood of God. Mal. 2:10: Have we not all one father? Hath not one God created us?

Q. What is the next great principle, implied in the first?

A. The Universal brotherhood of man. Acts 17:26: He hath made of one blood all nations of men?

Q. In studying the character of God from the Bible, what must we bear in mind?

A. We must bear in mind that the Bible is a collection of sacred writings, composed during a period of at least fifteen hundred years, and that it is progressive revelation, or unfolding, of the character of God, growing more complete from Moses to Jesus.

Q. What are the highest attributes ascribed to God in the Old Testament?

A. Power, Justice, and Goodness.

Q. Will you refer me to some passages which ascribe these attributes to Him?

A. Yes. First, as to Power: He is called the almighty 48 times in the Old Testament, as in Gen. 17:1: I am God Almighty; the Creator 33 times, as in Gen. 1:1: In the beginning God created the heavens and the earth.

Second, as to Justice: Deut. 32:4: For all his ways are justice. (See also Psa. 89:14; 19:7; Isa. 45:21.)

Third, as to Goodness: Psa. 145:9; Jehovah is good to all. Psa. 100:5: For Jehovah is good. (All just punishments are proofs of God's goodness. Psa. 62:12: For thou renderest to every man according to his work.) (See also Exod. 34:6,7; Isa. 54:7,8; Psa. 99:8; Jer. 9:23,24.)

Q. What still higher attributes are ascribed to God in the New Testament?

A. Love and Fatherhood.

Q. Will you refer me to some texts?

A. Yes. As to Love: Matt. 5:44,45: Love your enemies and pray for them that persecute you; that you may be sons of your Father who is in heaven; ... (See also John 3:16,17; Rom. 5:8 and 8:38,39; 2 Thess 2:16; 1 John 4:8,10 and 16.)

As to Fatherhood: God is called Father more than 250 times in the New Testament, as in Matt. 5:16 Even so let your light shine before men; that they may see your good works, and glorify your Father who is in Heaven. (See also Matt. 6:6; 7:11; 18:14; 1 Cor. 8:6, 6; Eph. 4:4-6.)[4]

This expository provided for Universalist children an understanding of the Universalist beliefs in a loving God who is like a Father and in the Bible as a collection of sacred writings and not the Word of God. In referring to the description of God as power, justice, and goodness, the pupil is given the information that it is possible to discover different writers' names for God and God's attributes. Orello Cone's higher biblical criticism scholarship and influence can be seen in Pullman's writing. For example, in the response to the question, "In studying the character of God from the Bible, what must we bear in mind?" Pullman answered that the Bible is a progressive revelation of unfolding of the character of God, growing more complete from Moses to Jesus. One of Cone's understandings from his studies was that revelation and humanity evolved together so that humanity would be capable of understanding and participating in God's revelation.[5] While this expository does not point out the literary sources that lay behind the examples of Scripture given, as it is written for young people, it is clear to those who have read Cone or studied the higher criticism.

Dr. Orello Cone had brought to bear the scientific method of inquiry in his work on the Higher Criticism in biblical studies. The theories of progressive education relating to religious education combined with the scientific method and encouraged a new focus in curriculum development and biblical study for the Universalists by the end of the 1890's and early years of the 1900's.

The Universalists' struggle to remain within the Uniform Lesson System is a study of the Universalist struggle to move to a more liberal theology within the denomination-wide movement while preserving their self-identification as an evangelical Protestant denomination. Tracing Universalists involvement in the Uniform Lesson System shows the struggle they experienced around this issue. Some of the struggle centered on the definition of the word "evangelical."

Russell Miller traces that struggle as it was interpreted by the evangelical Protestants and by the Universalists. Universalists used the word "Evangelical" synonymously with "orthodox." Orthodox referred to those denominations espousing the doctrine of endless punishment except for selected individuals who would be saved by faith and divine grace rather than good works. It applied to those who believed that grace was attained through belief in Christ as Lord and Savior and the unquestioned authority of the Bible. On the other hand, Miller notes, Universalist minister A. St. John Chambre wrote in defense of Universalists as evangelicals insisting that Universalists were evangelical in the historical sense because the words "gospel" and "evangelism" were synonymous, and that it was due to the misuse of the word by the orthodox that caused Universalists to be unacceptable to many of the evangelical Protestants.[6]

Miller writes, "Even though Universalists were sometimes temporarily accepted into the Protestant mainstream, there was always likely to be raised at least a shadow of doubt about their legitimacy as a completely Christian denomination."[7] Two instances demonstrate this "sometime acceptance." The first, as far back as 1873 when E.H. Chapin, Alonzo A. Miner, and W.H. Ryder attempted to attend the organizing meeting of the Evangelical Alliance of the American Sunday School Union, they were excluded from participation because, as Miller notes, "Universalists were not considered a truly evangelical denomination and therefore not a bona fide Christian body because they did not subscribe to the doctrine of endless punishment."[8]

Prominent figures in Universalist circles articulated the theology that engaged the evangelical/liberal dialogue among the Universalists. Chapin, Miner and Ryder were influential Universalists and their exclusion from such an organizing meeting was an overt rebuke against Universalists in general. Edwin Hubbell Chapin (1814-1880), junior (in the 1990s he would be called "associate") pastor at the School Street Church in Boston with the elder Hosea Ballou, was an ardent spokesperson in support of temperance, and a prolific hymn writer and supporter of Universalist theological educational efforts, especially at St. Lawrence and as president of Tufts. Chapin served his final pastorate at Fourth Universalist Church, also known as the Church of the Divine Paternity, in New York City from 1848 until his death in 1880. Alonzo Ames Miner (1814-1895) was minister to several Universalist churches; most notably, he was pastor for forty years at the Columbus Avenue Church in Boston, formerly the School Street Church. He was a member of the Massachusetts State Board of Education for twenty-four years, and a member of the Board of Trustees of Tufts University, becoming Tufts' second president, serving from 1862 to 1875. William H. Ryder, a prominent Universalist clergyman from the St. Paul's Church in Chicago, provided significant financial backing to Lombard College, Ryder Divinity School was named for him.[9]

Russell Miller notes that

> there was a common bond between Universalists and Protestant Christians, including those in the Evangelical Alliance....Universalists were included in the "Council of Twenty-five" when an American Congress of Churches met in Hartford, Connecticut in May 1885. James M. Pullman, then pastor in Lynn, Massachusetts, participated in a symposium on "The Attitude of the Secular Press towards

Religion," led by Washington Gladden, the well-known Protestant reformer....It took no less than thirty years of controversy before the Universalist Church was declared to be "evangelical" by the Sunday School Union in Brooklyn, New York, and hence eligible for full fellowship the same year [1915?]. It was not until 1920 that the state Sunday School Association in Massachusetts formally admitted Universalists....when the constitution of the organization was changed by striking out the term "Evangelical" and substituting, "Protestant Christian."[10]

This engagement was important to Universalists because it was through the Evangelical Alliance that the Universalists participated in the International Lessons System with participation on the Uniform Lesson Committee and in the use of the Uniform Lessons.

A discussion of the changes within the International Uniform Lesson System shows that even this system was not a static entity. As was shown in the discussion of the Universalist work in *The Sunday School Helper*, ideas of making Sunday school lessons more child-appropriate, Universalists were looking toward grading of their lessons. Frank G. Lankard details the initial move to develop graded lessons that was to have a direct impact on the Uniform Lesson Committee. It came from the Newark Association of Infant Sunday School Teachers in 1880 when they began to write lesson material for the very young, defined as children just beginning their Sunday school training. In 1894 the International Primary Union conducted a survey of over three hundred primary Sunday school teachers and submitted the results to the International Lesson Committee in 1894. The Lesson Committee accepted a resolution from the Executive Committee of the International Primary Teachers' Union recommending to the Lesson Committee that they select a separate International Lesson for the Primary Department. In 1895 the Lesson Committee issued a course, *Optional Primary Lessons for 1896*, published by the *Sunday School Times*. It was not accepted broadly.[11] Henry H. Meyer defined the Uniform Lessons departments as "Beginners (ages under six), Primary (ages 6 to 8), Junior (ages 9 to 12), Intermediate (ages 13-16), Senior (17-20), Advanced (ages 21+)." It is my assumption that the Infant School of the Newark Association was comparable to the Uniform Lessons' Beginners department.[12] According to Lankard,

The International Primary Union…in 1897 connected with the New Jersey School of Methods and issued a two years' course of lessons called, "Bible Lessons for Little Beginners," written by Miss Margaret Cushman (now Mrs. Haven). These lessons proved very much more popular than the primary course, "Optional Primary Lessons for 1896," and were adopted by many schools, making even more insistent in the denominations the demand for graded lessons. Continued activity on the part of the International Primary Union caused the International Convention in 1902 to authorize the Lesson Committee to prepare a two years' course.[13]

David L. Angus, Jeffrey E. Mirel and Maris A. Vinovskis in their book *Historical Development of Age Stratification in Schooling*, trace the development of age stratification in American society, specifically as it was developed in the public school system. They trace the development of the kindergarten, the movement from home education to school education and the work of Horace Mann that has been discussed earlier. Their contribution comes in the areas of the move from rural one-room schools to urban single-age, or grade, classrooms. William Torrey Harris' work in the Detroit school system is noted as an example of grading in the schools in 1842. Angus, Mirel, and Vinovskis provide the following definition of grading:

the Quincy Grammar School of Boston worked out a system of "Graded Instruction" that went well beyond the rough division into primary, middle, or grammar schools. As it developed and spread over the next couple of decades, the system had two features. First, the subjects to be taught were standardized with the material arranged in an orderly sequence of increasing difficulty. A group of subjects arranged in this way was then called a "course of studies." Second, teaching was subject to a "division of labor" in which each teacher would be responsible for teaching particular segments of material from the hierarchical arrangement of subjects. Once a school building was organized in this way, it was called a "graded school," and the children were assigned to different teachers depending on their level of past accomplishment."

In the most advanced graded schools, the whole course of studies was divided into segments representing one year's work on the part of the average child.

> It is important to emphasize that it was the curriculum and the work of the teacher that was graded, not the children. They were "classi-fied," that is, placed into classes based on what they had learned. Age was irrelevant....It is wrong then to assume, as a number of writers have, that the graded school was either intentionally or actually organized according to chronological age.[14]

As the years progressed into the 1900's the Uniform Lessons came under increased criticism with the influence of the graded structure of the common schools and the philosophy of the progressive education movement, which pressured the International Lesson System Committee to take seriously a plan to publish a graded series. However, as we have seen, and will continue to see in the graded efforts in the Uniform Lesson System and the Universalist lesson development, age was the prominent factor in dividing the material for use. The criticism most often leveled at the Uniform Lessons was the lessons' lack of material appropriate for different ages and grade levels of children. The fact that they were exclusively Bible-centered in curriculum material left out any social justice, temperance, or literature that would place biblical teachings within the context of the wider world. The lessons were considered to isolate the Bible from the relevant life of the child. The theories of the progressive educators demonstrated the psychological and behavioral efficacy of graded lessons, which the public school had responded to with great success. The teachers and workers in the local conventions began to urge for the Uniform Lessons System to follow the lead of the public schools.

In the early attempts at grading the materials for the younger children Lankard argued the mistake was made in not realizing that the content of the material needed to reflect the abilities of the younger children as well as the nature of the questions asked about the content. The questions were much too abstract for the very young and too simplis-tic for adults.[15] Robert Lynn and Elliott Wright concur. They write that

> it was educational absurdity to subject persons of different ages to the same lesson. What a child understands and needs — a....new word soon turned into a cliché in the lexicon of Protestant education — was not always fitting for adults.[16]

This argument was true of the early International Uniform Lessons Graded Series as well as very early grading efforts by individuals in the 1840s up through the time of the completely graded series developed in the 1910s by the International Sunday School Lessons System and other denominations. The Unitarians published the first graded manuals in 1852 and in 1909, a graded series, *The Beacon Series* which utilized progressive educational theory in its development.[17] The denominations using the Uniform Lessons, and now the Uniform Graded Series, published helps designed to meet the needs of the various age levels of the children. The Methodists had *The Berean Series*, the Congregationalist's *The Pilgrim*, Baptists *The Keystone*, the Presbyterians *The Westminster,* and the Universalists *The Murray Graded Series.*[18] While these supplementary materials were helpful, complete grading of the lessons could finally be ignored no longer. At last, it was understood that children learn, and need to be taught, differently than do adults.

By 1900 the powerful impact of the scientific method of inquiry and psychology prevalent in the progressive education theories could no longer be ignored by the International Lessons Committee. The influence in the field of religious education came from Edwin D. Starbuck, George Albert Coe and G. Stanley Hall. Hall is most noted for his work in the field of child psychology, Darwinian evolutionary theory, and child-centered education. He posited that as the child grows and matures, he or she, progresses through the evolution of the human race. Hall believed strongly that the school must be shaped to meet the developmental needs and abilities of the child, not that the child needed to be shaped to meet the demands of the school, as was the case in public schools in the 1800s and early 1900s.[19] Dr. Edwin D. Starbuck (1866-1947), an early scholar in the field of psychology of religion also exerted influence in the movement to graded lessons. He served as consulting editor for the Unitarian Department of Education when it formed in 1912. [20]

As noted by Henry Frederick Cope, who in 1907 became general secretary of the Religious Education Association, the Uniform Lessons broke down because of the "utter disregard of relative values in the biblical material." The Uniform effort was doomed from its inception when, in Cope's words, "the Sunday-school thus officially cut the [Bible] to pieces." Cope cast serious doubt whether at any time every person was, in reality, studying the same Scripture lesson at the same time all around the world. There was such insistence by the Lesson Committee to adhere only to the Scripture that no attention was given to current church history, ethical and social agendas, or the mission work of the denominations.[21]

Along with the influence of the Primary Union, another factor having a direct impact on the Lesson Committee's eventual decision to develop a graded series came from the Rev. Erastus Blakeslee, pastor of a Congregational church in Spencer, Massachusetts. In 1891 in Boston Blakeslee founded the Bible Study Union, an organization that included leaders in the field of progressive religious education, including George Albert Coe and Henry Frederick Cope. In 1910 the Bible Study Union began publishing as many as six courses for nearly every Sunday school year. In 1890 Blakeslee wrote a series of lessons on the Life of Christ.[22] It became a strong competitor of the Uniform Lessons and thus caught the attention of the Lessons Committee members. Supporters of Blakeslee's work were Episcopal bishop, Phillips Brooks, William Rainey Harper founding president of the University of Chicago; and Dr. Lyman Abbott (1835-1922), minister of the Plymouth Church in Brooklyn in the mid-1800's, an ardent spokesperson for evolutionary theory within Christianity, and in the words of Sydney Ahlstrom, "the virtual chaplain of Theodore Roosevelt's Progressivism." [23]

The work of progressives in the field of education were fostering a child-centered approach to education as formulated by such educators and philosophers as Horace Bushnell and John Dewey, Henry Frederick Cope and George Albert Coe. The religious, intellectual, and rational thinkers were the scholars, philosophers and theologians who incorporated the ideas of the German theologians, especially Friedrich Schleiermacher and Adolph Rischtl, philosopher Adolph von Harnack and the very early child psychology theories of Johann Pestalozzi (1746-1827) and Friedrich Froebel (1782-1852) into their liberal interpretation of biblical scholarship and the doctrines of human nature, God and history.[24] A theistic evolution of both God and humankind brought together science and religion on faith and intellectual planes and placed God immanently within the world. The methodology and importance of the child in the learning situation made the content-centered and biblical-centered curriculum of the Uniform Lessons difficult to defend.

The work of Swiss educator Johann Pestalozzi gained popularity in America in the 1860's. His teaching focused on the nature, or person, of the child, and on the development of empathy between the child and the teacher, thereby creating the optimum learning environment for the child, as well as the optimum teaching environment for the teacher. The influence of Horace Bushnell's culture of nurture further enhanced the centrality of the child in an environment of learning. Unitarian Elizabeth Palmer Peabody was a strong proponent of establishing the kindergarten in America as recommended in the work of Froebel. George Albert Coe influenced Sunday school pedagogy through his understanding of the psychology of educating and of the importance of methodology in educating for transformation, not only of the individual child, but ultimately, of society.[25]

> In his address, "Progressive Education and the Science of Education" John Dewey states succinctly the challenge of progressive education for the development of age-based groupings that eventually moved the Lessons Committee members of the International Uniform Lessons to adopt these practices. He writes:

> The [Progressive education school] takes for granted a common emphasis upon respect for individuality and for increased freedom; a common disposition to build upon the nature and experience of the boys and girls that come to them, instead of imposing from without external subject-matter and standards. They all display a certain atmosphere of informality, because experience has proved that formulation is hostile to genuine mental activity and to sincere emotional expression and growth. Emphasis upon activity as distinct from passivity is one of the common factors. And again I assume that there is in all of these schools a common unusual attention to the human factors, to normal social relations, to communication and intercourse which is like in kind to that which is found in the great world beyond the school doors; that all alike believe that these normal human contacts of child with child and of child with teacher are of supreme educational importance, and that all alike disbelieve in those artificial personal relations which have been the chief factor in isolation of schools from life. And in so far [as] we already have the elements of a distinctive contribution to the body of education theory: respect for individual capacities, interests and experience; enough external freedom and informality at least to enable teachers to become acquainted with children as they really are; respect for self-initiated and self-conducted learning; respect for activity as the stimulus and centre [*sic*] of learning; and perhaps above all belief in social contact, communication, and cooperation upon a normal human plane as all-enveloping medium.[26]

The challenge from these progressive theories and practices instituted in the public schools of the late nineteenth and early twentieth century was an extremely important one to the Uniform Lesson System. The framers and members of the Uniform Lesson Committee had dismissed outright any challenge from the Higher Biblical Criticism or the Darwinian theories of evolution to the theological, philosophical and educational beliefs guiding the Uniform Lesson approach. The Bible was sacrosanct. Yet the methodology and pedagogy of the classroom and of the structure of lessons was open to challenge, and challenge came strong and fast as the twentieth century unfolded. George Albert Coe and Henry Frederick Cope built upon the work of Froebel, Pestalozzi, Starbuck, Hall, Bushnell and Dewey to bring to bear the progressive education practices in religious education. Jack Seymour observes that the paramount influence on educational change within the churches came from the progressive movement.[27]

> The formation of the Religious Education Association in 1903 by George Albert Coe, William Rainey Harper, John Dewey, and others, gave the field of religious education a base from which to organize and focus its specific challenges to the Uniform Lesson Committee. By joining forces with the Primary Unions and harkening back to the words of Edward Eggleston, who felt the uniformity of lessons was a step backward in pedagogy, the coalescing of voices advocating for a more progressive form of religious education could no longer be ignored or dismissed.

At the General Convention of the International Uniform Sunday School Union of 1908, a new committee was formed to develop graded lessons. A disclaimer was also issued stressing the sound educational value of the Uniform Lessons, along with a resolution to create a graded series. The Lesson Committee still was reluctant to give its entire support to the changes indicated by progressive educational theories.[28]

For many progressive educational theorists, including Dewey, Coe, and Cope, a key issue lay in the fact that the Uniform Lessons had abandoned the missionary focus of the original Sunday school movement. The progressives in religious education had a new interpretation of "mission" and pressed their agenda to educate the whole child for the whole society, religious and secular.[29] The abandonment of the missionary focus of the early Sunday school movement had been the piece of the educational endeavor that reached out into the community and provided children and adults the opportunity to act on their faith in support of the less fortunate, as well as to spread the word of their faith. The progressive understanding of education was an enterprise involving the whole culture of society. The message given to children, youth, and adults in the Uniform Lessons was entirely biblical with only an occasional lesson on social concerns, especially that of "temperance" around alcohol consumption. Looking back from an experienced vantage point of the progressive movement, Universalist Professor of Religious Education at St. Lawrence Theological School, Angus Hector MacLean, summed it up well in the pamphlet "The Message is the Method" written for the Unitarian Universalist Association in 1962 from a 1951 article in *The Christian Leader*. For MacLean everything was the curriculum that was present in an educational experience, and what you and the children made of that experience was what made it educational. For MacLean, it meant that adults and teachers, all who interact with the child, must live out their religious ideals and beliefs so that their modeling, which is the message they really send, is the message the children comprehend. The progressive educational method for social transformation was the message.[30]

> The time had come for graded lessons. In 1908 the International
> Sunday School Union and the Uniform Lesson Committee approved
> plans for the International Completely Graded Series. Earlier, in 1901,
> the Universalists developed a graded series and in 1912 developed the
> Murray Graded Lessons published by the Universalist Publishing
> House.[31] The latter utilized the Beginners and Primary-level lessons
> from the International Completely Graded Series of the International
> Sunday School Union. The discussion of these developments consti-
> tutes the next three chapters.

ENDNOTES

1. John R. Sampey, *The International Lesson System: The History of Its Origin and Development* (Nashville: Fleming H. Revell Company, 1911) 154.

2. Robert W. Lynn and Elliott Wright, *The Big Little School* (New York: Harper and Row, 1971), 72-73.

3. Russell Miller, *The Larger Hope: The Second Century of the Universalist Church of America: 1870-1970* (Boston: Unitarian Universalist Association, 1985), 214, 215.

4. James M. Pullman and Frank Oliver Hall, *Bible Universalism In Questions and*

Answers (Boston: Universalist Publishing House, n. d., n. p.).

5. Orello Cone, "Science and Religion," Thomas B. Thayer, D.D., ed., *Universalist Quarterly: General Review*, n. s., 19 (1882): 90.

6. Russell Miller, *The Larger Hope: The Second Century of the Universalist Church of America: 1870-1970* (Boston: The Unitarian Universalist Association, 1985), 610.

7. *Ibid.,* 609.

8. *Ibid.,* 609, 610.

9. *Ibid.,* 14, 516, 380.

10. *Ibid.,* 610-611.

11. Frank Glenn Lankard, *A History of the American Sunday School Curriculum* (New York: The Abingdon Press, 1927), 274.

12. Henry H. Meyer, *The Graded Sunday School in Principle and Practice* (Philadelphia: Westminster Press, 1910), 154, 155.

13. Lankard, *History of Sunday School Curriculum*, 274.

14. David L. Angus, Jeffrey E. Mirel, Maris A. Vinovskis, "Historical Development of Age Stratification in Schooling," *Teachers College Record*, 90, no. 2 (New York: Columbia University, 1988): 217, 218.

15. Lankard, *History of Sunday School Curriculum*, 272.

16. Lynn and Wright, *Big Little School,* 81.

17. Henry Frederick Cope, *The Evolution of the Sunday School* (Boston: The Pilgrim Press, 1911) 125.

18. George Herbert Betts, *The Curriculum of Religious Education* (Cincinnati: Abingdon Press, 1924), 129.

19. Mary Boys, *Educating in Faith* (Kansas City, Mo.: Sheed and Ward, 1989), 46.

20. Betts, *Curriculum of Religious Education*, 151.

21. Cope, *Evolution of the Sunday School*, 109.

22. Ibid., 126.

23. Sydney E. Ahlstrom, *A Religious History of the American People* (New Haven: Yale University Press, 1972), 788.

24. *Ibid.,* 781.

25. Iris V. Cully, and Kendig Brubaker Cully, *Harper's Encyclopedia of Religious Education* (San Francisco: Harper and Row, 1990), 485, 486.

26. John Dewey, *Dewey on Education: Selections, Classics in Education No. 3* (New York: Teachers College Press, 1959), 115-116.

27. Jack Seymour, *From Sunday School to Church School* (New York: University Press of America, 1982), 1.

28. Meyer, *The Graded Sunday School in Principle and Practice*, 105.

29. Boys, *Educating Faith*, 50.

30. Angus Hector MacLean, *The Message is the Method* (Boston: Universalist Church of America, 1951), 24.

31. Clinton Lee Scott, *The Universalist Church of America, A Short History* (Boston: Universalist Historical Society, 1957), 49.

CHAPTER SEVEN
Graded Sunday School Lessons Finally Approved
The International Graded Lessons Approved

The influence of progressive education theory is seen in the Sunday school movement as the success of the public schools increased and set the stage for the development of grading in the Uniform Lesson System and Universalist's development of the Murray Graded Lessons.

The stated educational aim of the evangelical Protestant church school from its early development was to bring pupils to a conversion experience and then to deepen their conversion into a commitment to the Christian faith through study of the Bible. However, growing criticism coming from the churches, the progressive education movement, the critics of the Uniform Lessons who advocated for graded lessons, and biblical scholars indicated that this aim was not being met. By the twentieth century the International Uniform Sunday School Association found itself adopting insights from progressive education, which were setting the standards for what was considered good education in the public schools. Many changes began to be seen in the field of religious education, one of which was the training of Sunday school teachers in teaching skills with a serious attempt to bring them up to the perceived level of excellence of the public school teachers. A second change came in the movement toward grading in the curriculum of the church school.

Edwin Wilbur Rice notes in *The Sunday School Movement 1780-1917* that beginning back in the mid-1800s there had been attempts at creating graded lessons in Protestant education and that there was more than one interpretation and formulation of what "graded" meant. In some instances and lessons, the themes and teaching helps were graded, in others the grading referred to the texts upon which the lessons were based. In some of the rural and outlying schools where there were adults who had not yet learned to read, grading consisted of lessons to meet the needs of those adults. Rice also pointed out that in the Uniform Lessons the teaching methods were graded for the ages being taught even though the lesson essentially was the same for all levels and ages.[1]

By the end of the first decade of the twentieth century, the International Uniform Sunday School Association adopted insights from psychology and from educational theorists who insisted that graded lessons were required to effectively meet the needs of the children in the public schools as well as in the Sunday schools.[2] It was good pedagogy as well as good psychology, and it made possible a more nurturing environment in which children and teachers could interact. The graded content of the Sunday school lessons would make the biblical texts accessible and enable the children, youth and adults to learn about the Bible in greater depth and with more relevance to their everyday lives.

Within the International Uniform Sunday School Association the critical movement to a completely graded series occurred from 1902 to 1909, as is seen in the following outline of events presented by Henry H. Meyer in *The Graded Sunday School in Principle and Practice*. At the General Convention of the International Sunday School Association in Denver in 1902, the Lesson Committee prepared a two-year graded course for the Beginners that was authorized by the convention. A two year course for adults was, however, rejected at that same conference. The sense of the Lesson Committee was that the Uniform Lessons was still the best possible course of study for all ages, and also, Meyer notes, committee members incorporated the logical procedure of introducing grading into the Uniform Lessons from the primary level up to adults in sequence. The Lesson Committee, Meyer also notes, stated that the older students needed to be prepared for the introduction of graded lessons, so it was not logical to make an adult graded lesson available without the student having experienced graded lessons from childhood on. At the Toronto General Convention in 1905 permission was given to the Lesson Committee to plan advanced courses for adults as part of the movement toward full grading of the lessons.[3]

In 1903 the Religious Education Association had put a focused source of pressure on the International Sunday School Association to take on the publication of a completely graded series as soon as possible. The work of members of the Religious Education Association (George Albert Coe, Charles Foster Kent, Philip A. Nordell, Frank K. Sanders and H. A. Sherman and others) was to articulate the relevance of the educational philosophy of John Dewey and progressive education to religious education curriculum development, classroom structure and teaching methodology.[4]

Between 1903 and 1908 the International Sunday School Association responded to criticisms of a widespread ignorance of the Bible as reflected in the choppy treatment in the Uniform Lessons, of the lack of teaching skills of Sunday school teachers in comparison to public school teachers, and of the reality that several graded series of independent publishers were far superior to what the International Association had to date published.[5] One of these, as previously mentioned, was by Erastus Blakeslee. George Herbert Betts, in *The Curriculum of Religious Education,* notes that the Graded Lessons Series by Erastus Blakeslee had been issued by the Bible Study Publishing Company of Boston since 1888.[6] It was the great popularity of Blakeslee's lessons that caught the attention of the Lesson Committee and gave them further impetus to pay attention to the increasing evidence of the sound pedagogical and psychological grounding in graded lessons. The Protestant Episcopal and some branches of the Lutheran Church were also preparing lessons that were considered better than the International Uniform Lessons Series. Meyer notes that there was also a movement among some of these denominations to prepare a graded series in case the International Sunday School Association did not do so in the very near future.[7]

In London two meetings of the International Lesson Committee were held, in 1906 and 1907, to discuss the matter of graded lessons. It is noted by Henry Frederick Cope, in *The Evolution of the Sunday School,* that "several English educators had been added to that body and they stood for progress."[8]

When the General Convention of the International Sunday School Association met in Louisville in 1908 it authorized the Uniform Lesson Committee to develop and prepare a thoroughly graded lesson series. The publishers had been prepared for the vote and presented to the Lesson Committee a system of lessons for students ages seven to thirteen. These were adopted by the committee and published by 1909 in time for the fall classes. The response to these lessons was overwhelmingly positive.[9] The lessons met the criteria of the teachers who had been trained in the normal schools as well as the denominations which had already understood the need for progressive education theories of John Dewey, George Albert Coe and others.

In 1906 Erastus Blakeslee decided to write a completely graded series and called together as consulting editors Frank K. Sanders, George A. Coe, Charles Foster Kent and Philip A. Nordell, all of the Religious Education Association. Kent was author, with Henry A. Sherman, of the highly popular *The Children's Bible*. When Blakeslee died in 1910 this completely graded series was published by Charles Scribner's Sons, and H.A. Sherman became managing editor with Coe and Kent as consulting editors.[10] In the development of the Universalists' graded lessons, the writing of these men, Sanders, Coe, Kent, Nordell and Sherman, can be seen in the bibliographies as resources for the teachers in the Universalists' Murray Graded Lessons.

In some of the leading Sunday schools during the years following the issuing of the International Graded Lesson Series of 1908-1909 there was a refusal to use these lessons because they contained extra-biblical materials. This refusal came from those who firmly believed the Bible was the only source of truth and therefore the only resource suitable for church school study. Henry H. Meyer writes that an optional list of biblical lessons was substituted with the two sets titled "Extra-biblical Series" and "The Biblical Series."[11]

Universalists Develop Their Own Curriculum

During this time (1890 to 1910), the Universalists were also busy meeting the challenges of progressive education theories, the scholarship of the Higher Biblical Criticism, Darwinism and evolutionary theories, and the latest discoveries in the field of geology. Universalists also were beginning to express a desire for their curriculum to emphasize their own thinking, theology and values.[12]

In religious education the Universalists had participated in the evangelical Protestant's Uniform Lesson System since its inception in 1873. This system granted diplomas to teachers who successfully completed teacher training and certificates to pupils who completed the system's lessons. The Universalists had neither comparable diplomas nor certificates to award their teachers and pupils. Nor did they have a system by which to evaluate the work or to grant such diplomas or certificates. Through participation in the International Uniform Lessons System, Universalist teachers and pupils were able to earn these teacher certificates and pupil diplomas that were held in high regard, bringing honor and distinction to those who earned them.

The Universalists, while participating in the Uniform Lessons System, had also developed materials for their Sunday schools and families over the years. The Universalist Publishing House and various Sunday school or Sabbath school Unions and Associations in the State Conventions had published considerable material throughout the years: *The Sunday School Helper, The Christian Leader's* "Sunday School Search-

Lights" articles, *The Myrtle* (a Sunday-school paper first published in 1861 by an independent publishing house, the publication of which was transferred to the newly formed Universalist Publishing House in 1862, and which ceased to be published in 1924 as an economy measure by the publishing house), and catechisms as far back as Judith Sargent Stevens's (later Mrs. Judith Sargent Murray) in 1782 and Shippie Townsend's in 1787. As a biblically-centered religion the Universalists extensively and satisfactorily used the lessons of the wholly Bible-based International Uniform Lessons System for many years. With the "helps" developed by the Universalists throughout this time the system suited the Universalists well. *The Sunday School Helper* was first published in magazine form outside the denomination, was purchased by the Universalist Publishing House in 1873 and became a standard among the Universalist Sunday school publications put out by the General Convention.[13]

An 1888 Commission of the Universalist General Convention considered their response to the previously discussed 1873 exclusion from the meeting of the Evangelical Alliance, especially as it impacted religious education materials. The commission was made up of Universalist ministers: John Coleman Adams, editor of *the Sunday School Helper;* C. Ellwood Nash (1855-1932), who at the time was president of Ryder Divinity School of Lombard College until he became field secretary for the Universalist General Convention in 1904; Frank Oliver Hall, coauthor with James M. Pullman of several of the "expositories" (sic) for help with the Uniform Lessons; Elmer F. Pember, and Henry B. Metcalf, a leading layman from Rhode Island. The commission proposed that the International Lessons be used with an accompanying Universalist text to be prepared by the Rev. James M. Pullman. It was determined that the Uniform Lessons would continue to be used with Pullman's newly commissioned "expositories" and Adams's articles in the *Sunday School Helper*[14] This was done from the 1880's until the Universalists wrote their own graded lesson series in 1901.[15] Universalist youth were thereby greatly influenced by the theological views of the evangelical community through the use of the Uniform Lessons, but were given a Universalist "help" from Pullman and Adams.

In Volume XLVIII, Third Quarter, 1917, No. 3 edition of the *Sunday School Helper* Series the topics covered move from the book of Isaiah, Second Kings, Second Chronicles, Ezekiel, and Daniel. In this quarter of study they learned of Isaiah, Ahaz, Hezekiah, Sennacherib, Manasseh, Josiah, Hilkiah, Daniel, Shahrack, Meshech, and Abednego. The students were asked to complete passages that lifted up the significance of the lives, events, and significance of each of these people. The volume consists of twelve lessons with each ending with a Universalist Catechism.

The lessons are all Hebrew Testament passages while the Catechism material focuses on the life, teachings and death of Jesus in Universalist interpretation.

Universalist Catechism

XXVII: How was Jesus the son of man? *He shared our human nature and was subjected to its infirmities and temptations.* Heb. 4:15

XXVIII: Why do we specially exalt Jesus above other men? *For his spiritual endowments, his sinlessness, his sacrifice on the cross, his reappearance after death, his continual ministry in the earth.* Phil. 2:8, 9.

XXIX: How does Jesus save sinners? *By revealing the mercy of the Father and the attractions of a holy life; by the moral power of his love; by the imparting of his holy spirit.* John 4:9.

XXX: What is the Holy Spirit? *The Holy Spirit is the presence of God in the soul of man.* John 16:7.

XXXI: What is God's desire toward men? *He wills that all should be saved.* I Tim. 2:4.

XXXII: How is God accomplishing His will? *God through Christ is reconciling the world unto Himself.* 2 Cor. 5:17-9 (sic)

XXXIII: Will Christ fail to complete his divine work? *He will draw all men unto himself, he will find the last wanderer.* John 12:32 Luke 15:4

XXXIV: How is salvation to be found in Christ? *By believing in him, by following him, by opening mind and heart to his influence.* Eph 1:10

XXXV: What is our debt to Christ? *By giving his life for us he made us beyond measure his debtors.* 1 Peter 2:21-25

XXXVI: What should our response to Jesus' love for men? *We should confess his name and serve his cause.* Matt 10:32-33

XXXVII: What is our ground of faith that we shall live after our bodies die? *We are children and heirs of our Heavenly Father.* Rom. 8:16-17

XXXVIII: How has our heirship of immortality been confirmed to us? *By the resurrection and reappearance of Christ.* 1 Cor. 15:20. [16]

In each of the volumes of the *Sunday School Helper* Series for the senior lessons in 1916 and 1917 documented here the Universalist Catechisms ask and answer questions about the salvation of all through Christ. The questions and answers are repeated throughout the series as a repetition of the message that all will be saved through God's will of reconciliation through believing in Christ.

The lessons develop questions for discussion based on the biblical passage each session. In Lesson 1, July 1,1917 about Isaiah's Call to Service the questions strive to relate the text to the lives of the students. There are four: 1. How are we to suppose that Isaiah "saw" God? 2. Do you suppose he heard an audible voice? 3. How can we see God? 4. What is our world for such divine promptings?

These are followed by a section titled Light on Dark Passages where terms and things unfamiliar to the students are explained. The term is in bold and the explanation in regular type face. **I saw the Lord.** In mental vision. **Train.** The skirts of his robe. **Seraphim.** The only reference in Scripture to these celestial beings. They appear to have been the personification of the higher powers obedient to God. **Filled with smoke.** Smoke is usually associated with God's wrath, and may here be used to indicate the divine displeasure with Israel. **Terebinth.** The turpentine tree.[17]

During the late 1890's there was a growing a number of Universalists who wanted more liberal lesson content than was found in the International Uniform Lessons. Universalists were responding to the writing and scholarship of Orello Cone in Higher

Criticism, of Marion D. Shutter in evolutionary theory, and the work of John Coleman Adams and others who were articulating a Universalist theology influenced by these men, referred to as "the third stage of Universalist theology" by Lewis B. Fisher.[18] Throughout the ensuing years there were many commissions and much discussion of what, how and why to develop Universalist lessons.

Cone was part of the circle of Universalists ministers who were creating specifically Universalist religious education materials. His close association with John Coleman Adams (1849-1922), James M. Pullman (1836-1903), and Marion D. Shutter (1853-1939) gave a solid voice for the modernist and progressive ideas prevalent at the time. Adams, Cone, and Pullman published articles regularly in the *Universalist Leader and Quarterly*. Pullman and Shutter were active in the 1890's group of Universalists working for closer relationships with Unitarians, Ethical Culture, Reformed Jews, and liberal Protestants supportive of Higher Criticism and evolutionary theories. Pullman and Cone presented papers at the 1895 American Congress of Liberal Churches in Chicago.[19] Adams edited the *Universalist Helper*, for over fifty years (The Leader changed names in 1926 from Universalist to Christian, and in 1953, back to Universalist, most likely a reflection of the Universalists' balancing act between identification with the evangelicals in the 20s and 30s and accepting Universalism's liberal shift by the 1950s.)[20]

This circle of religious-education focused ministers concentrated their attention on the challenges to the old theologies of pre-biblical-criticism time. Universalists engaged in the scholarly discourse of scientific inquiry and modernist ideas being formulated in the mid to late 1800s. It was within this Universalist climate of rationalism, inquiry, and biblical critique that the discourse with science occurred, and in which Orello Cone, John Coleman Adams, James M. Pullman and Marion D. Shutter held central places.

With this scholarly basis for biblical interpretation and criticism, the Universalists developed their own lessons to complement and eventually replace the Uniform Lessons. The Universalists published a graded curriculum in 1901, a full seven years before the International Lessons Committee was able to produce such a resource:

> In 1901 the Commission [of the General Convention of Universalists]...recommended: for the Kindergarten Department the lessons prepared by Mrs. Maizie Blaikie Barney; for Primary grades, the lessons on the Life of Jesus written by Mrs. Marion I. Noyes; for

Junior grades, two series of lessons, the one on "Cardinal Values," and the other on "Topical Studies in the Teachings of Jesus," both prepared by Dr. [C. Ellwood] Nash; for Intermediate and Senior grades, Dr. [James M.] Pullman's, "Studies in Paul and the Life of Jesus," and a series of lessons from the Old Testament from the modern view-point, by Rev. F.W. Perkins....and it is also now publishing a new course of lessons edited by Rev. D. M. Hodge, Rev. F.W. Perkins, and Rev. J.F. Thompson. These last-named lessons are published in Manuals....These lessons are based on the best modern knowledge of the Bible, and we have no better denominational expression of the way the Church reads the Bible to-day in what we have called the third stage of our theology. [21]

These lessons and manuals are the earliest graded lessons documented for the Universalists, and they demonstrate Universalist participation in the movement to graded lessons in Sunday school material. The pressure to move to graded lessons from the Uniform Lesson System had been building for over two decades within the system itself. The Universalists were among the growing number of denominations that abandoned the Uniform Lessons due, among other things, to the system's reluctance to develop graded series.[22] The Universalists also moved away because of the International Uniform Lessons System's refusal to use the higher criticism in the biblical curriculum.[23] As stated above in the quote from the Universalist General Convention's Commission, Universalists were looking into the growing dissatisfaction with the Uniform Lessons and seeking in 1901 to have, as Fisher notes, a "series of lessons from the Old Testament treated from the modern view-point."[24]

As the various local Universalist Sunday School organizations began to merge into larger, and eventually into State Convention level, organizations, the work of developing curricula that met the criteria demanded by the times took place. These criteria were set by the progressive educators in the secular education field, by the modernist ideas of Higher Biblical Criticism, the scientific theories of Charles Darwin and others, and by the Religious Education Association's work in the field of religious education. Universalist theology also made its demands on Universalist biblical curriculum. Cone's work on a theistic evolutionary theology, whereby he wrote that evolution and Genesis are not in opposition to one another in the account of creation, gave to Universalists a theology in which humanity began as primitive creatures and

evolved into the higher, intelligent beings we now are. This theology no longer
affirmed a biblical creation story in which humanity was created in the image of God
and fell, thereby requiring salvation. Cone's theology held that humanity was ever
growing into the freely given salvation from God, or the First Cause, or Creator. Cone
espoused a "rational faith in historical Christianity."[25]

Massachusetts Universalist Sunday School Association Formed

The formation of Sabbath and Sunday school unions and associations began to slowly
take shape for Universalists. The process was slow and not at all easy. Russell Miller
documents the formation of the Massachusetts Sunday School Association and points
to several others in various Universalist State Conventions.

> [The Universalist Sabbath School Union] had been created in 1837 as
> the Universalist Sabbath School Association with Lucius R. Paige of
> Cambridgeport as the first corresponding secretary....[The Universal-
> ist General Convention had been encouraging] state Conventions to
> form local Sunday school associations, of which, there were seven by
> 1849....In several states, such as New Hampshire and Vermont,
> Sabbath School Associations, consisting of the pastors of all societies
> having such schools, and lay delegates from each, met simultaneously
> with the state convention....[In 1857 there were] thirteen Sunday
> School Unions scattered about the country, three of which were state
> organizations.[26]

The minutes of the Massachusetts Universalist Sunday School Association of 18 May
1910 document the formation of that Association:

> It was five years ago this month that the Universalist Sabbath School
> Union and the Essex Sunday School Union independently voted to see
> what steps could be taken toward closer co-operation of Sunday
> School workers in Massachusetts and form, if possible, a state Sunday
> School Association....this present organization was formed September
> 28, 1906. Rev. Vincent E. Tomlinson D.D. of Worcester was the first
> President.

The name chosen for this organization was, The Massachusetts Universalist Sunday School Association. It is interesting to recall at this time the purpose of the organization as embodied in the constitution. "The object of the Association shall be to promote the welfare of the Sunday School work in general and of Massachusetts Sunday Schools in particular. It shall maintain a central bureau for the distribution of information and advice on all matters pertaining to the improvement of Sunday School work"....

In the year 1908-09, as was reported at the last [Universalist General] convention, the Board [of the Massachusetts Universalist Sunday School Association] realizing that it was only lack of means that prevented [the directors of the Association] from fulfilling the obligation [of the Association's Constitution], decided to establish the office of field secretary and to make the office of the secretary the bureau of information. This was to help out the work of increasing the interest in Sunday School work and aid teachers and schools in promoting new methods. Mrs. E.M. Barney was engaged as field secretary. [27]

In these same minutes there was also recognition of the need for permanent office space for this newly created bureau of information and its newly hired field secretary, Mrs. Caroline C. Barney (Mrs. E.M. Barney). The Massachusetts Sunday School Association approached the Universalist Publishing House in Boston seeking a site for their headquarters. This was accomplished and Mrs. Barney began working from September to May each year. At the September 1909 meeting of the association it was voted that she attend the State Interdenominational Sunday School Convention at North Adams, Massachusetts, in October, and that her expenses be paid by the Massachusetts Sunday School Association. She was also authorized to attend the next meeting of the Religious Education Association held in Providence, Rhode Island. At the November meeting a vote was recorded "that there be a committee of four, of which the President E. B. Saunders and Mrs. Barney shall be members, to prepare a list of graded lessons which shall be recommended for use in our schools, and to have the same printed for distribution." It was also voted that Mrs. Barney invite teachers from Universalist Sunday Schools within a fifty mile radius of Boston to participate in a series of four Saturday afternoon teacher training sessions at the Universalist Publishing House. [28]

At the Massachusetts Universalist Sunday School Association's December 1910 meeting, it is noted that the Directors of the Universalist Sabbath School Union were asked to financially support the Association for the work done by Mrs. Barney, and they agreed to do so. [29]

During that same meeting of the Massachusetts Universalist Sunday School Association another discussion was recorded concerning the desirability of a graded series and of the Universalist Publishing House publishing it. A request was to be submitted to the publishing house's Publications Committee for consideration at their next regular meeting. The handwritten request, dated 29 March 1911, included these points:

> The Executive Committee of the Massachusetts Universalist Sunday-school Association is convinced that there is a widespread demand throughout our denomination for a series of graded lessons, prepared under Universalist auspices, and published with our imprint....Much of the material [currently in use] is excellent, and yet some of it is unsatisfactory because written from a point of view not entirely in accord with the ideals of the Universalist denomination. All would be delighted if such courses could be prepared by those filled with the spirit of our denomination.
>
> You may ask, "What is meant by graded lessons?" and "Are we not presenting such material in the present *Helper*?"[italics mine] We would reply, that, in the *Helper* [italics mine] at present are published the International Uniform Lessons, which provide for the use of identical material in every grade. By employing different editors an attempt is made to adapt this identical material for different grades....
>
> In the modern view the essential characteristic of a graded course is the selection of Biblical and other material adapted to the mind of the child in the various stages of normal development, together with the application of methods of teaching to the unfolding nature of the child. Our request, therefore, is that you shall make available for the Universalist Sunday-schools a similar progressive course....
>
> If deemed wise, all through the Beginners and Primary Grades the

International Graded Courses could be followed, thus enabling teachers to avail themselves of the many helps being published in connection with this series....[The Junior, Intermediate and Senior Lessons would be prepared independently of the International Graded Lessons by Universalist authors].

The [Universalist] editors are selected with regard to their fitness and qualifications for the material to be treated....[New graded lessons] should also be changed for pedagogical reasons.[30]

By their March 1911 meeting the Lessons Committee of the Massachusetts Universalist Sunday School Association reported that they had nearly completed their task of developing a plan for the creation of a graded series. In April the Publications Committee of the Universalist Publishing House recommended the gradual adoption of this plan for graded lessons. The Massachusetts Sunday School Association Lessons Committee minutes report the following actions:

that it had prepared a proposed curriculum. It was decided not to publish this at present, but to leave the matter with the [Publications] Committee [of the Universalist Publishing House]....Voted: That [the Lessons Committee] discontinue on May 1 the preparation of material for the Sunday School column of the *Leader*....Voted that the Lessons Committee be authorized to publish the curriculum at the discretion of the [Publications] Committee.[31]

At a special meeting held on 8 June 1911, of the directors of the Universalist Publishing House the following action was taken concerning the proposed graded lessons from the association's Lessons Committee:

1. That the Committee on Publication and the General Agent be authorized to arrange for the preparation and publication of a complete series of graded Sunday School lessons in general accordance with the prospectus of the International Lessons, but with independent Universalist treatment beyond the primary grade....

2. That this work be put in the hands of separate editors in different

grades and that an effort be made to have the material ready for publication September 1, 1912.

3. ....voted that the Agent be authorized to purchase the lessons of the International Course prepared for Beginners and Primary Grades....

Voted that the lessons be called "The Murray Graded Lessons;"....[32]

A few months later on 23 October 1911, at a meeting of the Publishing House Board of Directors, the Publications Committee reported they had taken the following action:

In accordance with your [the Universalist Publishing House Board of Directors] vote of September 18th the Publication Committee beg leave to nominate as editors of the Series of Sunday School lessons the following persons: For Editor of the Junior Grade Miss Mary L. Ballou; For Editor of the Intermediate Grade Professor and Mrs. Arthur I. and Alice L.G. Andrews; For Editor of the Senior Grade Miss Mabel I. Emerson.....We recommend the Publication of a brief biography of John Murray to sell.[33]

Another event took place in 1912 that solidified the Universalist move to go out on its own. In a letter from the Rev. Dr. George E. Huntley, professor at St. Lawrence Theological School, to the Sunday School Commission of the Universalist Church, dated 25 April 1912, he relates his experiences with the International Sunday School Association's Educational Committee. Excerpts from the letter explain the situation that the Universalists faced in regard to Sunday school curriculum development:

At the request of your secretary I give a brief account of my activities as your superintendent of Teacher Training....

I was instructed to arrange courses that would be approved by the International Association and win for graduates the International diplomas. It did not occur to me at first that the questions of fellowship would be raised and apparently it did not occur to any other Universalist workers.

My first endeavor then, was to select courses of study that should be
satisfactory both to the Educational Committee of the International
Association and to liberal and scholarly thinkers in our own schools.
I supposed that I could find suitable works among those already
accepted by the Committee and that in a month or six weeks I would
be ready to announce our courses. Examination of the approved
courses however showed that none of those in use in the Orthodox
churches would be available in our own. While the pedagogy was
good in many cases, the doctrines and the Biblical scholarship were
such that the books could not be recommended.

I next cast about for some published volumes to be suggested to the
Educational Committee with the hope that they would be approved as
a distinctly Universalist course....The section on the Bible by Dr.
Schauffler ought not to be used in Universalist schools. In the place of
that section I suggested Toy's "History of the Religion of Israel" and
Savage's "Beginnings of Christianity" as Shown in the Growth of the
New Testament." This course was rejected by the Educational
Committee, although part of the members approved of it "education-
ally". [*sic*]....

My next task was to select an Advanced Course –or is it to select it,
for the work is not yet done. The only trouble has been in regard to
the Biblical work....

I do not think that a more conservative or less scholarly volume
would be useful in our schools and I therefore have not known how to
proceed.

Moreover the question of fellowship has now been brought up. It
seems that objection is made not only to the suggested courses but to
any co-operation with Universalists. This was hinted so gently at first
that I did not understand, but in the latest letters has been clearly
stated. It seems that Dr. Hamill has had it in mind to bring up at a
directors' meeting the whole question of the relation of the International Association to the Universalist Church, but that the pressure of

other business has prevented him from doing so....

The suggestion that we may arrange independent courses and grant
our own diplomas is interesting. One or two facts in connection with
it, however, should be considered. One is that almost all my corre-
spondents had asked first of all for courses that would result in the
International diploma. Another is that independent action will call
for much time and expense.[34]

This situation ended the Universalist's participation in the work of the International
Educational Committee and further spurred the Universalist's writing of the Murray
Graded Lessons.

The Murray Graded Lessons Published

The Murray Graded Lessons were published in 1912 and included three groups: the
Junior Course for ages 9 to 12, the Intermediate Course for ages 13 to 16, and the Senior
Course for ages 17 to 20. As previously documented in the 29 March 1911 Massachu-
setts Sunday School Association minutes, the International Graded Series for Beginners
Course, ages 4 and 5; and the Primary Course for ages 6 to 8 continued to be used to
avoid having separate Universalist lessons created.

The International Graded Lessons were written in the same form as
were the old Uniform Lessons. The International Lessons Committee
prepared a detailed outline of each course but left the selection and
preparation of the textbooks to the individual denominations or
publishing houses. They provided fifty-two lessons containing new
content, beginning in October and going until the end of June, with
the July and August lessons being supplementary in nature and not a
required part of the year's overall goals. The September lessons were
a preparation for the coming year's work. The Bible was the major
resource used but also materials were included from missionary literature, temperance information, church history and stories from nature.[35]

The Murray Graded Sunday School Lessons followed this pattern of lessons with the
exception of the Junior Course which had forty-six lessons rather than fifty-two. The

rationale given in the *Junior Teacher's Book* was to allow the teachers six sessions for extra reviews, observance of Christmas, Children's Sunday and other holidays that do not have the usual routine of schedule.[36] In the Murray Lessons' listed reading material for the teachers and for use with the children are many resources from the 1909 Beacon Series of the Unitarians as well as several from Universalist sources such as James M. Pullman, Frank Oliver Hall, Orello Cone and Lewis B. Fisher. The Murray Lessons also include Memory Hymns as an additional means of helping the children learn the Scripture passages. The lessons included art projects, such as making collages from cut-up magazines or drawing and coloring their own pictures. The suggestion of making books from the hymn words and using them for Christmas presents, or taking them to hospitals or shut-ins, or donating them for use in mission work demonstrates an experiential pedagogy of doing as well as listening and seeing. The social action aspect was brought in as the child was encouraged to think of ways to make life a little happier for those who suffer. The suggestion was also made to encourage the pastor to use the hymns in the church service when the children were to be present. The lessons consist of one- year sessions that are closely related to one another and form one continuous and unified Bible study.[37]

An advertisement in the 12 July 1930 Christian Leader *for The Murray Graded Sunday School Lessons* provides the following outline of the entire series:

> The Junior Course for pupils 9 to 12. A four-years [*sic*] course issued in two parts to each year.
>
> OUTLINE OF THE LESSON SUBJECTS
>
> FIRST YEAR (For pupils nine years of age):
> PART I   Stories of the beginnings.
>   Stories of the Patriarchs. 20 Lessons.
> PART II   Stories of Joseph. Stories of Moses.
>   Stories Jesus Told. 26 Lessons.
>
> SECOND YEAR (For pupils ten years of age):
> PART I   Stories of the conquest of Canaan.
>   Incidents in the life of the Lord Jesus. 22 Lessons.
> PART II   Followers of the Lord Jesus (Missionary).

Stories of the Judges. 24 Lessons.

THIRD YEAR   (For pupils eleven years of age):
PART I   Stories of the Kingdoms of Israel and Judah. 20 Lessons.
PART II   Stories of the Kingdoms of Israel and Judah
             (continued). 11 Lessons.
                 Responsibility for one's self and for others
             (Temperance). 4 Lessons.
                 The Exile and Return of the People of Judah.
             11 Lessons.

FOURTH YEAR (For pupils twelve years of age):
PART I   The Gospel according to Mark. 25 Lessons.
PART II   Studies of the Acts. Later Missionary Stories.
             21 Lessons.

Memory hymns and Bible drill are included in each year's course as supplementary work.

The Intermediate Course for pupils thirteen to sixteen. A four-years [*sic*] course issued two parts to each year with 26 lessons in each part.

LESSON SUBJECTS

FIRST YEAR (For pupils thirteen years of age):
PART I   Leaders of Israel.
PART II   Leaders of Israel.
             American Religious Leaders.

SECOND YEAR (For pupils fourteen years of age):
PART I   Early Christian Leaders.
PART II   Later Christian Leaders. Missionary Leaders.

THIRD YEAR   (For pupils fifteen years of age).
PART I   Studies in the life and character of Jesus.
PART II   Studies in the life of Jesus.

Missionary activities at home.

FOURTH YEAR (For pupils sixteen years of age):
PART I   Studies in the Teachings of Jesus.
PART II   The Teachings of Jesus.
        Christian Work Abroad.

The Senior Course for pupils seventeen to nineteen and over. A three-years [*sic*] course issued in two parts to each year.

LESSON SUBJECTS
FIRST YEAR:
PART I   The World a Field for Christian Service.
PART II   Problems of Youth in Social Life.
        The Book of Ruth.
        The Epistle of James.

SECOND YEAR:
        The History and Literature of the Hebrew People.

THIRD YEAR:
        The Literature and History of New Testament Times.[38]

The Murray Graded Sunday School Lessons are located at Meadville Lombard Theological School's Fahs Center and in the archives at the Andover-Harvard Library of Harvard Divinity School. The most complete set of the Murray Graded Lessons available in these libraries is the Junior Course written by Miss Mary L. Ballou. Missing from the Junior Course are the three *Junior Teacher's Books* for the Second Year, Part One, the Third Year, Part One, and the Fourth Year, Part Two.

ENDNOTES

1. Edwin Wilbur Rice, *The Sunday School Movement 1780-1917, and the American Sunday School Union 1817-1917* (Philadelphia: American Sunday School Union, 1917), 310, 311.
2. George Herbert Betts, *The Curriculum of Religious Education* (Cincinnati:

Abingdon Press, 1924), 137-140.

3. Henry H. Meyer, *The Graded Sunday School in Principle and Practice* (Philadelphia: Westminster Press, 1910), 102, 103.

4. Betts, *Curriculum of Religious Education*, 408, 409.

5. Frank Glenn Lankard, *A History of the American Sunday School Curriculum* (New York: Abingdon Press, 1972), 274.

6. Betts, *Curriculum of Religious Education*, 408.

7. Meyer, *The Graded Sunday School*, 106.

8. Henry Frederick Cope, *The Evolution of the Sunday School* (Boston: The Pilgrim Press, 1911), 120.

9. Betts, *Curriculum of Religious Education*, 147.

10. Betts, *Curriculum of Religious Education*, 150.

11. Meyer, *The Graded Sunday School*, 311.

12. Russell E. Miller, *The Larger Hope: The Second Century of the Universalist Church in America: 1870-1970* (Boston: Unitarian Universalist Association) 1985), 215.

13. *Ibid.*, 214.

14. Clinton Lee Scott, *The Universalist Church of America: A Short History* (Boston: The Universalist Historical Society, 1957) 48, 49.

15. *Ibid.*, 48, 49.

16. *The Sunday School Helper Series Senior Lessons Vol. XLVIII Third Quarter No. 3* (Boston: Universalist Publishing House, 1917) full pamphlet

17. *Ibid.*, 1

18. Lewis B. Fisher, D.D., *A Brief History of the Universalist Church* (Boston: Young People's Christian Union, 4th ed., rev., 1903 or 1904), 131.

19. Miller, *The Larger Hope, The Second Century*, 126, 127.

20. *Ibid.*, 248, 250.

21. Fisher, D.D., *Brief History of Universalist Church*, 130-131.

22. Betts, *Curriculum of Religious Education*, 144.

23. Lankard, *History of American Sunday School Curriculum*, 269.

24. Fisher, *Brief History of Universalist Church*, 130-131.

25. Orello Cone, *Gospel Criticism and Historical Christianity* (New York: GP Putnam's Sons, The Knickerbocker Press, 1891), vii.

26. Russell Miller, *The First Century of the Universalist Church in America: 1770-1870* (Boston: Unitarian Universalist Association, 1979), 280-281.

27. *Massachusetts Universalist Sunday School Association Minutes* [18 May 1910], Andover Harvard Archives, bMS 285.1, 77-80

28.*Ibid.*, 77-80.

29.Massachusetts Universalist Sunday School Association Minutes, Special Report to the Universalist Publishing House [December 1910], Andover Harvard Archives, bMS 285.1.

30.*Ibid.*

31.*Massachusetts Sunday School Association Minutes* [15 March 1911], Andover Harvard Archives, bMS 285.1, 102-112.

32.*Handwritten Minutes of a Special Meeting of the Board of Directors*, of the Universalist Publishing House [8 June 1911], Andover Harvard Archives, bMS 369/2, vol. 3,) 65-66.

33.*Universalist Publishing House Minutes Records*, 1862-1962 (inclusive) HU HOLLIS # ACZ8674/mss, (Andover Harvard Archives, Theol. Ms BMS 369), 70.

34.George E. Huntley, Letter to the Sunday School Commission of the Universalist Church, [25 April 1912].

35.Betts, *Curriculum of Religious Education,* 362-385.

36.Mary L. Ballou, "Junior Teachers Book," *Murray Graded Sunday School Lessons* (Boston: The Universalist Publishing House, The Murray Press, 1912), 5.

37.*Ibid.*, 5.

38.The Christian Leader, "The Murray Graded Sunday School Lessons" (Boston: The Universalist Publishing House, [12 July 1930]

CHAPTER EIGHT
The Murray Graded Junior Lessons

The Murray Graded Sunday School Lessons were examples of the influence from the Higher Biblical Criticism, evolutionary theory and progressive education. They embody Universalist theology and provide for the children lessons in the values and beliefs central to Universalism in 1912.

Mary L. Ballou of West Somerville, Massachusetts, was an active religious educator and youth worker in the Boston area. In the 1 January 1905, "Semi-annual Report of the National Secretary and Committee" to the National Executive Board of the Young People's Christian Union (YPCU) it is reported that she was hired by the National Junior Organization to write the junior column in the *Onward* and was paid $25.00 per year for this service. At the 4 July 1908 meeting of the YPCU board she was appointed superintendent of Junior Methods for the coming year. At the 10 July 1912, Twenty-fourth Annual Convention of the Young People's Christian Union she gave a report of the Junior Union in her capacity as national superintendent of juniors. At the same meeting she was elected to the YPCU national board and conducted the Junior Union Conference. At the 18 May 1910, Annual Convention of the Massachusetts Universalist Sunday School Association meeting she delivered the intermediate department report. She was listed as a life member of the Massachusetts Universalist Sabbath School Union in 1923-1924.[1]

The outline of the junior course is nearly identical to that of the International Graded Series junior course as recorded by John Richard Sampey in *The International Lesson System, The History and Origin of its Development*. This chapter provides a comparison of the Murray Graded Lessons Junior Series with its counterpart in the International Graded Series. The one exception where the Murray Series varies is in the third year where the International series includes a fourth lesson titled "Introduction to New Testament Times" which the Murray Series does not.

The foreword to the *Junior Teacher's Book* for the first year, part one, is basically the one used in the International Graded Lessons with a few exceptions. The stated purpose of the graded lessons is printed in the beginning of each *Junior Teacher's Book* in both the International Graded Series and in the Murray Graded Lessons. They are identical to the International Series' Junior Course with the exception of one phrase added by the Universalists.

The first statement of purpose in the International Course reads, "To know God as He revealed Himself to us in nature and in Christ." The Universalist statement of purpose reads, "To know God as He revealed Himself to us in nature, *in the heart of man*, and in Christ" (italics mine). The italicized phrase is not included in the Murray Senior Course, and the Murray Intermediate Course statement of purpose is altogether different.[2]

In the listing of material chosen for the junior lessons of the International and Murray series the explanation of how these materials were chosen is the same with the exception of the italicized phrase added by the Universalists. "The truths are presented in lessons from the Bible, and are illustrated by lessons from nature, from the history of missions, and from the temperance [movement] *and other humane movements* (italics mine)." One other difference between the stated purpose and the construction of the lessons is seen in the following statements from each. The International Lessons state, "As each year's work is adapted to the interests, capacities and needs of the pupils of that year, the Lessons can be made most effective when taught by the class teachers." The Murray Lessons state, "..., but an effort had been made to adapt each year's work to the interests, capacities, and needs of the pupils of that year."[3]

In each of these instances the Murray Lessons include a broader understanding of the individual's role in the process of education. The "heart of man," "other humane movements" and a commitment to a more child-centered pedagogy are early indications of the difference in the two lesson series.

Following the outline and stated purpose of the lessons, the Murray Lessons *Junior Teacher's Book* has a section on the characteristics of the age group being taught. For the Junior Course the section is called "The Junior Period." It includes "junior characteristics," "junior interests," "junior habits" and "how to help the junior spiritually." It suggests also that the junior teacher be knowledgeable of the childhood years that precede the junior years, and the adolescent years that follow, so as to better understand the pupils as they move through the years between nine and twelve. While the content of the Murray Graded Lessons is Bible-centered, the pedagogy is more child-centered. The pupil participates in the learning process through art projects, music, social action activity and workbook assignments done during the week in their *Junior Pupils' Book.* The teachers' instructions include directions to ask the pupils for their understandings of things and for their participation, not only through recitation of the memory verses and answers to questions from the pupil's books, but through critical thinking responses to open-ended questions. The teacher is also instructed to relate the biblical story to the everyday life of the children in the class.

An example of open-ended presentation and questions requiring critical thinking by the pupils can be seen in this exchange from the *Junior Teacher's Book*, Lesson 21, "Stories of Joseph."

> Have pupils find the Psalm [121] in the Bible and read the first two
> verses. When Joseph lived these words had not been written. If Joseph
> could have said them to himself during the long, hard journey to
> Egypt, do you think they would have comforted him?...When no
> pursuers came from Jacob's tents and the pyramids of Egypt came in
> sight Joseph might have said, "I cannot see that God is helping me; He
> is not doing what I ask Him to do for me." But I think instead of this
> the boy continued to talk with God, to thank Him for every little
> blessing, and to ask for His help in each day's trials. And I think
> Joseph felt that God was truly helping him, although he could not see
> just how it was being done.
>
> God has a plan for your life, just as He had for Joseph's. He is
> watching over you to help you through all the hard places and
> unhappy places. He wants you to talk with Him about everything
> which comes into your life. This Psalm is one of the loving messages
> He has put into the Bible to help us when trials come.[4]
>
>   Psalm 121:
> I lift up my eyes to the hills—
>   from where will my help
>   come?
> My help comes from the LORD,

who made heaven and earth.
He will not let your foot be
    moved;
    he who keeps you will not
      slumber.
He who keeps Israel
    will neither slumber nor sleep.
The LORD is your keeper;
    the LORD is your shade at your
      right hand.
The sun shall not strike you by
    day,
    nor the moon by night.
The LORD will keep you from all
    evil;
    he will keep your life.
The LORD will keep
    your going out and your
      coming in
    from this time on and
      forevermore.[5]

This exchange and Psalm provide the pupil with an experience in the Universalist belief that God is love, and a God who loves His children as professed in the 1803 and 1899 Professions of Faith. "We believe that there is one God, whose nature is Love," and the First Principle of Universalist Faith, "The Universal Fatherhood of God."

Following the list of characteristics of the children in the *Junior Pupil's Book* is a bibliography of additional books recommended for the teacher's reference to enable her or him to be better prepared to teach the lessons. Included in the list are a good *Teacher's Bible* (American revision preferred), a Bible atlas, the *Cambridge Bible*, *Biblical Geography and History* by Charles Foster Kent, *The Spiritual Life* by George Albert Coe, and *A Study of Child Nature* by Harrison.

Following the bibliography is a section of simple rules for storytelling, information about missionary education and church support, and how to prepare a lesson. The last two suggestions for storytelling are to avoid telling a story for the sake of a story, but to tell it for the truth it will teach and to give the pupils a chance to tell the Bible stories themselves. For missionary work the *Junior Teacher's Book* instructs the teacher to develop the understanding by the children of what, to whom and why they are giving money to mission work. Learning about missionary work and the opportunity for children to make financial contributions instills in the children the financial habits that will lead to future financial support for the church. Teachers are to help children learn that support means service as well as money, and children need to be given opportunities to do what they can for their home church. In the section on lesson preparation, it is highlighted to "think of what the pupils already know which will lead up to the lesson....Study and plan the lesson with each pupil in mind, his virtues, faults, limitations, possibilities. Remember that each needs instruction and inspiration."

The next sections of the *Junior Teacher's Book* include the "Class Program," and "Home Work." The class program section begins, "The teacher should be the first member of the class to be found in her place in Sunday school...Example speaks louder than words." The homework was to be done in each child's *Junior Pupil's Book*, and children were to practice recitation and memorization of the Bible passages used in the class each week. As the child progressed in ability to read, the passages were to be read before the class rather than as review following the Sunday class. The goal was to prepare the children to engage the biblical passage during the Sunday school lesson rather than memorize it after the lesson had been taught. It was an educational method that had the potential of engaging the pupil at a more personal level with the biblical passage during the lesson. It is suggested that the teacher also fill in a pupil's book and on a semi-annual basis hold an exhibition of the pupil's books for the parents and the full congregation to view and praise.

At the conclusion of the lessons in the *Junior Teacher's Book* is a section titled "Helps in Teaching 'Our Bible'." This section provides techniques in presenting the Bible and in giving a critical interpretation of biblical content. The first two lessons in the "Our Bible" section offers instruction on how the Bible is constructed in books and two testaments. Lesson 3 begins the critical understanding of the content. For example, in Lesson 3 of the *Junior Teacher's Book,* as the children read from Psalms, Exodus and 1 Samuel, it is suggested the teacher say, "Each one sounds as if it was from a different kind of book, doesn't it? Yes, the books in the Bible are not all alike; some are books of history, some contain poetry, and several other forms of literature are to be found there. We can divide them as John did his." This teaching of the literary nature of the books of the Bible reflects the use of literary source criticism in this course.

The International Graded Lessons gave very little assistance for teachers, providing simply a listing of aims for the course and titles for the biblical stories contained in each text. Lesson 1of the International Graded Lessons Junior Course lists the following:

I. Stories of the Beginnings.

1. In the Beginning. —Teaching Material: Gen.1:1 to 2:3. Pupils' Reading: Gen. 1:1-5. Memory Text: In the beginning God created the heavens and the earth. Gen. 1:1.

2. The Garden of Eden. Teaching Material: Gen. 2:4-25. Pupils' Reading: Gen. 2:15-25. Memory Text: And the LORD God took the man, and put him into the garden of Eden to dress it and keep it. Gen. 2:15.

3. Hiding From God. — Teaching Material: Gen. 3:1-24. Pupils' Reading: Gen. 3:1-15. Memory Text: Can any hide himself in secret places so that I shall not see him? saith the Lord.

4. Cain and Abel. — Teaching Material: Gen. 4:1-26. Pupils' Reading: Gen. 4:3-15. Memory Text: Love suffereth long and is kind; love envieth not. 1 Cor. 13:4a.

5. Review.

6. The Building of the Ark. — Teaching Material: Gen. 6:5 to 7:5. Pupils' Reading: Gen. 6: 13-22. Memory Text: Thus did Noah; according to all that God commanded him, so did he. Gen. 6:22.

7. The Flood and the Rainbow. — Teaching Material: Gen. 7:6 to 8:22; 9:12-19. Pupils' Reading: Gen. 8:6-19; 9:12-19. Memory Text: I do set my bow in the cloud, and it shall be for a token of a covenant between me and the earth. Gen. 9:13.[6]

The Murray Graded Lessons' Junior Course, Part One, also has seven lessons. Rather than listing only the teacher materials, pupil readings and memory text, the Murray Lessons also lists additional Scripture readings and non biblical readings for the teacher. Examples of the non biblical readings include, from the lesson on Cain and Abel, *Man Without a Country,* by Nathan Hale, and *Paradise Lost* by John Milton. In

Lesson 15 of the First Year, Part One, on Abraham willing to offer Isaac, the poem *Victim* by Alfred Lord Tennyson is suggested as non biblical reading. As can be seen on the following page, the aim of each lesson is stated along with the Memory Verse in contrast to the International Graded Series listing of general aims for the entire Junior Course portion. Following this listing is a section in the *Junior Teacher's Book* on working out the lesson with the class, which is essentially a suggested method of presenting the lesson, or a lesson plan. It includes the story and the questions to be presented in the class and tips for the teachers on how to present the material. For example, it suggests the teacher "Have book ready to open at the first title page for coloring and let pupils read 'Stories of the Beginnings.' Pupils tell where found." The "Our Bible" for lesson one begins the process of the lesson plan.

Following is a listing of the Murray Graded Lesson's Junior Course, First Year, Part One, Lessons 1 through 7 that correspond to the International Lessons profiled above:

Stories of the Beginnings

Lesson 1. — In the Beginning.
Memory Verse. - In the beginning God created the heavens and the earth. Gen. 1:1. Pupil's Reading. — Gen. 1:1-31.
Teaching Material. — Gen. 1:1-2:3.
Additional Scripture. — Psa. 8; Psa. 147; Psa. 148; Job 38 and 39.
Helpful Reading. — Genesis, by *Dods*, chap. 1. "The spacious firmament on high," *Addison*. The Creation, in "On Holy Ground," *Worcester*.
Aim. — To present the thought of God as the Creator of all things, a Being wise, powerful and loving.

Lesson 2. The Garden of Eden.
Memory Verse. — The Lord God took the man and put him into the garden of Eden to dress it and to keep it. Gen. 2:15.
Pupil's Reading. — Gen. 2:1-25.
Teaching Material. — Gen. 2:4-25.
Additional Scripture. — Psa. 104; Psa. 90: 1,2,17; Eze. 31:3-9; Matt. 6:28-30; 1 Thess. 4:12.
Helpful Reading. — The Garden of Eden, chap. 1, *Hodges*. Poems of

Labor, *Whittier*. Ethics for Children, Third Year, *Cabot*.

Aim. — To show that God gives each person a work to do in the world. To inspire each pupil to do his work with joy.

Lesson 3. Hiding From God.

Memory Verse. — Can any hide himself in secret places so that I shall not see him? Saith the Lord. Jer. 23:24.

Pupil's Reading. — Gen. 3:1-6; 8-10; 12-14.

Teaching Material. — Gen. 3:1-24.

Additional Scripture. — Prov. 20:11; 1 John 3:20, 21 and 1:9; Psa. 139:11-12; Psa. 32.

Helpful Reading. — The Garden of Delight in "Old Stories of the East," *Baldwin*. A Drama of Exile, *Mrs. Browning*. Paradise Lost, *Milton*.

Aim. – To show that breaking God's law brings punishment.

Lesson 4. Cain and Abel.

Memory Verse. — Love suffereth long and is kind; Love envieth not. 1 Cor.13: 4a.

Pupil's Reading. — Gen. 4:3-15.

Teaching Material. — Gen. 4:1-26.

Additional Scripture. — Heb. 11:1-4; Prov. 3:9; Luke 11:45-54; Micah 6:6-8.

Helpful Reading. — The Two Brothers in Old Stories of the East. Man Without a Country, *Hale*. House with the Bible, chap. 12, *Geikie*.

Aim. — To lead pupils to feel that it is better to have love in the heart than evil feelings.

Lesson 5. The Building of the Ark.

Memory Verse. — Thus did Noah: according to all that God commanded him, so did he. Gen. 6:22.

Pupil's Reading. — Gen. 6:9,10; 14-22; Gen. 7:1-5.

Teaching Material. — Gen. 6:5-7: 5.

Additional Scripture. — Heb. 11:7; Josh. 24:14, 15; Psa. 1;1 John 5:3,4; Rev. 2: 7, 17, 26, and 3:12, 17.

Helpful Reading. — The Garden of Eden, chap. 2. The Flood of

Waters, in Old Stories of the East. Genesis, by *Dods*, chap. 5.
Aim. — To encourage the pupils to do right in the face of ridicule.

Lesson 6. The Flood and the Rainbow.
Memory Verse. — I do set my bow in the cloud, and it shall be for a token of a covenant between me and the earth. Gen. 9:13.
Pupil's Reading. — Gen. 7:6-10, 17-21; 8:1-4, 6-12, 15-22; 9:12, 13, 17.
Teaching Material. — Gen. 7:6-8, 22; 9:12-17.
Additional Scripture. — 1 Kings 8:54-61; 2 Peter 3:9; 1 John 2:25; Psa. 111.
Helpful Reading. — On Childhood, *Wadsworth*. To the Rainbow, *Campbell*. Also see suggestions for last lesson.
Aim. — To show that God had an everlasting covenant with His children: God is to bless; the children are to obey.

Lesson 7. Looking Back.
Pupil's Reading. — Gen. 1:1-5, 31; 2:15-17; 4:2-5; 8:6-12, 22.
Teaching Material. — Genesis, chapters 1-9.[7]

Taking each lesson once again and looking at how the lesson was developed and how the biblical material was utilized in the "Our Bible" teacher's instructions, it can be seen how Mary L. Ballou developed a Universalist curriculum that responded to progressive educational ideas, including child psychology and the modernist impulses of Higher Criticism and the science of geology. There is no explicit teaching of Universalism, but the content has a decided Universalist flavor as will be seen in the full development of these seven lessons.

Lesson 1, "In the Beginning," in the *Junior Teacher's Book* begins with telling the children what they can expect during the morning.

> The Book about which we have been talking is full of many wonderful stories. I suspect you know many of them now, but we shall learn to find them and to read them for ourselves in these new Bibles that we have.

> The first stories that we are to find are stories about the very beginnings of things, ever and ever so many years ago.[8]

The children are then instructed to look in the "Our Bible" section for a quick fill-in-the-blank review of the books of the Bible used in each lesson. The first lesson gives general information about the two Testaments of the Bible, with the individual books being referred to as a library of books. In the *Junior Teacher's Book* there is a picture of a bookcase with the books of the Bible arranged on the shelves of Old Testament books in categories of Law, History, Poetry, Minor Prophets, Major Prophets and a shelf of New Testament books that are divided into categories of History and Epistles.

The children open their Bibles and read the verses as they are able while the teacher tells the story. The teacher explains the word Genesis as meaning "beginnings." The teacher is told to "Tell the story in the words of the Bible, with little addition or subtraction, letting the children feel the majesty of the marvellous [*sic*] poem." It is suggested that the teacher read Genesis 2:1-3 to complete the story. The children are given their pupil books and shown the first page, which contains blank lines for the child to write the Memory Verse. The teacher suggests the child color in the first letter block with crayons or water colors. The teacher explains that each child is to write in their book the answers to what happened on the first, second and third days of creation. "Ask what was done on the first day and tell pupils they are to write in the blank spaces two or three words to tell what was done on each 'day,' a word that has been explained as meaning in this story, 'a long period of time.'" This particular phrase indicates the influence of evolutionary thought as developed by Orello Cone and Marion D. Shutter to wed theology and evolution into a single and whole story of creation. Cone posited that because God's revelation must be understood by humanity, both revelation and humanity must evolve together.

As part of the understanding that God is creator, powerful and loving and the one who has made the earth and sky, light and darkness, the concept of being given gifts by God is presented, and the suggestion of saying, "thank you" to God for these gifts leads the children into a time of prayer.

> A wise teacher will strive to enter into the prayer life of her pupils.
> Prayer seems a very intimate and personal thing, even to a child, and
> the teacher who shares in directing the same, normal prayers of her
> pupils can usually be free to talk with them on whatever subject that
> may be necessary no matter how closely it may touch the child's
> personal life.[9]

With this instruction for the teacher, Mary L. Ballou has given the child and the teacher a basis for developing the relationship between them, and to foster within the classroom a sense of trust between child and teacher, with the Bible as the source of the good news of a loving God. In the work from the "Our Bible" activities, the children begin to learn how to read the Bible and thereby gain a level of comfort with it. The goal is for them to know how to read the Bible, to feel competent to read it, and to find the passages they want in it on their own so that it becomes a part of their experiences and their lives.

Lesson 2, "The Garden of Eden," begins with a review of Lesson 1. It is the time when the teacher will learn how well the children can or will be able to do the homework and how she/he as teacher can foster the necessary cooperation of parent and child in the work. As part of the review of the first week's work it is suggested that "We can enrich the child [sic] life by connecting the Bible with music, art, literature, nature, and human life, as occasion offers." It suggests the teacher bring in Haydn's *Creation* to quote or play on a piano (since recording devises [sic] were not available) or to read or sing Addison's hymn "The Spacious Firmament on High."

Lesson 2 is then launched by talking about a garden, preferably a garden that one of the children has at home. The lesson suggests taking a few minutes talking about gardens in general and what is required in upkeep and the needs for water and sunshine. The children then find the story of the Garden of Eden in chapter two of Genesis. The teacher tells them, "This is another of the old, old stories of the world, told first before any books were written. Once upon a time, said the ancient story-teller, there was no one living on the beautiful earth which God had made, no one to take care of the plants and animals." Here again is reflected the influence of source criticism and literary criticism in the lessons. As discussed earlier in this dissertation, German theologian Hermann Gunkel and Universalist scholar Orello Cone believed in the existence of an oral tradition behind the biblical writings, and this theory is expressed by Mary Ballou in this lesson. The genre of the story, whether myth or saga or history, gave the scholar or teacher the information required to ask of the story appropriate questions and interpretation. According to Gunkel the Garden of Eden story is a saga and therefore not entirely historically factual, it is "another of the old, old stories of the world."[10]

As the children read this story of creation the following advice is given for the teacher in the *Junior Teacher's Book*:

(If any pupil scornfully says, "I know that isn't true," explain that
these are the ancient stories of the Jewish people, as all races have
stories of their beginnings. They are not always intended to be literal
statements of fact; but the Bible stories differ from others in connecting events with God. Moreover, in each story there is a truth to be
found. Usually young Junior children do not criticize in this way, but
care must be taken, for the sake of future faith in the Bible, to teach
many lessons as stories with truths in them, rather that as actual
occurrences.).[11]

This interpretation of the biblical stories is seen in the liberal theology of the time,
notably in the writing of Albert Schweitzer and Harry Emerson Fosdick.

Lesson 2 continues by reinforcing the idea that everyone must work and that we all
have duties to perform, just as Adam and Eve did in the Garden of Eden. The Bible
drill is used in this lesson to teach the fact that there are 39 Books in the Old Testament. This was a repetitive reciting of the books of the Bible in correct order. An
example of such drill for Lesson 2 asks the teacher to say:

Let us see how much we can say about the Bible without looking in
our notebooks. The Bible is a _____? Book made up of books. Yes;
let us say the whole sentence together. Once more. All who can tell
me something else about it may fold their hands. What do you want to
tell, Jennie? Let us say together what Jennie told us.

The lesson ends with the following poem intended to reinforce the stated aim to show
that God gives each person a work to do in the world.

Labor
"Labor is worship!" the robin is singing;
"Labor is worship!" the wild bee is ringing.
Listen; that eloquent whisper up-springing

Speaks to thy soul from out Nature's great heart.
From the dark cloud flows the life-giving shower;
From the rough sod blows the soft-breathing flower;

From the small insect the rich coral bower;

Only man in the plan shrinks from his part.
Frances Sargent Osgood [12]

This poem is an example of the naturalistic theologies of the early 1900's. Unitarian Robert S. Corrington, associate professor of philosophical theology at Drew University, writes of naturalism as being best described in four forms. The forms he identifies are "Descriptive" Naturalism, "Honorific" Naturalism, "Process" Naturalism and "Ecstatic" Naturalism. Each of these forms differs in what each stresses, but through all of them nature reveals the sacred as an integral component of nature. Of these forms he writes,

> It should be noted at the outset that each form of naturalism insists that there can be no special realm of the supernatural that somehow remains disconnected from nature itself. Insofar as the supernatural is still affirmed it is done so as one dimension with the rest of nature...."Descriptive" Naturalism stresses the primacy of material and efficient cause within a vast cosmic structure that is indifferent to human aspiration, even if it allows for the growth of the good within fragmented human communities...."Honorific" Naturalism places special priority on the role of the spirit in either creating nature or in quickening natural possibilities toward an ideal consummation....."Process" Naturalism focuses less on a ubiquitous and omnivorous spirit and more on plural centers of power and awareness that interact to sustain an evolutionary cosmos...."Ecstatic" Naturalism combines several of the elements of the previous three forms but that transforms all of them by its radical insistence on fundamental division within nature itself...Ecstatic naturalism affirms with descriptive naturalism that nature is often indifferent to the aspirations of the human process.[13]

Universalists were finding affinity with the naturalistic theologies and it is reflected here in the work of Mary Ballou.

Lesson 3 "Hiding from God," focuses on the need to obey; when one does not, punishment will follow. It begins with a Bible lesson on how to arrange all the books of the Bible into the Bible Bookcase and is a repetition as was done in Lesson 1. The teacher begins by asking the children if any of them have so many books they need a bookcase to keep them in. The teacher is instructed to say, "Name several books that children this age would be reading to illustrate how one might have enough books to need a bookcase and then talk about how one might sort these books." The teacher then has the children open their Bibles to the book of Psalms, then to the book of Exodus and finally to First Samuel. The teacher then comments on how these books all sound very different from one another. Reflecting the use of literary criticism in studying the Bible, the children are taught to notice the differences in style and form of the stories. They are asked to note how different the books look and sound and how reading them provides an understanding of these differences. It gives the message to the pupil that the Bible has many authors and is part of the Hebrew people's culture and society. The children begin to draw their own Bible bookcase as a method of learning the names and places of the thirty-nine Old Testament books in order of sequence in the Bible and in classification as laws, history, poetry, major prophets, and minor prophets.

Next the teacher talks about laws and asks what laws God gave Adam and Eve to obey. The story relates how Eve was tempted by the snake to eat the fruit of the tree of knowledge of good and evil. The children are then asked, "Does a voice ever seem to tell us that it will do us no harm to disobey?" The story's message of guilt is placed, through questions by the teacher, within the context of a child who becomes conscious of having done wrong and what that feels like. Issues of blaming others, feeling better once someone knows the truth, and having the ability to choose right from wrong are all brought out by the teacher. It ends with the message that God forgives those who repent of wrongdoing. Here the lesson emphasizes a Universalist, loving, forgiving God who, while demanding obedience from humankind, is a God of love, rather than a God of vengeance. This message of John Murray, Hosea Ballou, and George deBenneville is given within the context of a child's need for forgiveness when he or she has disobeyed.

Lesson Four, "Cain and Abel," focuses on this biblical story with the aim of leading the children "to feel that it is better to have love in the heart than evil feelings." The Bible section again focuses on learning the names and order of the books of the Old Testament by having the children work on their bookcases. The names of the books are explained in terms to which the children can relate. Exodus is "going out," Leviticus contains the laws of the people, Numbers is a census of the people, and Deuteronomy is a repetition of the laws so the people will remember them better.

It is suggested that the teacher talk about how God watches over us in a loving way, rather than watching in order to catch us in times of disobedience. The story of Cain and Abel reinforces the idea that we have choices to make and that Cain made a wrong choice just as had Adam and Eve in the last lesson. The concept that each individual is capable of making responsible as well as irresponsible choices teaches the pupils that humanity has a part to play in how their relationship with God will develop. The idea of being worthy of salvation by God was an important value for Universalists, and making good choices and doing good deeds was taught. John Coleman Adams writes of the Universalist doctrines of rewards and punishments as they were formed out of the theology of Hosea Ballou, which grounded the ethics of Universalism into the 1900's. He writes:

> The one impregnable position in life is to be right with God. To be right and to have a heart full of love, is to be able to face pain, privation, persecution, and yet all through them to be strong and victorious.....As there is no heaven for the healthy man greater than the blessedness of health, so there is no heaven for the loving and the good which can by any possibility be more blessed than just the state of being good and loving....So our heaven is not a ready-built place awaiting our souls hereafter; it is a "building of God." Which we, with all other children of the Father, are slowly fashioning out of our own hearts and wills.[14]

This theology held that reward and punishment were of this world, and humanity was a participant in the heaven and hell of his or her life. When a man or woman repented of their sins and chose to follow God's will then they were worthy of the salvation waiting for them from God. He or she would have become "worthy" of salvation. This was a human responsibility. To achieve this state one must develop as good and strong a character as one can.

The teacher is instructed to impart an understanding that Cain brought his offerings before God with an unwilling heart, in contrast to Abel who brought his with a willing heart. This is done to make plausible God's rejection of Cain's offering. Once again the Universalist message of a loving God is reinforced, although it is not explicitly stated. It is important to note that the teacher is instructed to provide a reason for God's rejection of Cain's offering. Without such an explanation the pupil could hear that God is vindictive and unreasonably mean and unjust, as Calvinist interpretations asserted. The lesson ends with the teacher talking with the class "about unkind thoughts that may come into the minds of boys and girls...[and to]...tell how kind, loving thoughts may be used to drive the bad thoughts away." The following poem attributed to John Wesley is presented for the children to learn by repetition:

> Do all the good you can,
> To all the people you can,
> In all the ways you can,
> As long as ever you can.[15]

Lesson 4 concludes with plans for a social justice project such as a Thanksgiving basket for a needy family. A prayer is learned that will help begin to "lighten" the story of Cain with the thought of the sinless child Jesus whose example, it is hoped, the children will come to follow.

Lesson 5 "The Building of the Ark," has as its aim to encourage the children to do right in the face of ridicule. The lesson story and focus of the morning tells of the building of the ark by Noah. Because junior-age children enjoy repetition, the Bible session goes through the naming of the books of the Bible on the shelf of the Bible bookcase once again. The Bible story begins with the death of Moses and the leadership of Joshua. The concept of a family as a tribe of many, many people is explained as they learn that in the time of the Judges each family was led by a judge, and the families turned to the judges for settlement of disputes and for advice on making good choices. The children then find the books of First and Second Samuel in their Bibles. Samuel is presented as someone known for making good choices. The "Our Bible" section is a repetition of the previous four lessons, and the goal is for the children to learn in sequence the names of the books of the Bible in the span of the year's study, while the main lesson each Sunday focuses on one story for in-depth study.

The lesson on Noah begins with the idea that people go about their lives not listening to the voice of God or thinking about whether they are doing things that will please God. During the story, as Noah is building the ship, the children and teacher talk about what it is like to know what is the right thing to do even while others, not understanding, make hurtful comments of ridicule, and how hard it is to keep on doing what is right. The lesson affirms, however, that in the end the good choices will be rewarded. This concept reinforces the Universalist belief that people are capable of making choices and acting responsibly in accordance with what God wants them to do.

Lesson 6 "The Flood and the Rainbow," is about the events at the conclusion of Noah's story. The idea of covenant is developed, and it is hoped that the children come to understand that "God is to bless; the children are to obey." The Bible lesson is of First and Second Samuel and the formation of the Kingdoms of Israel. The lesson moves through First Kings to Chronicles. In many lessons the Bible section covers areas that are not covered in the main lesson which enables the teacher to cover more of the biblical passages during the class time and provide the pupils with a complete overview of the Bible each year. It is jarring, however, to move back in time from the Bible session to the main lesson in this particular lesson. In the previous five lessons there was a connection between the passages in the themes of the stories and events of the main lesson and the "Our Bible" work. Lesson 6 does not make such a connection, and the two parts of the lesson do not constitute a solid cogent lesson for children or adults.

When the teacher begins working with the main story of the flood, she/he is instructed to,

> Review what was told last week and go on with a graphic story of the flood, avoiding descriptions of the horrors incidental to it but making vivid the days of continuous rainfall, the steady rise of water, the isolation of the little company in the ark. What a sea of water Noah looked out upon! How glad he must have been that he obeyed God![16]

The idea of covenant in this lesson is explored in some depth as a promise between God and humankind. The rainbow is the sign of the covenant, and the children are encouraged to give thanks to God when they next see a rainbow in the sky.

Lesson 7 is a review titled "Looking Back." The review process consists mainly of repetition of the memorization that has taken place throughout the first six lessons.

The Lessons Committee, asserting that children love repetition, encourages teachers to present biblical passages that can be memorized and repeated over and over, much to the children's delight and accomplishment. It is suggested that they be given the opportunity to recite for the congregation during a worship service. The teacher is reminded that in any review the questions must deal with the underlying truths of the stories, not the literal component of the stories.

For homework leading into Part Two the children are asked to read about the Patriarchs. Nothing is said in the teacher's instructions to help in explaining where Cain found a wife if Adam and Eve and their two sons Cain and Abel were the only humans God had created on earth. I cannot imagine a child not wondering how this wife got there or from where she might have come.

It is obvious that Mary L. Ballou has utilized the scholarship of the higher criticism as she explicitly notes where literary and source criticism is used in the Bible passages she draws on in the lessons. She teaches Universalist values and beliefs through the examples she gives for the pupils to study, and in the questions she asks. The characteristics of the pupils presented in the *Junior Teacher's Book* demonstrate her understanding of the educational needs of the young people who will be studying these lessons. Ballou has shown how the Murray Graded Junior Lessons reflect the Universalist response to the challenges of Modernism.

ENDNOTES

1. *The Christian Leader* (Boston: Universalist Publishing House, 12 July 1930)

2. Mary L. Ballou, *Junior Teacher's Book*, First Year, Part One, *Murray Graded Sunday School Lessons* (Boston: Universalist Publishing House, Murray Press, 1912), First page of Foreword.

3. John Richard Sampey, D.D., LL.D., *The International System: the History of Its Origin* (New York: Fleming H. Revell Company, 1911), 285.

4. Ballou, *Junior Teacher's Book*, 93.

5. *Holy Bible*, The New Revised Standard Version with Apocrypha, *Psalm 121* (Nashville: Thomas Nelson Publishers, 1989), 571.

6. John Richard Sampey, D.D., LL.D., *The International System The History of Its Origin*, (New York, Fleming H. Revell Company, 1911), 313.

7. Ballou, *Junior Teacher's Book*, 25-35.

8. *Ibid.*, 25.

9. *Ibid.*, 27.

10. Walter Harrelson, *Interpreting the Old Testament* (New York: Holt, Rinehart and Winston, 1964), 31.

11. Ballou, *Junior Teacher's Book*, 29.

12. *Ibid.*, 29.

13. Robert S. Corrington, "Ecstatic Naturalism and the Transfiguration of the Good," *Empirical Theology: A Handbook*, ed. Randolph Crump Miller (Birmingham:, Ala. Religious Education Press, 1992), 204.

14. John Coleman Adams, D.D., *Universalism and the Universalist Church* (Boston: Universalist Publishing House, The Murray Press, 1915), 46-47.

15. Ballou, *Junior Teacher's Book*, 32.

16. *Ibid.*, 34.

CHAPTER NINE
Murray Graded Intermediate Lessons

The next graded level in The Murray Graded Sunday School Lesson Series is the Intermediate Course. Today few of the intermediate lessons exist at the Andover-Harvard or Meadville Lombard libraries. The only *Intermediate Teacher's Book* available is for the second year, part one. The only *Intermediate Pupil's Books* are for the first year, parts one and two; second year, part one; and third year, part one. Because the second year, part one, is the only one with both an *Intermediate Teacher's Book,* and an *Intermediate Pupil's Book* I will explore these lessons in order to illustrate the educational philosophy and theology underlying the Murray Graded Lesson Series. I will demonstrate the influence of the Higher Biblical Criticism, progressive education theories, and evolutionary theories influencing Modernism.

The authors of the intermediate course are Mrs. Alice L.G. Andrews assisted by her husband, Professor Arthur I. Andrews. They were both listed as life members of the Massachusetts Universalist Sabbath School Union in 1923-1924.[1] Alice Lazelle Gladding Andrews served as the President of the Ferry Beach Ladies Aid Society from 1936 to 1937 and served in the Society for several years. She was active in the First Universalist Church of Providence where she was a teacher in the Sunday school. She died July 28, 1958. Dr. Arthur Irving Andrews's Obituary in the New Hampshire Sunday News, Manchester, N.H. May 1, 1960 edition stated that he was widely published in the international field and is listed in *Who Was Who Among North American Authors 1921-1939.* He was born March 27, 1878 in Providence, Rhode Island and died April 27, 1960. He was Associate Professor of History 1911-1912, Professor of History 1912-1915; Professor of History and Public Law 1915-1926 at Tufts University, Professor of Diplomacy at the Charles University of Prague 1921; Professor of European History at the University of Maryland 1926-1927; Professor of History at the University of Vermont 1927-1928 and was decorated by the Kingdom of Yugoslavia for "continued and noble activity in the field of international understanding." He earned an AB from Brown University in 1901 and his PhD from Harvard in 1905. He married Alice Lazelle Gladding June 16, 1907. Arthur and Alice Andrews are buried in the

Sway Point Cemetery in Providence, RI. And like Alice he was active in the First Universalist Church in Providence.

He launched the Institute of World Affairs at Ferry Beach and served as its Dean from 1935 to 1940.

The lessons of the Murray Graded Intermediate Course follow those of the International Intermediate Graded Lessons course. There are five lessons in both courses of the second year, part one, "Christian Leaders," beginning with the heading "Jesus, the Leader of Men." The five lessons are: "Jesus, the Conqueror of the World"; "Jesus Victorious Over Temptation"; "Jesus Mastering Others"; "Jesus Triumphant Through Self-Sacrifice"; and "Jesus Inspiring His Followers."[2]

The Murray Lessons' *Intermediate Teacher's Book* contains an introduction of the graded lessons in general and the intermediate lessons specifically. The International Series Lessons begins with statements that the aim of this course is "To present the ideals of the Christian life, as exemplified by Jesus himself and by leaders whom he inspired, and to secure pledged allegiance to his service." This is followed with an outline of the titles of the lessons for four years.[3] An introductory paragraph in John Richard Sampey's book on the International Lesson System, states that the intermediate ages of thirteen, fourteen, and fifteen years are ones of hero worship, with the pupils interested in character as well as conduct. Therefore, biographies of biblical persons deemed of worthy character and conduct are presented to give a concreteness to the problems and ideals of these characters within the lessons. Regarding the goal of the international intermediate lessons the introduction states that "It is impossible to picture a character without the historical setting, but the history is simply the background. Moral questions are involved in life studies, but the purpose is to present them in the concrete as embodied in conduct."[4]

The Murray Intermediate Lessons are designed around the understandings that young people, ages thirteen to fifteen, are in a time of rapid growth and physical, mental, emotional and spiritual development. The introduction to the *Intermediate Teacher's Book* states:

> Ambitious ideals play an important part in the great decisions which are made in this period of life. Therefore it is most essential at this

time to create high ideals and noble ambitions....Now they are to
study the leaders in Bible and church history, not what they did nor
what they taught, but what they were. The historical setting is of
course necessary, but only as much is used as is needed to bring out
the character of the individual....The aim is to create in the pupil an
approval of and desire to emulate the good and a disapproval and
dislike for the evil.[5]

The introduction then provides a description of the *Intermediate Pupil's Book* and an
outline of the *Intermediate Teacher's Book,* along with information about supplemental
material for the implementation of the lessons to their fullest potential. Maps of
Palestine in Jesus' day are printed in the teacher's book, as well as stereographs of, for
example, the mountains of Judea from the Plain of Jericho, and a description of
stereographs and where they can be purchased. "A stereograph is made with a camera
which produces at the same moment two negatives that are as exactly alike as the
impressions received by a [person's] two eyes. Seen through the lenses of a stereoscope
things stand out solid as in nature, in natural sizes at natural distances."[6] The effect
would be similar to pictures of today that you put close to your nose and then slowly
move it away until the vision from each eye crosses, creating a three-dimensional
picture.

In the *Intermediate Teacher's Book* there are suggested additional readings for the
teacher, to assist her/him in preparing more in-depth information in the lesson. The
Universalists were responding to an educational methodology that broadened the
pupil's learning through connections of their Sunday school lessons and their everyday
lives, here specifically in the realm of literature. Some of those listed are: "Youth" by
G. Stanley Hall, "Historical Bible" by Charles Foster Kent, and "Every Day Ethics" by
Cabot.[7] Next in the teacher's book comes a section on suggestions for the teacher on
the specifics of teaching and lesson planning:

Successful work in the Sunday School depends not so much upon
textbooks as upon the teacher himself....The aim is to make these men
and women of the Bible real people, and so to interpret their lives that
the pupil will be impressed by their character, be taught by their
mistakes, and inspired by their victories. The subject for study is not
so much the facts of these lives as what lies behind the facts, the hopes

and fears, the aspirations and achievements, the motives and ideals,
the failures and victories.

There are suggestions of other visuals in the form of postal cards, pictures and magazines that can be used with the lessons. Names of the publishing companies of these
pictures and cards are also listed. There is a substantial listing of recommended books
for the teacher on pertinent issues of teaching. G. [Stanley] Hall's *Youth* and Forbush's
Church Work with Boys are two. There are also some providing additional information
for lesson enrichment such as [Charles Foster] Kent's *Historical Bible*; Geikie's *New
Testament Hours*, volume two and *The Apostles*. A lengthy listing of books in which to
find maps of biblical lands, for example, Charles Foster Kent's *Biblical Geography and
History* and Smith's *Historical Geography of the Holy Land* concludes the introduction
for the teacher. This course consists of fifty-two lessons as does the International
Graded Intermediate Series. All fifty-two lessons are listed by title for a quick reference to the Christian leaders who will be covered during the year. These leaders
include Jesus, Martha, Mary, Stephen, Saul, Mark, Luke, Augustine, Chrysostom,
Boniface, Luther, and Wesley. The only Universalist listed among the mission Lessons
is Clara Barton. Clara was the founder of the American Red Cross and an active
laywoman in social service for Universalists. The omission of the Universalist leaders
and theologians John Murray and Hosea Ballou, along with the inclusion of religious
leaders Luther, Calvin and Wesley, seems to hinder the purpose to lift up Universalist
ideas, leaders and history in the form of extra biblical material. Michael Servetus,
though Unitarian, would also have been a logical inclusion due to his interactions with
Calvin during the Reformation. Servetus serves as one of the defining Unitarians in the
1550s as Protestantism was taking shape in Central Europe. By this time, following
Ballou's *Treatise on Atonement*, published in 1805, Universalist theology was unitarian
in nature, making Servetus's ideas important for Universalist young people to hear.

As stated earlier, an in-depth development of the second year, part one of the Murray
Graded Intermediate Lessons will be covered, including the first five lessons that
constitute the section on Jesus.

> The Scripture references for these five lessons are:
> 1. "Jesus, the Leader of Men": John 1:1-8 and Philippians 2:5-18.
> 2. "Jesus Victorious Over Temptation": Matthew 4:1-11 and John 6:15.
> 3. "Jesus Masters Others": Luke 4:14-30; John 7:37-52; and Mark 11:11, 15-18.

4. "Jesus Triumphant through Self-sacrifice": Mark 8:27-9:1; 15:16-39.
5. "Jesus Inspiring His followers": John 15:1-8; Acts 1:6-9; 2:1-47.[8]

The Murray Graded Intermediate Course second year, part one "Jesus, The Leader of Men," begins with the first lesson, "Jesus, the Conqueror of the World." The central thought that begins the lesson is "To Jesus as king of kings, the revealed of God, should be paid all reverence and homage." The Scripture references are John 1:1-8 and Philippians 2:5-18. A statement of the intent of the entire five lessons in part one and of this first lesson's specific aim is clearly written for the teacher, as follows: "These five lessons are intended to present Christ as a new divine and inspiring force in the life of man. The aim of this lesson is to picture him as a new kind of king." The lesson is providing the pupils with an understanding of a loving, forgiving god who sent Jesus to bring a message of obedience to hope and love that will bring in the Kingdom of Heaven, or Kingdom of God. The idea of the Kingdom of God for the Hebrew people is explained as the expectation of the Hebrews that God would rule over them in the Promised Land thereby fulfilling the Covenant between them and God. The Hebrew idea of the Kingdom of Heaven was that God would, through the Covenant, make Heaven on earth. This lesson introduces the idea of Jesus as a king who is not a political ruler who will establish a kingdom, but one who will inspire men and women, boys and girls, to live lives exemplified by His own. The Universalist God of love could be known through Jesus and by loving him. Jesus would be a king of a spiritual kingdom ruled by a God of love.

John Coleman Adams writes:

> With the advent of the Larger Faith has come also to the hearts of
> Christian men [sic], the understanding of the great plan and enterprise
> of Jesus Christ in the world. It was to establish the Kingdom of God. It
> was to organize all souls and all moral forces into a society whose
> will should be the will of God. This was the chief theme of his talk to
> men,—parable, precept, preaching, prayer. The central doctrine of the
> son of God is that this world and all worlds where sentient beings
> dwell are at last to come into harmony with the will of God; that men
> are to form a great fellowship, whose law is love and whose ideals are
> freedom, truth, righteousness and peace. This kingdom is to be spread
> and established by the power of the Divine Spirit in Jesus the Christ. Its

work and sway begin in the individual heart, and require the personal allegiance of the individual to the great Head of the Kingdom.[9]

Adams, in his reference to "all worlds where sentient beings dwell," demonstrates the influence of scientific inquiry and scholarship on the thinking of Universalists of the early 1900's. It is a very advanced concept for the time. God is "God" of the vast Universe, not just planet earth. And God is "God" of all sentient life, not just human beings.

> The lesson, "Jesus, the Conqueror of the World" taught that Jesus was greater than the greatest king, that he had dignity and strength of character that exerted a powerful influence over all with whom he came in contact, and which made his death the greatest of victories. Jesus was the revealer of God, and as we know and love Jesus we know and love God.[10]

It is suggested in the lesson that pupils read the seventh chapter of Daniel, which tells of Daniel's dream whereby the domination of foreign powers is overcome by the people of the holy one of the Most High. The main lesson continues to tell of the messianic hope of the Jewish people, of the oppression of Roman rule over the Hebrew people and of the ministry of John the Baptist who foretold the coming of the Messiah. The instructions for the teacher emphasize the need to clearly develop the understanding of the Messiah that most of the people of that time and place expected, and what Jesus' understanding of the Messiah was. The Hebrew people believed the Messiah would deliver them from oppressive foreign rulers. The Covenant between them and their God would be brought about by the Messiah. The teachers are to explain that Jesus understood himself as the one who revealed God to the people, the one who brought the message of how to love one another so as to bring in the Kingdom. As Alice and Arthur Andrews wrote, for Jesus, the Kingdom of God was far from a political entity, it was a spiritual kingdom that was within the hearts of all God's children. The lesson discussion centers on an understanding of the meanings of the words and images of Life, Light and the Word. As light is required for seeing Jesus was the light showing, or for seeing, the love of God.

Excerpts of the extra-biblical reading are printed in the *Intermediate Teacher's Book* from Rush Rhees, *The Life of Jesus of Nazareth,* and Marcus Dods, *The Gospel of Saint John.* Each of these selections discusses the concept of the indwelling God, the distinctions between the Kingdom of Heaven and the Kingdom of God as Jesus preached them and as the people of the time anticipated them as being, and of the theology of God as the Father. The indwelling God of the current day was shown to be an example of what Jesus taught as he preached about the inner light. The lesson is teaching the Universalist value of developing an inner spiritual life that is exemplary of Jesus' life and that will bring the pupil to a deeper understanding of a loving God. The idea of God as Father provides for the pupil a belief in a God who loves them as a father loves his children.

The *Intermediate Pupil's Book* for this lesson, "Jesus, the Conqueror of the World," relates the same concepts in language, images and definitions understandable to a youth of fourteen. The material is divided into five sections: "The Hope for a Messiah"; "A New Kind of King"; "Source of Christ's Power"; "The Revealer of God"; and "The Mission of Jesus." The first section explicitly delineates the differences between the earthly king who would conquer the Romans and bring in the Jewish Covenant of the Promised Land and the Chosen People, and Jesus' Kingdom of God, which was a spiritual Heavenly Kingdom. The pupils are told of the historical setting of Palestine at the time of Jesus' birth. The Roman Empire was supreme and the times had been hard for the Hebrew people. The historical setting of this political rule set the background for the lesson. The influence of historical criticism gives the teachers needed information to make the distinctions between the types of kingdoms the people hoped for and the one Jesus preached. The new kind of king was divine and loving. In section two, "A New Kind of King," the source of Christ's power was in God's manifestation of Himself in Jesus, and Jesus showed all that one needed to know about God. The third section, "Source of Christ's Power," the Revealer of God was Jesus as the word of God. It is to be explained that

> a word is an expression of thought. By words a person expresses what
> is in his mind and heart and so reveals what he is....The word of God,
> therefore, is the expression of God. We have never seen Him, yet
> through His word, Jesus, we know the kind of person He is. What
> Jesus is, God is. Jesus was described as full of grace and truth. By
> grace is meant God's overflowing love toward his undeserving
> children. Truth is reality. Jesus, then, is full of loving kindness and is
> the true expression of the character of God.

In this third section, the idea of children being "undeserving" of God's love seems out of place in a Universalist curriculum. This may be a reflection of the thinking by Alice and Arthur Andrews that responded to the evolutionary formulation of creation. It may have some grounding in the idea put forth by Orello Cone and evolutionists that humanity was created along beside all other living creatures and is evolving into worthiness of God's love. It may have come out of G. Stanley Hall's ideas that children evolve through all the stages of human development in their individual lifetime, beginning with primitive existence and moving toward human maturity. It may have come from an understanding of Hosea Ballou's sovereignty of God theology, that even though, or if, we are undeserving of God's love, God will love us anyway. Whatever the source, it seems to this author to be out of place and incongruent with fundamental Universalist theology of the day.

The message of God's character as revealed by Jesus is a significant part of a Universalist conception of a loving God. Although at no time in this lesson is there instruction for the teachers that refers to specific Universalist theology, it is implied in the emphasis on the power of love in the character of God as revealed by Jesus. The idea of the Kingdom is set within the historical context of the political situation of the Roman Empire's rule over the land. The history of the Hebrew people and their conquerors set the background for how the idea of a Messiah developed in the minds and hearts and spirits of those who understood themselves as a Chosen People of God. The final section, "Mission of Jesus," develops the idea of Jesus as the light over the darkness of injustice, hatred and impurity. Jesus' mission was to bring a guiding light into the darkness of sinfulness and of the ignorance of God. It concludes with six questions for the pupil to study and answer:

1. What were the expectations of the Jews?
2. What kind of a Messiah did they want?
3. How did Jesus differ from this?
4. Why did John call Jesus the Word?
5. What is the purpose of light?
6. How is Jesus the Light of the World?

The notebook work tells the pupils to
1. Design a title page for "Jesus the Conqueror of the World."
2. Write the first chapter on the "Mission of Jesus."[11]

The International Uniform Lessons utilize much of the same material for their first lesson in the second year, part one. There is a slight difference in the amount of biblical passages listed. Whereas the Murray Lesson suggests reading John 1:1-8, the international lessons suggest all of John 1. The Murray suggests using Philippians 2:5-18 and the international ones suggest only 2:5-11 and 15-18.[12]

The missing verses in the International Lessons, 12 to14 contain ideas Universalists would wish to have the children learn.

> 12: There, my beloved, just as you have always obeyed me, not only in my presence, but much more now in my absence, work out your own salvation with fear and trembling; 13: for it is God who is at work in you, enabling you both to will and to work for his good pleasure.

> Do all things without murmuring and arguing.[13]

Lesson two, "Jesus, Victorious Over Temptation," explores how powerful a temptation it must have been for Jesus not to succumb to the expectations of the Hebrew people for a triumphant and conquering earthly Messiah. The central thought to be presented by the teacher is that "We must master ourselves before we can influence others." The definition of temptation is explored, making clear it is not sin, but a situation involving a choice between two strong alternatives. One course of action is unworthy or wrong: "It is not temptation unless the wrong course makes a strong appeal and causes struggle." The examples given as choices that would be unworthy or wrong focus on the idea of the Kingdom that had been developed in earlier lessons. The ambition and power motives of the Roman Emperor Julius Caesar or Alexander the Great are cited as unworthy ones for being a leader of people. Jesus was tempted to gain fame and control by using his powers for selfish ends. The teacher is instructed to remind the pupils that overcoming temptation is one aspect of building character.

The pupils are asked to discuss the differences between the ambitions of the Roman Emperor Caesar and Alexander the Great with the ambitions of Jesus. The concept of the temptations is developed to demonstrate the reality of the struggle and the nature of the powers at play. The teacher is instructed to explain the reality of the choices between winning power to rule like Caesar and create a political kingdom for them and Jesus' concept of the Messiah as bringing in a spiritual kingdom. Selections from biblical scholarship in the *Intermediate Teacher's Book* provide the teacher with a passage from G.H. Gilbert's *The Student's Life of Jesus*. In it Gilbert explains that Jesus' temptations were spiritual and inner struggles to take up the mantle of the Hebrew Messiah or to hold fast to his understanding of God's call to establish the Kingdom of God as Jesus understood it to be. It "is not a historical description of outward situations and spoken words, but a poetical representation of inward, spiritual experiences." By presenting the material from Gilbert as an interpretation of the narrative, the pupils were to be led away from a literal interpretation of the Bible. By relating the temptations as comparisons to the political kingdom of the Roman Empire as found in the Gospels, Gilbert sets the struggle in an historical context. This historical context shows the pupils how the Hebrew people understood the struggle, and it provides a concrete metaphor to enable young people to grasp an abstract idea. The three temptations from Satan in the wilderness challenge Jesus to struggle between following the physical lure of earthly power or the spiritual power of God.

The material in the *Intermediate Pupil's Book* treats the time of Jesus in the wilderness and the three temptations he faced. The stories are developed as spiritual struggles and do not mention Satan at any time. As in the Intermediate Teacher's Book, the temptation comes from within Jesus' mind and spirit. It is made clear that accepting earthly power would be easier and less costly to Jesus than would the spiritual power required to bring in the Kingdom of God. When Jesus comes out of the wilderness his resolve is set and he is able to follow God's will as his own. Because Universalists believed there was no hell, the concept of Satan would not have been relevant. A person's "hell' was earthly, just as sin and restitution was always redemptive, not vindictive or vengeful as Satan's was in Calvinist theology. The power of the spirit that resists earthly temptations is inner, and its reward comes from following God's will as one's own.

The pupils are asked to answer six questions during the week:
1. What was Jesus to do?
2. How was he to be a different king from Caesar?
3. How was Jesus tempted to use his power for selfish ends?
4. How was he tempted to disregard God's laws?
5. How was he tempted to lower his ideal and become the kind of Messiah that was wanted?
6. What helped him to overcome temptation?[14]

The notebook instructs the pupil to write in their own words the second chapter on "How Jesus Conquered Temptation." In this way pupils were given the opportunity to internalize their understanding of the underlying truth and message. In the "Suggestions for Teaching" in the *Intermediate Teacher's Book,* the teacher is instructed to remember that "The notebook work can be done better during the week following the lesson upon which it is based, as the ideas in the pupil's mind have then taken more definite shape. The writing will be done by the pupil at home and will serve to impress upon his mind the important points of each lesson." This pedagogical teaching method is an attempt by the authors to be more child-focused in his or her learning of difficult abstract concepts.

The central thought of lesson three, "Jesus Mastering Others," is that "Righteousness gives us inestimable power and influence over others." This lesson aims toward an understanding of the significance of an individual's inner dignity and resolve to do what is good. The Scriptural passages of Luke 4:14-30; John 7:37-52; and Mark 11:11, 15-18, tell the stories of Jesus overcoming anger, evil and greed through his inner power and conviction to follow the will of God as he understood it. The *Intermediate Pupil's Book* lists the Memory Verse as Matthew 5:44 "Love your enemies and pray for those who persecute you."

The story of Jesus in the Temple is the lesson used to present the concept of the power of inner strength. Jesus knew that what he saw in the temple courtyard, with the money changers and merchants conducting earthly commerce and defiling the purity of the temple, was wrong and a profanity to God's House. In his commitment to God he did not hesitate to act on his understanding of the wrong he saw. Instead of doing nothing he plunged into action overturning tables and doing what he could to clear the temple courtyard. His powerful presence and action were observed with awe and fear. The lesson points out how often one is aware that something is wrong and should be challenged, but the spirit is fearful and therefore one does not act. It requires tremendous courage and self-mastery to face great opposition to do what is right. Self-mastery requires people to be in control of their actions and how their actions are governed by their knowledge of right and wrong. The lesson in the *Intermediate Pupil's Book* states that:

> By his love, his sympathy, his unselfishness, his kind acts, he made
> some people his friends and influenced them to try to live like him.
> But these same qualities made other people his enemies. They were

jealous of him or they disapproved of his message. Yet, even these were sometimes controlled by the strength of his personality.[15]

There is a list of seven questions for the pupil to answer during the week.

1. How did Jesus win friends?
2. How did he make enemies?
3. What overawed the mob at Nazareth?
4. What prevented the soldiers from seizing Jesus?
5. Why did he say the temple had been made a den of thieves?
6. What enabled him to drive out the traffickers without interference?
7. Can righteousness today hold in check the evil passions of men?[16]

The Notebook assignment was to write a third chapter in the Pupils' own words on "How Jesus Held His Enemies in Check."

While this homework draws on the pupil's critical thinking, imagination and experiences, there is little in the way of encouraging him or her to relate the story to their own lives. The message of the power of inner strength and resolve that exemplified Jesus' life is clear, but it would be difficult for youth of fourteen to imagine or think he or she could have such strength as is shown in the stories. This course is much more Bible-centered than child-centered, although the pupil's book is written at a level easily understood by a fourteen-year-old. In the context of this entire curriculum it is not easy to imagine what a child-centered lesson might look like. It would need to begin with the pupil's understanding of issues of power and ambition and how decisions they have made relate to those issues. The biblical stories would be used to reinforce the learning about those issues and to put forward the example of Jesus as the model who best exemplifies the successful resolution of the issues.

Lesson four, "Jesus Triumphant Through Self-Sacrifice," begins with the central thought that "The supreme test for us, as followers of Christ, is our readiness for unselfish service and willingness for self-sacrifice." The Memory Verse for the pupil is Mark 8:34, 35, "He called the crowd with his disciples, and said to them, 'If any want to become my followers, let them deny themselves and take up their cross and follow me. For those who want to save their life will lose it, and those who lose their life for my sake, and for the sake of the gospel, will save it.'"

The teacher begins the lesson with questions that elicit critical thinking about Peter's response, "You are the Messiah," in answering Jesus' question, "Who do you say that I am?" The connection is made to the earlier lessons that explored the identification of Jesus as the earthly Messiah and the temptation to be a Caesar-like ruler. The biblical story is interpreted as showing that Jesus has succeeded in instilling the knowledge of the difference between an earthly kingdom and the Kingdom of God when Peter is able to say on his own that Jesus is "The Messiah." The teacher points out the teaching of Paul in First Corinthians 13 that the greatest thing in the world is love and that Jesus held the allegiance of his followers by his love. Jesus did not need to hold his followers with threats or force. He showed them how to lead by example and loving respect for each one. By reading Mark 10:42-45 it is made clear that service is the ultimate expression of love. Jesus taught that being in service to others is at the center of how one is to live one's life. Service to God and others is the highest form of obedience to God. The idea of self-sacrifice as service is shown to be the means by which one can live one's life in the example of Jesus. One is to give up all ties to earthly goods and possessions and follow a life of service to others.

In Universalist theology this would be an important lesson on how to respond to universal salvation. If there is no threat of hell then one must learn to live a good and righteous life because that is the highest response to God that one can give. In learning to lead by the example of Jesus, the pupil is helped to understand what is required of him or her by God.

When the teacher begins to discuss the crucifixion as the ultimate self-sacrifice he/she is given the example of a soldier who gives his life for his country. For some the self-sacrifice might be in areas of ease or comfort or wealth that can be shared with those who lack them. The pupil is asked to name examples of what self-sacrifice might be either for them or for someone they know. The teacher is instructed to convey the understanding that the cross is a symbol of triumph of self-sacrifice (bringing in the Kingdom of God) rather than a symbol of defeat. *The Intermediate Pupil's Book* expresses the teaching well. The message of the crucifixion is written in this way:

> Christ knew that to found a lasting kingdom it was necessary to win
> the love of his followers, and the way to win love was to love and to

serve. There can be no true love without service. So Jesus spent his life doing good....His supreme gift to mankind was his life. He sacrificed it willingly that all might have more abundant life. He called upon his disciples to take up the cross and follow him, that is, to live a life of self-sacrifice if they would be his friends. Jesus had founded his kingdom upon love, and loving service was required from those who would share its blessings.[17]

The lesson concludes with questions and the notebook work of writing the story of the fourth chapter, "How Jesus Conquered by Self-Sacrifice."

1. What was Peter's great confession?
2. Why did this mean more now than when he first hailed Jesus?
3. Why was it hard for the disciples to believe Jesus must die?
4. Did knowledge of approaching death affect Jesus?
5. Why could he not save himself from this fate?[18]

Lesson five, "Jesus Inspiring His Followers," begins with the central thought that "God needs human agents to carry on his work and summons all men to become his helpers." The Memory Verse for the pupil is John: 15:4. "Abide in me as I abide in you. Just as the branch cannot bear fruit by itself unless it abides in the vine, neither can you unless you abide in me." Other Scriptural readings listed for the teacher to read in preparation for the lesson are John 15:1-8; Acts 1:6-9; 2:1-47.

The teacher's task in this lesson is to help pupils understand the need to work and live one's life in the example of Jesus in order to bring in the Kingdom of God. The pupil is given the message that the way to live such a life is to follow the teachings of Jesus and to follow his example of sacrifice and good works. Through a spiritual connection to Jesus one will find the strength and courage to live a productive life. If the pupil lives such an exemplary life, and if all people were to do so, then the Kingdom of God would be established. The teachings of Jesus in John 15:1-8 tell the pupil to abide in Jesus and through Jesus they will then abide with God. The book of Acts tells the pupil to follow the example of Jesus, and to spread his teachings throughout the world. The Holy Spirit is the spirit of God indwelling within each person who is a follower of Jesus; it is the idea of the kingdom being in the hearts of people. The indwelling spirit is a person's innermost nature, the reality of each individual. The Holy Spirit is God's spirit and, shows it the way to new power.

The *Intermediate Pupil's Book* emphasizes the inner kingdom and spirit as the source of power that comes from the Holy Spirit. The lesson relates the story of Jesus telling the disciples that the Kingdom is in the hearts of people and that the spiritual kingdom was what Jesus brought to being, and now they too have an ability to work to spread this kingdom. "The spirit of Jesus dwelling in them [the disciples] gave them courage and power and eloquence, and was an inspiration for all to follow his steps." This message is now for the pupil to understand as his or hers to take up in their lives.

The questions for study are:

1. What commission did Jesus give his disciples? (Matt. 28:19, 20).
2. What was to give them the power to do this?
3. What was the immediate effect of the coming of the Holy Spirit?
4. How were the disciples to be witnesses of Christ?
5. How are Christians today to be his witnesses?[19]

The Notebook work is to write the fifth chapter on "How Jesus Inspired His Followers to Conquer."

It is regrettable that other teacher's books are not available in the two libraries consulted for this book. The other teacher's and pupil's books might have provided the opportunity to expound more explicitly on Universalist theology undergirding the Murray Graded Intermediate Lessons. Jesus' messages of love and the inner spirit are important components of Universalist thinking. Jesus message of love and of God the Father could have been explicitly shown to be what Universalists believe about the transformative power of love and of God as a loving God, much like a father as Jesus taught.

The only other extant books of the Intermediate series available at Meadville Lombard or Harvard Divinity School are the *Intermediate Pupil's Book* of the first year, part one, "Leaders of Israel"; the *Intermediate Pupil's Book*, first year, part two, "Leaders of Israel and American Religious Leaders"; and the *Intermediate Pupil's Book*, third year, part one, "Studies in the Life and Character of Jesus." The first year books deal with the leaders of Israel and explore Jewish history beginning with the political and geographical situation in the Middle East in the time of the Babylonian, Assyrian and Egyptian Empires. The first lesson in part one ends with this paragraph on the religion of the Ancient World: "The worship of many gods and with the gradual uniting of the people into cities and nations created the gradual uniting of the powers of their gods into more and more powerful Gods." This statement demonstrates the use of historical criticism in setting the biblical stories within the context of Middle Eastern history and of the existence of other religious myths prevalent at the time. It is a relating of an historical perspective on the development of the monotheistic theology of the Hebrew people. The second lesson of part one begins the story of Abraham, and the lessons follow the Hebrew people's history of Isaac, Jacob, Joseph, Moses, Joshua, Gideon, Ruth, Samuel, Saul, David, Solomon, Jeroboan and Elijah. The first year, part two begins with Elisha, the divided Kingdoms of Israel and Judah, Amos, Hezekiah, Isaiah, Jeremiah, Daniel, Esther, Haggai, Nehemiah, and Judas the Maccabee, concluding with John the Baptist. The remainder of the lessons in year one, part two, are on American religious leaders. Covered in these lessons were such figures as "John Robinson, The Independent Minister of the Pilgrims"; "Roger Williams, The Champion of Religious Freedom"; "John Eliot, The Apostle to the Indians"; "William Penn, Who Founded a State Upon Peace and Good-Will"; "Jonathan Edwards, Whose Intellect Broadened Religion"; "Samuel J. Mills, A Pioneer in Missionary Work"; "Frances E. Willard, Who Strove for Purity and Temperance"; "Edward Everett Hale, Who Influenced For Broad and Hopeful Religion"; (it is mentioned in the final sentence of this lesson on Hale that he was a Unitarian.). "John Murray, Who Planted the Seed"; "Hosea Ballou, Who Watered the Plant"; "Alonzo Ames Miner, Who Helped the Harvest to Ripen"; and "Isaac Wallace Cate, D.D., Guidance in the Japan Mission."

The lessons on the Universalists, Murray, Ballou, Miner and Cate tell the stories of how these men became Universalists and how they lived their lives in service to God and to Universalism. Murray, Ballou, Miner and Cate, all ministers, were instrumental in founding, defining, expanding and propagating Universalism. The story, "John Murray, Who Planted the Seed," tells how Murray found Universalism in the teaching of James Relly in London, and then came to America and planted the seed of Universalism. The pupil's study questions ask them to tell of the change of his religious beliefs while he lived in London, what happened when he landed in Good-Luck, what was his reception and what was the result of his labors in America. They learn that Hosea Ballou (1771-1846) learned to read by reading the Bible until he had nearly memorized it. His father was a strict Calvinist Baptist minister, and Hosea was relieved when he first heard Rev. Caleb Rich preaching Universalism. Ballou was a common school teacher during the week and a preacher on the weekends as he gained in prominence as a spokesperson for Universalism. In 1812 he became pastor of the School Street Church in Boston, where he served thirty-four years until his death. It is noted that he wrote many treatises and articles as editor of the *Universalist Leader.* The pupils are asked to answer questions about how Ballou became a Universalist, what kind of man he was, what he did for the denomination and how he came to be called "Father Ballou." Alonzo Ames Miner (1814-1895) was raised by Universalist parents in New Hampshire. He began his ministerial life as a circuit-riding preacher while teaching school during the weekdays. He was ordained by the New Hampshire State Convention in 1839. His final pastorate was at the School Street Church in Boston, which later became the Columbus Avenue Church in 1872, as a colleague of Hosea Ballou. He served there forty-seven years until his death. He was an avid worker on behalf of temperance and abolition. He was a founder of the Universalist Publishing House and served as the second president of Tufts College. Isaac Cate, D.D., was instrumental in developing the Japan Mission for the Universalists. He was a 1889 graduate of Tufts. It is regrettable that the *Intermediate Teacher's Book* for these lessons is not available for study.

The stories of the Universalist leaders provide for the pupils a solid foundation for understanding the history of the Universalist religion in America. These stories, however, are about these Universalist ministers and their work, without much attention given to the theology of Universalism. It is possible the theological presentation was done by the teachers in drawing out the messages of Ballou's character, Miner's devotion to service, Murray's theology and Cate's life of service in foreign missionary work. The Intermediate Lessons on American religious leaders are focused on the adventures and characters of these persons, thereby providing examples of leaders to emulate.

The third year, part one *Intermediate Pupil's Book,* "Studies in the Life and Character of Jesus," are a repeat in greater depth of the second year, part one "Christian Leaders" lessons discussed earlier in this dissertation.

Alice Andrews, with assistance from Arthur Andrews has written a course implicitly rich with Universalist theology. The pupils received a solid grounding in Universalist ideas and beliefs throughout the course. The examples of Universalists whose lives are models of those who have lived out the values of Universalism provide us with a pedagogy influenced by the progressive education ideas of John Dewey, George Albert Coe and others. They have utilized higher criticism and evolutionary theory in the biblical material. The pupils would now be prepared to study Universalism and biblical materials in more depth as they enter the senior course.

ENDNOTES

1. Universalist Sabbath School Union minutes, 1923-1924.

2. Alice L.G. Andrews, assisted by Arthur I. Andrews, *The Murray Graded Sunday School Lessons: Intermediate Course* (Boston: Universalist Publishing House, The Murray Press, 1912), "Intermediate Teacher's Book," Second Year, Part One; "Intermediate Pupil's Book," Second Year, Part One, 1, 4, 7, 11, 13.

3. John Richard Sampey, D.D., L.D., *The International Lesson System: The History of Its Origin and Development* (Nashville: Fleming H. Revell, 1911), 329.

4. *Ibid.*, 285.

5. Andrews and Andrews, *The Murray Graded Sunday School Lessons*, "Intermediate Teacher's Book," iii.

6. *Ibid.*, vi.

7. *Ibid.*, vi

8. *Ibid.*, 1, 4, 7, 11, 13.

9. John Coleman Adams, *Universalism and the Universalist Church* (Boston: Universalist Publishing House, The Murray Press, 1915), 104.

10. Andrews and Andrews, *Murray Graded Sunday School Lessons*, "Intermediate Teacher's Book," 2.

11. Andrews and Andrews, *The Murray Graded Sunday School Lessons*, "Intermediate Pupil's Book," 5.

12. Sampey, *International Lesson System*, 333.

13. *Holy Bible*, The New Revised Standard Version (Nashville: Thomas Nelson Publishers, 1989), 197.

14. Andrews and Andrews, *The Murray Graded Sunday School Lessons*, "Intermediate Pupil's Book," 8.

15. *Ibid.*, 9

16. *Ibid.*, 11

17. *Ibid.*, 13.

18. *Ibid.*, 14.
19. *Ibid.*, 16.

CHAPTER TEN
Murray Graded Senior Lessons

The senior course is a powerful example of the goals of the Murray Graded Lessons. Progressive education theories are clearly demonstrated in the understanding that the author, Mabel I. Emerson, provides teachers in the introduction to the course. She has incorporated higher criticism in the presentation of the biblical material, and Universalist thinking is interjected into the questions asked at the conclusion of each lesson. Emerson was a visionary and a credit to Universalist religious education.

The Murray Graded Senior Course was written by Dr. Mabel Irene Emerson. Her obituary appeared in the October 1952 *Christian Leader*:

> Dr. Mabel I. Emerson, well known and loved Universalist, died in her
> home in Wrentham, Massachusetts, August 7, [1952]. Dr. Emerson was
> ninety-one.

> Dr. Emerson lived for many years in Roxbury and was an active member
> of the Grove Hall Universalist Church. Twenty years ago she retired
> after a career of nearly a half century of teaching in Boston. At the time of
> her retirement Dr. Emerson was head of the old Boston Normal School.

> Dr. Emerson was one of the first women graduates of Tufts College.
> Following her graduation from Tufts, she did graduate work at both
> Harvard and Boston University for her Doctorate in Philosophy. She was
> the author of text books on education which became standard instruction
> in many training schools.

> Throughout her professional educational career, Dr. Emerson found time
> to do a great deal of most valuable research and writing for Universalist
> Church Sunday Schools. Within recent years she wrote her last booklet
> for Universalists, a charming "Advent Devotional Manual."[1]

Most of the teacher's manuals and student books for the senior course are available in the libraries of Harvard Divinity School or Meadville/Lombard. Missing are the *Senior Teacher's Manual* for the second year, part two, and the third year, parts one and two.

The International Graded Lessons profiled in Sampey's book *The International Lesson System: The History of Its Origin and Development* included only the first year of the senior course.[2] George Herbert Betts, in his book *The Curriculum of Religious Education*, indicates that eventually there were three years of the senior lessons for the International Graded Lessons with at least one more year of advanced study. The titles of the courses are the same as those of the Murray Graded Sunday School Lessons, however, there are differences within the individual lessons of the two series. The International Lessons have the standard fifty-two lessons per year whereas the Murray Lessons have only forty.[3]

The stated aims of the International lesson's senior course are: "To lead the pupil to see life in proper perspective from the Christian point of view, and to aid him in finding his place and part in the world's work." A second aim was

> To lead the pupil, through frank conference on himself, his limita-
> tions and his relations to the Kingdom of God, to a realization of the
> claims of Christ as Savior and Lord, and of his service as the true basis
> of successful living.[4]

The International Lessons senior course was written to help those persons who had not already done so to undergo a "personal surrender to Christ as Saviour and Lord." The clear aim of the International Graded Uniform Lessons is to emphasize the Christian-centered message of conversion and commitment of one's life to Christ. The first seven lessons are under the heading, "Opportunity, Inspiration and Challenge of the World Today."

> The lesson titles are
> 1. The Kingdom of God on Earth. — (a) The Prophetic Vision. (b) Jesus' Ideal of the Kingdom. Biblical material: (a) Isa. 2:2-4; 4:2-6; Rev. 21: 1-8;22:1-5; (b) Luke 4:18-21; 10:25-28; Matt. 11:2-6.
> 2. The Needs of the World. — Physical, Mental and Spiritual Welfare. Biblical Material. - Matt. 9:35-38; Luke 4:16-21; Mark 6:34;

James 1:27; Acts 4:32-37.

3. How the Needs of the World Are Met. — (a) By Personal Sacrifice and Principle. (b) By Division of Labor. (c) In Modern Life by the Home, Church, Voluntary Agencies, Civic Agencies. Biblical Material: Matt.: 16:21-28; Rom. 12:9-21; Acts 6:1-6; Tim. 1:3-5; 3:14, 15; Eph. 4:11-16; Rom. 13:1-8.

4. The Standard of Success. — Biblical Material: Matt. 6:19-34; Prov. 3:13-20; Luke 12:13-21.

5. The Challenge of the Individual. — Biblical Material: Gen. 12:1-3; Deut. 31:23; Josh. 1:1-9; Matt. 4:19; 5:13-16.

6. The Kingdom and The World's Work. — Biblical Material: Eccl. 9:10a; Prov. 22:29; Matt. 25:14-30; Gal. 6:7-10.

7. The Significance of Youth, of the Strategic Relation of Youth to Life and the World's Needs. — Biblical Material: Eccl. 11:9 to 12:1; 1 Tim. 4:12; Kings 3:5-15; 12:1-11; Daniel 1.[5]

The sources for the International Intermediate Graded Lessons, John Richard Sampey and George Herbert Betts, do not provide the details of how the content and method of the lessons attempted to fulfill its aims.

The senior course of the *Murray Graded Sunday School Lessons* has two aims stated in the first year, part one *Senior Teacher's Manual*:

The Senior Course will aim to accomplish two things, namely:
1. To give the pupil the true meaning of life, and to assist him in finding his place as a Christian in the world.
2. To give him a knowledge of the Bible, both of the Old and New Testaments, not only from the standpoint of history and literature, but also from the standpoint of a Universalist.[6]

The Bible Readings for Lessons I to XX of the first year, part one cover two major biblical themes:

The Training of Moses for His Life Work: Ex. 2:1-4:18; Acts 7:20-36; Heb. 11:23-29.

The Training of Paul for His Life Work: Acts 22:1-21; II Cor. 11:22-
12:10; Gal. 1:11-2:10.[7]

The Murray Graded Lessons *Senior Teacher's Manual* provides the teacher with
information about the characteristics of young people age seventeen, for whom the
first year is written and intended. This information includes:

> In this self-assertive period, the ego is the most prominent feature of
> life. They are now entering the late adolescence stage, and through no
> little struggle have attained a certain degree of self-reliance. They seek
> companionship, and prefer to work with others, and to co-operate
> with them for some definite end. They are full of resourcefulness, and
> aspire to leadership. This is the age, too, when the conscience is
> thoroughly awakened, and criticism is keen and unsparing, but it is
> the period, also, when life presents wonderful vision....In the "lexicon
> of youth there is no such word as fail," hence, here lies the great
> opportunity of teacher and the church to present to these young men
> and women the need of active, enthusiastic workers in the world, and
> to provide for them occasions for definite concrete service.
>
> These lessons, while based upon biblical material, must of necessity
> be intimate and personal....The teacher should remember, too, that
> these young people crave sympathy and are eager and willing to be
> guided when once their confidence is gained.[8]

The years of the senior course, seventeen to twenty-one, are powerful times in the lives
of adolescents and young adults, and the International Lessons interpret this as the
perfect time to seek conversion experiences. The Murray Lessons, in contrast, interpret
this period of life as the perfect time to awaken within the pupil the means with which
to find himself (herself) and make him/herself "felt" in the wider world. It is the time
"to present to these young men and women the need of active, enthusiastic workers in
the world, and to provide for them occasions for definite concrete service."

An overview of the lessons in the senior Murray Lessons is presented for easy reference.

First Year, Part One: "The World a Field for Christian Service,"

Lesson One: "The Threshold of Life"
The Biblical Material is Matt. 9:36-37; Luke 10:1-11; John 4:35-38
The Aim of the lesson is "To establish a bond of sympathy between teacher and pupil which is based on like experiences; and to create in the pupil a sense of responsibility as he faces the problems of life."

Lesson Two: "The Needs of the World"
The Biblical Material: Physical needs; Matt. 4:23-24; Acts 4:32-37. Mental needs: Prov. 4:1-9,. Spiritual needs: Luke 4:16-21; Mark 6:34. Social needs. Luke 3:10-14
The Aim of the lesson:"To help the student to distinguish between the desires and needs of man, and to aid him to recognize his responsibility in helping to meet these needs."

Lesson Three, "How the Needs of the World Are Met"
The Biblical Material: Matt. 16:21-28; Rom. 12:9-21; Luke 9:1-6; Acts 6:1-6; II Tim. 1:3-5; 3:14, 15; Eph. 4:11-16; Rom. 13:1-8
The Aim of the lesson: "To give the student a vision of the innumerable agencies for the upbuilding of man, and to enlist his co-operation."

Lesson Four, "The Kingdom of God on Earth"
The Biblical Material: Luke 4:18-21; 10:25-28; Matt. 11:2-6; 20:1-16; 25:14-30; Gal. 6:7-10
The Aim of the lesson: "To give the student an idea of what the kingdom of God on earth is, and to inspire him to become a worker in it."

Lesson Five, "The Challenge to the Individual"
The Biblical Material: Gen. 12:1-3; Deut. 31:23; Josh. 1:1-9; Matt. 4:19; 5:13-16
The Aim of the lesson: "To help the pupils to recognize the call of the world as a sacred duty to be fulfilled."

Lesson Six, "The Standard of Success"
The Biblical Material: Matt. 6:19-34; Prov. 3:13-20; Luke 12:13-21

The Aim of the Lesson: "To establish in the student's mind a standard that may be used as a test of success in any phase of life."[9]

The overall theme for the first year, part one, "The World a Field for Christian Service," and the first lesson is "The Threshold of Life." The Bible material is Matt. 9:36-37; Luke 10:1-11; John 4:35-38. The aim of the lesson is "To establish a bond of sympathy between teacher and pupil which is based on like experiences; and to create in the pupil a sense of responsibility as he faces the problems of life." It is recommended that this lesson be considered an introductory lesson and used as a basis of establishing trust and confidence between the teacher and the student. Dr. Emerson provides the teacher with a listing of the topics to be covered in each lesson, with the caveat not to follow it rigidly. Emerson hopes the teacher will remain open to spontaneous discussions that often arise with this age group. The teacher is advised to read as many of the suggested readings listed at the end of the lesson as is possible so as to be better prepared to work with the material in depth and to develop a greater ability to relate the material to the lives of the students. Some of the books listed at the end of the first lesson include *The Making of Character* by John MacCunn, LL.D., *The Next Great Awakening* by Josiah Strong, *Education in Religion and Morals* by George Albert Coe and *Practical Idealism* by William DeWitt Hyde. This reading would provide the teacher with a greater understanding of the developmental level of the students as well as deeper insight into their thinking.

This first lesson begins with a "Blackboard Plan," or what would be known now as an outline of the lesson which is then developed throughout the class time. Each of the lessons begins with this "Blackboard Plan" which lets the students know what will be happening each Sunday. This age group, seventeen to twenty-one, likes to know what and why they are doing things. The plan is a clear building from where the individuals have been in his and her development to the teaching of how each individual can be of service to God and the world. Following is the "Blackboard Plan" for lesson one:

I. *Looking Backward.*
1. Self- Assertive period. Know-it-all. Growth of self-reliance.
2. "World," means home, school, church, one's friends.
3. Interests are those that give pleasure to self.

II. *Looking Forward.*
1. Co-operative period. Desire for leadership. Great resourcefulness.

2.   "World," larger horizon , extends beyond one's home and
     friends.
3.   Interests those that lead to achievement.

III. *What Is The "World?"*

Differs with different people. Environment, education, and tempera-
ment determine the definition of it.

IV. *The World A Field for Work.*

1.   For self. Earning a living. A chance to make something of one's self.
2.   For others. Helping maintain the home, family. Devotion to a cause.
Note: Highest type of work is done when influenced by high ideals.

V. *The World as a Field for Christian Service*

Matt. 9: 36, 37; Luke 10: 1-11; John 4: 35-38
God has need of *you* and *your* service.[10]

Dr. Emerson suggests the teacher use this outline as a means of highlighting the basic
issues in young people's growth. The Blackboard Plan is a quick reference for the
teacher in this regard. The teaching begins with the image of the student standing on
the threshold of his or her life "eager to explore the mysteries of the great world
beyond." "The Looking Backward" section acknowledges where the student has been
in his or her personal growth and recognizes the struggles it has taken to reach this
stage in their lives.

The *Senior Student's Book* is powerful in its development of this first lesson. The
students are affirmed in their abilities and the book is written directly to them. Dr.
Emerson's insights into the life of seventeen-year-old young people in 1912 are clear
and right on target. She acknowledges the ability of the student to critically think
about their lives so far, how they can understand who they are at this point in their
lives, and how they can impact their development into the future. I have included the
entire narrative of this first lesson for students because it is remarkable in its pedagogy
and sensitiveness to the lives of the adolescent. This is the only instance so far in the
Murray Graded Lessons where the material is written directly to the student. It is
affirming and provides information a seventeen-year-old would have experience with
and questions about. Dr. Emerson writes in the *Senior Student's Book*:

At the age of seventeen you have practically reached your full physical development. The brain has completed its growth, and the body has attained its full height and weight. Outwardly you are men and women, but in reality you have yet to experience all that makes up life as men and women understand it. You are standing, as it were, on the threshold of life.

As you glance back over your past, you see at once that you were born into this world without your consent; that you were given surroundings over which you have had no control; that you have had certain tendencies that have been difficult for you to master. When you were a child, of course your interests, like that of every child, were centered in your home, day school and Sunday school, your small circle of friends, and, most of all, in yourself. Did it ever occur to you that the way you have lived in the past, will be a powerful influence on your future? Have you been handicapped by ill health? Have you had the advantage of an education? Have you chosen worthy companions? Have you read good books? Have you conquered your bad habits, learned to restrain your tongue, and acquired habits of courtesy and self-control? How can you overcome any of these disadvantages now? If you have had a "good start" in life, should more be expected of you than from those less favored? Try and think what place you fill in God's great plan.

Just now it is more interesting to you to look forward than back. There are many avenues open to youth. Have you decided your life-career? Have you any natural bent? What should guide in the choice of vocation? Who can be your best advisor?

You long to get out in the world and take part in its life. What is the "world" to you? How large is it, not in actual area that you can learn from any geography, but how large is your notion of it? Have you ever traveled? Have you read about people in other lands? How small is the world to you, how close do these people lie to your interests? Can they help you, and can you serve them? Read the *Geographical Magazine* to enlarge your horizon.

The world is a place for service. Remember it is your attitude toward things, rather than the conditions which surround them, that determines the effect of those conditions upon you. What is your attitude toward work? Whose interests do you consider most, yours or your employers? How much does your work influence your life in the home? In society? In the church? How much does your life in the home, in society, and in the church influence your work? Can you earn a living and still maintain a Christian ideal of life?

Read the Bible text given for study. Can you "earn a living" and still have time for other work? What does your neighborhood offer in the way of Christian service? Are you a helper in the church? Do *you* feel responsible for any share in reaping God's harvest?[11]

A poem ends the student's first lesson.

It matters little where I was born,
            Whether my parents were rich or poor,
      Whether they shrank from the cold world's scorn
            Or walked in the pride of wealth secure;
But whether I live an honest man,
            And hold my integrity firm in my clutch,
      I tell you brother, plain as I am,
            It matters much.
From the Swedish. [12]

The student is asked to think critically about privilege and responsibility, about natural advantages of health and handicapping conditions (whether physical or cultural), about the foundations for making choices in their lives, and about what impact these things have on who they are at this time. They are asked to think about the influence of their past on how they will engage the future, and to think about the service they will do in the world. The suggested readings are diverse and include *What Are You Doing Here?* by Unitarian minister Abram Conklin, *The Faith that Makes Faithful* by Unitarian ministers William C. Gannett and Jenkin L. Jones, and *The Day's Work — (The Ship that Found Herself)*, by Rudyard Kipling. The biblical passages of the gospels Matthew, Luke and John provide an understanding of compassion for the needy. Matthew 9:36-37 speaks of Jesus having compassion for the crowds who had gathered to hear him because they were "harassed and helpless like sheep without a shepherd." The message of the need to go forth into the world and work on behalf of the people is shown in Luke 10:1-11, which begins, "After this the Lord appointed seventy others and sent them on ahead of him in pairs to every town and place where he himself intended to go." John 4:35 tells that the labors of one will be for the reaping of another and in that cooperation they both will rejoice.

Of the seven questions suggested to be explored with the students, the teacher's book concludes with "Does the Universalist Church, as a part of the world, offer to young people any opportunity for Christian service?" Here Emerson is hoping to make the connections between the student and Universalist service work with the Gospels. She wants to make it clear that service is an important value for Universalists and that each student can find opportunities within the Universalist Church and the wider world to live out their Universalist values and the Gospel teachings of Jesus.

Dr. Emerson understands the characteristics of her pupils and constructs a lesson implicit and explicit in Universalism. She first presents the characteristics of the students for them to read in a form that speaks directly to them, affirming them as individuals growing into adulthood. She then provides biblical texts to highlight the message of how to understand the need for service to others in the world. She then asks questions that will direct the students to how to become involved in Universalist service and church work.

Lesson Two of the first year, part one, is titled "The Needs of the World." The biblical material covers four areas: (1) Physical needs: Matt. 4:23-24; Acts 4:32-37. These passages teach the students of the healing powers of Jesus and of the giving of what was owned to the Apostles to be distributed to all, especially to those in need. (2) Mental needs: the biblical passages of Prov. 4:1-9, relates a father's advice to his son to seek wisdom and insight. (3) Spiritual needs: Luke 4:16-21; Mark 6:34. These passages tell of Jesus in the Temple as a youth, and Mark tells of Jesus when he was an adult, teaching the multitudes who seemed lost. (4) Social needs are told in Luke 3:10-14, which relates the need to take only what you need and give willingly to those in need, even to give two when one is needed. The stated aim of this lesson is "To help the student to distinguish between the desires and needs of man, and to aid him to recognize his responsibility in helping to meet these needs." Emerson develops the biblical messages of the physical, mental/educational, spiritual and social needs of each person. What one needs is what will sustain one's life - such as food, water, shelter, and clothing - and enable him or her to then go out into the world in service to others. What one wants can lead to reaching for better ways to do things or the development of new ways of doing things that make life easier and for an engagement in interesting investigations. But such wants, while they make life richer in many ways, are not what sustains our existence.

Lesson two explores the reality of the physical need for food, clothing, and shelter, mental needs for education, spiritual needs to know God and practice one's faith and the social needs to overcome poverty and sin, described as selfishness, greed and injustice. The distinction is made in each section of the lesson, as discussed in the first lesson, between desires and needs. The lesson is careful to note that as people become used to having the things they need it becomes possible to obtain the things they desire until these things become perceived as needs. Things like nice clothing have the ability to add to one's sense of self-esteem. A series of questions is asked: "Why is it necessary to dress well? Is anything more required than mere neatness of attire? Does a man's character influence his dress? Does dress influence a man's moral nature?"[13] These questions encourage the student to not only think critically about why they choose to wear what they do, but also what will be the consequences as well, and how those consequences will impact their character. In the section on social needs there are the teachings about temperance. A note to the teacher reminds him or her that "The Universalist Church recognizes all healthy and normal amusements under proper conditions." There were Temperance lessons included in this series although not in this year. They were the only social issue lessons to be included in the *Murray Graded Sunday School Lessons,* and are found in the International Graded and Uniform Series as well.

The student's lesson had begun with the acknowledgment that the biblical passages may not seem relevant to the students' lives in the modern world, but they are asked to think about the needs of modern life and biblical life to find similarities. This referred to the needs in all times for the classification of food, shelter, and clothing. The student's book discusses the difference between desires and needs and the student is encouraged to look at their desires in the light of how these might move him or her to a more unselfish life. As the student looks at the spiritual needs he or she is asked if they can tell if their church needs them. The lesson does not give any answer to this question, but one might conclude that the student would know by how accepting the congregation was of his or her participation in the life of the church. A student might know the church needed him or her by the opportunities provided for him or her to find meaningful work in the church and in the service it gave to the community. They are asked in conclusion to read James 1:27, which reminds them that "Religion that is pure and undefiled before God, the Father, is this: to care for orphans and widows in their distress, and to keep oneself unstained by the world." The setting is laid for the third lesson.

Lesson three, "How the Needs of the World Are Met," has the aim, "To give the student a vision of the innumerable agencies for the upbuilding of man, and to enlist his co-operation." The biblical material includes: Matt. 16:21-28; Rom. 12:9-21; Luke 9:1-6; Acts 6:1-6; II Tim. 1:3-5; 3:14, 15; Eph. 4:11-16; Rom. 13:1-8. These biblical passages provide the teachings and examples of Jesus and the Apostles as they took up the work of the world. The message is clear that spiritual faith is required to engage in the work of the world. The teacher is instructed to tell the students, "all movements for the betterment of mankind have had their origin in Christianity;"

This third lesson shows that the home, school, church, government and social agencies are the places where the student may exercise the needs of the body, mind and spirit. The "Blackboard Plan" for lesson three outlines these places. "The home meets the physical needs, school and colleges meet mental needs, the church meets spiritual needs, government, social agencies, and philanthropies meet social needs, Christian ideals the motive power." The home is where one is fed, clothed and sheltered. The school is where one learns and gains the education required to participate productively in the world. The church is where one worships and finds spiritual sustenance. The government and social agencies are where one finds opportunities to participate in social service on behalf of others. Emerson encourages the teacher to trace the making of a pair of boots as an example of the cooperative effort required by many people in many stages of the process. Cooperation with one another is required to accomplish the aims and goals of a world where the Christian life can be fully lived. The lesson teaches that sacrifice of one's individual desires is part of what it means to cooperate. Each person is encouraged to discover what it is that they do best, and to do it. They are asked what philanthropic work the Universalist Church is engaged in and how they may become involved.

Lesson four, "The Kingdom of God on Earth," has the stated aim, "To give the student an idea of what the kingdom of God on earth is, and to inspire him to become a worker in it." The biblical material is: Luke 4:18-21; 10:25-28; Matt. 11:2-6; 20:1-16; 25:14-30; Gal. 6:7-10. The passages in Luke relate the stories of Jesus in the Temple reading the Torah telling of the coming of the anointed one to proclaim "the year of the Lord's favor." Jesus tells those assembled, "Today this scripture has been fulfilled in your hearing." In Luke 10 Jesus teaches what one must do to earn eternal life, "You shall love the Lord your God with all your heart, and with all your soul, and with all your strength, and with all your mind; and your neighbor as your self." Matthew 11:2-6 instructs the disciples to tell John the Baptist, who is in prison, that Jesus is the one whose coming John has foretold. Matthew 20:1-16 tells of sowing of the spirit and reaping eternal life, Matthew 25:14-30 is the story about investing the talents given to each of us and using them to increase the benefit of that talent in the world and thereby spreading the work of God, and the sending forth of each to teach as we are called and to do the work of God in the world.

The first paragraph of this lesson in the *Senior Teacher's Manual* provides the teacher with some excellent tips on presentation and methodology. The tips acknowledge the need for the teacher to be didactic when new material is introduced to the students. The tips then encourage the teacher to return initiative to the students as soon as possible so as to nurture their own inquiring minds.

> Up to this time most of the lesson period has been given to free discussion by the pupils. It is hoped that the habit of discussing definite questions will become a fixed one. Occasionally there will be some lessons in which the teacher will be obliged to assume distinct leadership because of his [sic] superior knowledge and experience. As soon as possible, however, he should bring the discussion method into prominence, in order that the pupils may be led to make decisions for themselves.[14]

The Blackboard Plan is written on a blackboard or large piece of paper for the class to see and refer to during the class period. "Pupils can hold a lesson in mind much longer if they can see as well as hear. It will also help to hold rambling minds to a continuity of thought." With the Blackboard Plan visible the teacher can concentrate on the content of the lesson and the students can easily know what to expect during the morning. This, ideally, will enable both teacher and students to more fully concentrate on the content of the lesson. Emerson asserts that students this age, seventeen, like to know what is going to happen and they like to have a sense of their having some control over how things develop. This plan gives them the opportunity to do just that. The Blackboard Plan for lesson four is as follows:

I.   Introduction.
     Connect with last lesson.
II. The Kingdom of God.
1.   Ancient idea.
2.   Jesus' idea
3.   Modern idea.
III. Practical not theoretical.
IV. Workers not idlers.
V.   Inspiration in being a worker with God and for God.[15]

Following the Blackboard Plan the fourth lesson develops the following concept:

> The idea of the early Hebrews was that the kingdom of God meant a glorified national life. It meant that the Jewish nation was to be free from any foreign yoke of oppression and governed only by the laws of an unseen God. This kind of independence was to be brought about by a Messiah who should lead the Jews to triumphant victory. The effect of such teachings resulted in making the Jewish race very intolerant and exclusive.
>
> Jesus' idea was that the Kingdom of God included the whole human race; that God was the father of all men [*sic*], and that all men were brothers; that kingdom was one of love shown by deeds of mercy; that self sacrifice and service were necessary to all members of the kingdom. "This universalistic idea was hateful to the Jewish leaders, and Jesus was put to death."[16]

It is surprising to read this sentiment here and difficult to determine why the material was presented with this slant. If Emerson's intent was to develop a sharp contrast between Jewish teachings and the teachings of Jesus, she might better have focused on the idea of the kingdom being spiritual rather than material as the Alice and Arthur Andrews had done in the Intermediate Lessons.

Emerson continues in the lesson by explaining that he modern day understanding of the Kingdom of God "is one in which individuals and society live in harmony with God's laws." By the 1910s, as will be seen in following the lesson's quote, a "New" Universalism had become wide spread and is seen in the Murray Lessons as has been demonstrated in discussions of the development of the importance of character in many of the lessons. In section three of the lesson it states:

> This modern idea of the kingdom of God is not visionary, but entirely possible. The kingdom of God is not a place set apart for a future existence, but it is a very real part of every day life. It is not a theory to be discussed by ministers in the pulpit, but a life to be lived by everyone. It means personal responsibility and active co-operation.[17]

This teaching, presented by Emerson, of the modern idea of the Kingdom of God is grounded in Universalism and in the modernist thinking of the time. Russell Miller notes in his discussion of the American Congress of Liberal Religious Societies which became the Congress of Religion, that "Here was the articulation of a truly world religious concept which was to capture the imagination of the supporters of the 'New' Universalism that had by then (1895) become visible."[18] The supporters of the "New" Universalism were James M. Pullman, John Coleman Adams, Orello Cone, Marion D. Shutter and others and was, as stated above, by the 1910's widely accepted in Universalist circles. Miller writes:

> The key word of the New Universalism was "character"....Individuals entered the next world with the goodness or badness in which they died. None were saints, none were devils. Salvation was not achieved by "going to Heaven," but by the development of good character, the results of which were a human and not a divine responsibility. The old theological scheme, incorporating in it the mythological fall of Adam, was being replaced by the theory of evolution....The duty nearest at had was, rather, to labor for the present good, not to speculate and dogmatize upon the events of eternity.[19]

This view of the biblical message of the Kingdom of God is interpreted as God being immanent in the world and of humanity's responsibility to work to make a better world expressed by the modernist concept of the "Social Gospel" as the means by which the kingdom will be made manifest. Ultimately, this better world could be seen concretely in each person's move to develop his or her "good character."

> The questions at the end of this lesson invoke reflection upon the effect of religion on a student's everyday life upon ways the idea of the Kingdom of God has changed throughout the centuries, and upon the ways that the doctrines of Universalism have affected all creeds. Emerson was suggesting that eventually Universalism's message has changed the creeds of Christian Protestantism. It is a clear claim of Universalism related to the message of the Gospels. Salvation and the Kingdom of God are for everyone. The obligation is for each to accept their part and to live to the fullest of their capacity and not to turn away from the call to work on behalf of the kingdom.

The questions listed in the *Senior Teacher's Manual* are:

1. What is the effect of a religious belief on the life of a nation?
2. In what respect were Jesus' teachings in advance of his time?
3. How does the modern idea of the kingdom of heaven differ from that of medieval times?
4. How has the doctrine of Universalism affected all creeds?
5. What is the difference between working for the kingdom and working for your living? Can you do one without the other?
6. Can you illustrate the universal law, "Use or lose?"
7. Are there any special ways in which young people can help establish the kingdom?
8. What does your church do?
9. Can you practice Jesus' teaching in your community?[20]

Lesson four concludes with a quotation with no author listed. In part it reads:
> The essence of the kingdom is character; the perfection of the kingdom, the fullness of the stature of Christ; the rewards of the kingdom, dominion and ever increasing power for service.[21]

Lesson five, "The Challenge to the Individual," has as its stated aim, "To help the pupils to recognize the call of the world as a sacred duty to be fulfilled. The biblical material: Gen. 12:1-3; Deut. 31:23; Josh. 1:1-9; Matt. 4:19; 5:13-16. Genesis 12:1-3 begins the message of leaving home to answer a call to duty in the story of Abram being called by God. Deut. 31:23 tells of Joshua being given the leadership of the Hebrew people after the death of Moses, and Joshua 1:1-9 tells of Joshua following God's command and crossing the Jordan. Matthew 4:19 tells of Jesus' urging the fishermen to follow him and 5:13-16 is the teaching of Jesus that you are to let your light shine before others so your good works will be seen and followed and glory will be given to God.

The fifth lesson begins by suggesting the connection between the young person's desires to try his or her strength in feats of prowess and the challenge of the call to do God's work in the world. By relating the lives and deeds of Abram, Joshua, and Jesus the teacher is encouraged to show that the work of Christian duty is as challenging and demanding for the students as it was for these ancient figures. The distinction is made between fame and service to a cause. Youth of this age are often more lured by the idea of fame than they are by hard work that offers no public recognition and rewards. The understanding that the challenge comes from God and the rewards are spiritual is difficult to establish. It is acknowledged in the student's book that this is a *thinking* lesson and the student is to think about and answer for him or herself the questions posed in the *Senior Student's Book,* and they are asked to be prepared to defend their attitude toward the life issues and problems posed in the questions.

> The Blackboard Plan for lesson five is:
> I.   Introduction
> II. Forms of the challenge
> 1.   Desire to found a family
> 2.   Desire for success in business.
> 3.   Desire for self-realization
> 4.   Desire to serve others.
> III. Strength of challenge depends on physical, mental and spiritual equipment of the individual.
> IV. Challenge is from God.[22]

Lesson five develops, according to Emerson, the normal desires of young people as being the desire for a home, success in business, self-realization and service to others. It then moves into the call to service, to answer the call from God to respond to the challenge to participate in the responsibility to make the world a better place in which to live. The lesson's questions connect the sacrifices of Abram, Joshua and the Disciples as they responded to the challenges from God to follow the call to service. The *Senior Student's Book,* asks:

> Every young person longs to make a name for himself. Ought you to consider fame more than service? The former means being known the world over, the latter may offer nothing but hard work with obscurity. What challenge lies in that fact? Do you know any men [*sic*] who became famous and still were full of good works?[23]

The lesson concludes with a poem by Episcopal Bishop Phillips Brooks:

> Do not pray for tasks equal to your powers.
> Pray for power equal to your tasks!
> Then the doing of your work shall be no miracle,
> But you shall be a miracle.

Lesson six, "The Standard of Success" has the stated aim, "To establish in the student's mind a standard that may be used as a test of success in any phase of life." The biblical materials are Matt. 6:19-34; Prov. 3:13-20; Luke 12:13-21. Matthew 6:19-34 convey the messages that the value of spiritual treasures in heaven is greater than earthly treasures of wealth and material things, and the value of wisdom is greater than fame and fortune. The verses contain the stories of the slave trying to serve two masters, God and wealth, and the lilies of the field who do not worry about their arraignment. Proverbs 3:13-20 speaks of the happiness of those who gain wisdom and understanding that is more precious than jewels. Luke 12:13-21 tells of the rich man who stored his riches away from the world and refused to share with those in need.

The Blackboard Plan for the lesson is to explore what constitutes wealth and what standards are used to measure true success. It looks at the commonly accepted standards of wealth, fame, service and character. Wealth is measured by the amount of material possession and money one has stored away. Fame is gained through the distinction one has gained among others. The students then compare those standards of success taught by Jesus with those of the modern day, concluding the lesson with a true standard comprised of placing important things first. Emerson suggests the teacher present four elements considered to be worthy measurements of success: purpose in life, effort put into one's work, personal character, and a degree of permanency in the work one does. The students are asked to make a list of persons they consider successful and to think about the standards they used for their choices. They are reminded of those who have achieved fame through service: Florence Nightingale (1820-1910), who was an English nurse who reformed hospital conditions and procedures; Universalist Clara Barton (1821-1912), who was the founder of the American Red Cross; Scottish missionary, David Livingstone (1813-1873), who explored the inner continent of Africa; Belgian Roman Catholic Father Damien (1840-1889), who served as a missionary to the lepers of Moloki; and Congregationalist Jane Addams (1860-1935), a social worker who established the settlement house, Hull House in Chicago. The pupils are then asked to consider those who are of great character but who have gained no renown. What are the qualities of the characters of each of these groups of "successful" people? Wealth, fame, service, and character are the four criteria named in the lesson that have been commonly accepted as the standards for success. But Jesus offered another, that of the strength of the soul. The message presented is that when one develops and strengthens one's inner life, one's soul, then one is better prepared to develop to the fullest one's outer life. It is suggested they at this point re-read Matthew 6:33: "But strive first for the kingdom of God and his righteousness, and all these things will be given to you as well." The question is then posed: "Is there not an implication there that he who develops his inner life will become more capable of enlarging his outward life?"

This lesson promotes the understanding that for the modern day the standards of success must, as Jesus taught, have something to do with one's purpose in life and include wisdom, effort, and quality of character. The final standard for this different notion of modern day success is the permanency of the results of the work. The *Senior Teacher's Manual* concludes the lesson with the following questions.

1. What do you mean by success?
2. May a man possess wealth and still be a failure?
3. May a man be poor and yet be considered a success?
4. Is fame necessary to success?
5. In what way may people in humble walks of life become successful?
6. May a person be successful in some things and a failure in others?
7. How much does personality count in a successful life?

8. Was Jesus a success?
9. How much to Christian ideals affect the measuring standard of success?
10. Do Christian ideals help or hinder a successful business career?
11. What constitutes a successful church?
12. Has your church produced any successful men or women?
13. How may young people contribute to the success of the church?[25]

A final quote in the *Senior Teacher's Manual* by a Senator Hoar provides a summary for this lesson. "The great things of this world have been done by men of ordinary capacity who have done their best."

The *Senior Student's Book* asks twelve questions. I have chosen to list five from those twelve as examples that relate directly to the student's capacities and abilities for success.

4. A pupil may sometimes be very brilliant in school, but is never heard of after his graduation; is such a one a successful pupil?
9. What work of the Y.P.C.U. can be counted successful?
10. Can you lead a Christian life and be successful in business?
11. Do high ideals help or hinder successful careers?
12. Are you putting first things first?[26]

The lessons seven, eight and nine deal with physical, intellectual and spiritual efficiency. I have chosen not to discuss them in detail in consideration of the length of this dissertation. Lesson ten is divided into two parts, one for boys and one for girls. The boys are offered a lesson on "Opportunities for Service Through Industrial and Agricultural Life" and the girls, "Domestic Arts." Lesson eleven is for both boys and girls on "Business Life." In this lesson the students are asked to list all the occupations open to both men and women. The *Senior Student's Book* lesson eleven has the wonderful comment about the possible occupations available to both young men and women of the day: "You will be astonished at its length." Lesson twelve is on "Professional Life." The professions, which include physicians, teachers, journalists and scientists, are described as available for men and women, though some are referred to as being for men, such as doctors and lawyers, and some predominately for women, such as teaching.

Lesson thirteen is on "Public and Social Life." The *Senior Student's Book* asks,

> Can young men and women practice Christian ideals in public and
> social life? What does the church expect its young people to do?
>
> The Young People's Christian Union is one phase of social life. In
> what way does the Y.P.C.U. help young people to practice the
> teachings of Christ? Are you a better voter, and a more intelligent
> worker, because of your church affiliation?[27]

Lesson fourteen is on "Good Citizenship and Service Through Civic Agencies." It
relates the work of the Y.P.C.U. to students' lives and to that of the wider community.
It asks them to obtain information of civic outreach by Universalist churches in Boston
and Chicago.

A brief backtrack is needed here to tell of the Y.P.C.U. Lewis B. Fisher notes, in *A
Brief History of the Universalist Church,* that

> However well the Sunday-school does its work, there is a gap between
> it and the Church organization when the youth feels too old for the
> former and no vital interest in the latter. To pilot young people safely
> across this perilous gap, Rev. F. E. Clark, pastor of Congregational
> Church in Portland, Maine, organized in 1881 a Young People's
> Society Christian Endeavor (Y.P.S.C.E.).[28]

Fisher devotes a full chapter to the development of the Universalist's Young People's
Christian Union and its relationship to the Y.P.S.C.E. After several attempts to
organize around a missionary goal modeled after the Young People's Society of
Christian Endeavor (Y.P.S.C.E.) the organizing meeting of the Universalist Young
People's Christian Union (Y.P.C.U.) took place in Lynn, Massachusetts, in 1889. The
General Convention of Universalists was scheduled to meet in Lynn that year and the
organizers of the youth wisely added their first meeting to take place the day before
the General Convention was to start. Fisher writes:

> The call to come to Lynn in 1889 went out, and they [the youth] did
> come....The young people of the land sent up to Lynn that year 131

delegates representing 56 young people's societies from 13 States, and
they held their first meeting Oct. 22, 1889. After a brief meeting of
praise and prayer, the task of organizing was begun. The name,
National Young People's Christian Union of the Universalist Church
was adopted. In later years when Canada and Japan were heard from,
the Union became known as the Central Union, and the society is
always known as the Y.P.C.U....The constitution, adopted the next
day, stated the object of the organization to be "To promote an
earnest Christian life among the young people of the Universalist
Church, and the sympathetic union of all young people's societies in
their efforts to make themselves more useful in the service of God.[29]

The Y.P.C.U. began publishing its own newspaper the *Universalist Union*. In 1894 the
Universalist Publishing House took over its publication, dividing the profit or loss
with the Y.P.C.U. This paper changed it name to *Onward* and was in publication until
1945 when, as Russell Miller notes, it merged with the Unitarian youth organization's
publication to become *The Young Liberal*. That paper lasted only two years.[30]

At the tenth anniversary meeting of the Y.P.C.U. Dr. James M.
Pullman's address of welcome was, according to Fisher, long remembered. Fisher quotes the first paragraph:

And what is Universalism? It is belief in a capable God, who does not
let his worlds run away with him; an adequate God, who is equal to
the solution of his problem, and is able to conduct his universe to the
good he aims at without the intervention of an eternal catastrophe:
therefore all evil is vulnerable, and every soul is savable.[31]

In 1894 the Y.P.C.U. added a Junior Union Department to meet the needs of younger
youth. The work of its Mission Department was one of the crucial areas of the
Y.P.C.U.'s work. Several churches were built and founded by the efforts of the
Y.P.C.U. through its collection of money and youth working in service to the church.

Lesson fourteen of the Murray senior course stresses the importance of civic duty and
citizenship done with an understanding of how their faith, and the teachings of the
Bible grounds that work. The students are referred to copies of the *[Universalist] Leader*

and *Onward* to read articles on information about Universalist work in civic and mission fields. They are encouraged to join actively in the work of the Young People's Christian Union. The teacher is instructed to order leaflets from the publishing house on different mission activities of the Universalist Church of America.

Lesson fifteen is on "The Christian Ministry and Its Assistants." The stated aim of the lesson is "To show the importance of Christian preaching and teaching, and to inspire the students to engage in pastoral work." Dr Emerson considered this to be one of the most important lessons in the senior course. She finds an opportunity here to appeal for those who have the ability, capacity and inclination for ministry to be encouraged to consider the calling. Those who do not have the inclination for ministry they are encouraged to consider the work of assistant pastors or Sunday school teachers, both of which are held in high regard as fields of involvement in the church. It is noted in the *Senior Teacher's Manual* that the Universalist Church's ministry is open to both men and women. It is not, however, so mentioned in the *Senior Student's Book*. The question posed to the students elicits the qualities they hold important for a minister to have to be successful.

The *Senior Student's Book* has a series of quotes at the end of the lesson. It is regrettable that the names of the authors are not included for they are wonderful quotes that illustrate important Universalist themes. One quote advocates the power of Universalist principles in character formation and social action when it says, "The Universalist Church is about its real business when it is free to use its principles in character building and social reconstruction, and no longer has to fight for the theological right to exist."[32]

A second theme related to ministry is found in the quote that says, "The logic of Universalism is not only academic, it is practical; and the mighty movements for human uplift which are to-day stirring the world have no logical support in old-fashioned orthodoxy, but are the material manifestations of Universalism." And the third quote expresses that "The Universalist Church as an organization may never attain to great numbers and vast wealth, any more than did the earliest Christian Church, but like that earliest church, it is to be one of the chief factors in the world's redemption, and the bringing in of a real kingdom of heaven."[33]

These quotes provide the message that Universalism is a religious faith built on the character of its followers, the commitment to social justice and belief in a God who is merciful and forgiving. Universalists' centuries-old message of salvation and belief in the teachings of Jesus to build a world on an ethic of love will endure, according to Emerson, even though the denomination itself may never gain strength in numbers. It is the aim of the lesson to give the message to the young people that their commitment to Universalism is important for the future, and if they are so called, the church's ministry and Sunday schools need them to teach and preach the Universalist faith.

The final five lessons will not be critiqued in-depth out of consideration for the length of this book. As with the junior and intermediate courses, I have only discussed the first few lessons to provide an overall picture of how these lessons were developed and what Universalist principles and beliefs have been presented. These final lessons present the missionary work within the Universalist Church. The lessons are titled "Home Missions"; "Foreign Missions"; specifically the Japan Missionary work; "How to Choose a Vocation"; "Qualifying for Efficiency"; and "Dedicating One's Opportunities."

While many of the lesson titles are the same for the International Graded Lessons the aims of each of the year's cycles are more focused on, "It is urged that the social aspect of these lessons as a point of contact and the outlook on life be utilized to emphasize the necessity for personal surrender to Christ as Saviour and Lord."[34]

> At its Semiannual Meeting, December 30, 1910, of the International Sunday School Lesson Committee, in response to the request of a large constituency, appointed a Special Committee, not to revise the Graded Lessons, but to prepare Biblical Lessons to run parallel to al the so-called extra-Biblical Lessons in the Graded Series....The special Committee prepared its report, and it was submitted to the entire Lesson Committee, and passed upon by correspondence, March 14, 1911.[35]

As seen by this action, the International Sunday School Lesson Committee went in an opposite direction from the Universalists as they developed the Murray Graded Sunday School Lessons with considerable extra-biblical material. As noted earlier in this dissertation, George E. Huntley had tried to introduce liberal biblical materials to the Lesson Committee in 1911-1912 but was unsuccessful in doing so. The Universalists were moving into more liberal theology and biblical interpretation through the work of Orello Cone,

John Coleman Adams, Marion D. Shutter and others who had made overtures to the American Liberal Congress of 1894.[36]

ENDNOTES

1.The Christian Leader, *Obituaries, Dr. Mabel I. Emerson* (Boston: The Universalist Publishing House, October 1952).

2.John Richard Sampey, *The International Lesson System, The History of Its Origin and Development* (New York: Fleming H. Revell, 1911), 343.

3.George Herbert Betts, *The Curriculum of Religious Education* (Cincinnati: Abingdon Press, 1924), 386, 387.

4.Sampey, *International Lesson System,* 343.

5.Sampey, *International Lesson System,* 343, 344.

6.Mabel I. Emerson, *The Murray Graded Sunday School Lessons,* The Senior Teacher's Manual , First Year, Part One" (Boston: The Universalist Publishing House, The Murray Press 1912), 3.

7.*Ibid.,* 3.

8.*Ibid.,* foreword.

9.*Ibid.,* 5, 10, 14, 19, 23, 27.

10.*Ibid.,* 6.

11.Emerson, *The Murray Graded Sunday School Lessons,* "The Student's Book, The Senior Course, First Year, Part One," 5, 6.

12.*Ibid.,* 7.

13.Emerson, *The Teacher's Manual,* 13.

14.*Ibid.,* 19

15.*Ibid.,* 19, 20.

16.*Ibid.,* 20.

17.*Ibid.,* 21.

18.Russell Miller, *The Larger Hope: The Second Century of the Universalist Church in America 1870-1970* (Boston: Unitarian Universalist Association, 1985), 131.

19.*Ibid.,* 135-136.

20.Emerson, *Senior Teacher's Manual,* 21, 22.

21.*Ibid.,* 22.

22.*Ibid.,* 23, 24.

23.Emerson, *Senior Student's Book,* 14.

24.*Ibid.,* 15.

25.Emerson, *Senior Teacher's Manual*, 31.

26.Emerson, *Senior Student's Book*, 17.

27.*Ibid.*, 35.

28.Lewis B. Fisher, D.D., *A Brief History of the Universalist Church,* 4th ed., rev. (Boston: Young People's Christian Union, 1904), 138.

29.*Ibid.*, 142, 143.

30.Miller, *Larger Hope: The Second Century*, 211.

31.Fisher, *Brief History of Universalist Church*, 145, 146.

32.Emerson, *Senior Student's Book*, 39.

33.*Ibid.*, 39, 40.

34.Sampey, *International Lesson System*, 343.

35.*Ibid.*, 349.

36.Miller, *Larger Hope, The Second Century*, 140.

CHAPTER ELEVEN
Conclusion

The Murray Graded Sunday School Lessons were in use from 1912 into the 1930s. They had been written to reflect Universalist theology and the influences of Modernism's Higher Biblical Criticism, evolutionary theory and progressive education ideas.

In the *Christian Leader* issue of 21 October 1933 the executive board of the General Sunday School Association of the Universalist Church, in its report read at the Annual Convention in Worcester, Massachusetts, October, 1933, recommended that the use of the Murray Graded Lessons be ended. This report came under the sub-heading "Courses of Study," and gave the executive board's response to questions from the local churches about what were the best courses for children and youth in the Sunday school:

> To the best of our ability we answer them. But as we do so we realize what it would mean to each school if this whole matter of instruction were approached from the point of view of the needs of the pupils themselves. During the past decade the public schools have taken great strides in making their programs pupil-centered rather than material-centered. Much has been written advocating the same procedure for religious education. But down in the church school, with its volunteer, untrained leadership, such changes come about very slowly.

> That there is great need for better courses of study presenting the liberal point of view in religion we are all aware. Recognizing the worth of Dr. [Gertrude] Earle's course on the "Beginnings of Universalism," issued in 1931, a recommendation was made at our last convention that the Publishing House put out several teaching units on suggested subjects. This request has not been overlooked. The Publishing House was consulted regarding it. But for financial reasons it could not be granted this year.

At the present time the *Helper*, published quarterly, and the Murray
Graded Lessons are the only teaching materials which bear our
denominational label. The latter, written in 1910, [*sic*] with the
exception of one or two courses, are no credit to us today. As an
Association we have long since ceased to recommend them. Another
request at our last convention, that the *Helper* no longer confine itself
to uniform lessons, was referred to a committee of which Dr.
[Gertrude] Earle, the editor, was chairman [*sic*].[1]

The Universalists had by this time moved toward child-centered curriculum philosophy and away from a Bible-centered one. The theology of the Murray Lessons, while in
the main stream of the 1910s, was no longer reflective of Universalism in the 1930s.
Universalism as a Christian expression and centered on the Bible were no longer the
central concerns by 1933 as the Universalists had been moving into more liberal
theological thinking and were influenced not only by the earlier modernist ideas of the
higher criticism, evolutionary theories and the Social Gospel, but also by the humanist
movement and a closer affinity with the Unitarians. As seen in the following article in
the *Christian Leader* of 1933, the ties with Unitarians was a factor in the abandonment
of the *Murray Graded Sunday School Lessons*, although Universalists maintained a
theistic emphasis on God.

In the 21 October 1933 issue of the *Christian Leader* it was reported that the General
Sunday School Association was affiliated with the Religious Education Association
and that Mr. Ratcliff was sent by Tufts College to attend the REA annual meeting in
Cincinnati the previous May [1933] as a representative of the G.S.S.A. This affiliation
further moved Universalists away from the Murray Graded Lessons to a more liberal
content and progressive methodology in curriculum development. This affiliation
served as well to strengthen the move of the Universalist Church of American more
firmly into liberal circles and further away from the evangelical circles.[2]

The 1933 *Christian Leader* also contained the following article under the heading,
"With the Unitarians":

The relations between the Department of Religious Education of the
American Unitarian Association and the G.S.S.A. are most friendly.
During the year Miss [Susan] Andrews and Miss [Harriet G.] Yates

became members of the Unitarian Curriculum Commission. The purpose of this group is to make a thorough study of the Beacon Press text books with a view to revising them that they may be less material-centered. This is not a task to be done lightly or speedily. And when attempted by a group of persons whose daily programs are full, it must needs progress slowly.

Certain helpful bulletins have been published by the Department of Religious Education (Unitarian) this year and in each case we have been consulted regarding them. Upon request, Mrs. Galer has prepared one on the Bible in the church school, which will be printed this fall. Already we have placed with Beacon Press our order, that this may be available to our churches as well.

We have cooperated with the Unitarians in other ways also. At the May meetings in Boston Miss Andrews led a discussion group and in July conducted a daily conference at the Religious Education Institute at the Isles of Shoals. In the last annual report of the Department of Religious Education, Unitarian, is this statement, under Cooperation: "Our principal and most rewarding cooperation has been with the General Sunday School Association of the Universalist Fellowship."

For our part we can truly say that our associations with the Unitarians have been enjoyable and profitable. If, in our sharing, we have given to them we have also received much in return.[3]

Theologically Universalists had moved further away form the Christian Winchester Profession of 1803 and its revised version of 1899. As the 1930s progressed Universalists were challenged from within to articulate their theology in light of the influences of Modernism, the humanist movement and increased affinity with the Unitarians. These influences had shifted Universalist theology to the point that a new statement of faith was required:

In 1935 Universalists once again re-wrote their profession of faith. The bond of Fellowship was ratified unanimously in 1935, with only 91 of the 125 delegates voting, and with a minimum of discussion and no debate. [Frederick] Perkins (1870-1943), distinguished Universalist clergyman and scholar, was so amazed that the revised statement had gone through two convention sessions without a dissenting vote that he suggested the fact be inscribed on his tombstone.....Universalism had evolved over the years from a gospel of individual salvation to "a social proclamation of the Kingdom of God." In spite of changing emphases, the theistic character of the denomination was once again asserted, and secular humanism was rejected. "We cannot have the Kingdom of God and leave out God."[4]

The 1935 Washington Profession or the Bond of Union stated,

> The bond of fellowship in this church shall be a common purpose to
> do the will of God as Jesus revealed it and to co-operate in establish-
> ing the Kingdom for which he lived and died.
> To that end we avow our faith in
> God as Eternal and All-conquering Love,
> The spiritual leadership of Jesus,
> The supreme worth of every human personality,
> The authority of truth known and to be known,
> And in the power of men of good will and sacrificial spirit to over-
> come all evil and progressively to establish the Kingdom of god.[5]

These theological changes moved Universalists closer to Unitarian affiliations and with the liberal religious connections. This was reflected in the work of religious education. The work of the Universalists was now being regarded as a valued contribution and held in respect by Unitarian colleagues in the field. From the 1930s on this cooperative work increased and many Universalist children growing up in the 1940s experienced the New Beacon Series, published by the American Unitarian Association in their Sunday schools.

To bring the movement in religious education to its conclusion as a distinct Universalist effort a very brief synopsis of the move to merger with the Unitarians is necessary. From here on the Universalists and the Unitarians began a cooperative effort in the field of religious education. In 1953 the Council of Liberal Churches, a joint organization of Unitarians and Universalists, was formed to administer the public relations, publications, and education materials of the two denominations. The departments of religious education of the American Unitarian Association and the Universalist Church of America [The General Sunday School Association had become a department of religious education of the UCA in 1948] became one Division of Education with the Rev. Ernest Kuebler as its director. In 1959 the Rev. Dr. Dorothy Tilden Spoerl, a Universalist, was appointed its first full time curriculum editor following the retirement in 1954 of part time editor, Sophia Lyon Fahs.

From that time forward Universalist religious education was no longer an entity of its own, but in a partnership with the Unitarians. Since 1961 with the merger of the two denominations, the Unitarian Universalist Association's religious education offices came into being to develop religious education curricula and publications. In 2003 the Department of Religious Education changed its name and focus to that of Lifespan Faith Development Staff Group and began the process of publishing Unitarian Universalist curricula that is faith based.

The Murray Graded Sunday School Lessons demonstrate how Universalists met the challenges of the modernist movement. They responded to the changes within their faith as they moved through their controversies with revisions to their Profession of Faith. These new theologies were reflected in the Murray Graded Sunday School Lessons as well as within the denomination as a whole.

The example of how Universalists met these challenges and maintained their move forward into the twentieth century provides us with insight into how we might face the twenty-first century with its conservative challenges to our liberal faith.

It is important for us to read and heed our history. Many of the ideas and methods employed in the Murray Graded Lessons can give us a deeper respect for our Universalist ancestors and our Universalist heritage. They were participants in the rise of the Sunday school movement and contributed significant scholarship to it. It is a heritage of which Unitarian Universalist can be proud.

As Unitarian Universalists we ask ourselves, "Where have we been in our history and how did we as Universalists respond to the events of those times?" We have responded to an angry God with a loving God. We have asserted that God is One. We have affirmed Jesus as teacher and prophet of God. We have affirmed the capacity and worthiness of humankind, of truths known and to be known and that all religions have some truth but no one religion has all the truth. We have moved with an evolving culture and increased knowledge with reason and faith, hope and tolerance, love and freedom.

What have we embraced in our Universalist past as Unitarian Universalists that can be embraced by the generations of today and tomorrow? We can embrace the ethical teachings of the world's religions, the transformative power of love, the belief in human potential, the necessity to co-create good, justice and mercy and the need to gather in community. We have embraced the ability to disagree in love and tolerance, to nurture individual differences and communal caring, to be prepared for change and to engage in scientific inquiry while honoring our spiritual need.

The Murray Graded Sunday School Lessons moved Universalists away from evangelical Protestantism to liberal higher critical interpretation in a biblical curriculum. They moved Universalists away form the Uniform Lessons to progressive education's graded, more child-friendly lessons. The Murray Lessons moved Universalists to an explicit connection with Universalist values, practices and beliefs, and they affirmed the Universalist beliefs in God as love, Jesus as teacher and exemplar of ethical behavior, in the human ability and responsibility to service as duty and to truths yet to be known. This history has demonstrated that Universalists "Do Not Stand, We Move."

In conclusion we ask these questions of future readers of this book. What are the religious and theological questions that challenge our religious education efforts for children, youth, and adults in the twenty-first century? Will the response to those questions impact our future as powerfully as the decisions around the development of the Murray Graded Sunday School Lessons did for our Universalist ancestors? If so, then we need to know that history.

Where have we been in our history and how did we respond to the events of those times? What have we embraced in our past as Unitarian Universalists that can be embraced by the generations of today and tomorrow?

ENDNOTES

1. *The Christian Leader*, Report of the Executive Board of the General Sunday School Association of the Universalist Church of America (Boston: Universalist Publishing House, [21 October 1933], 1331.

2. *Ibid.,* 1332.

3. *Ibid.,* 1332.

4. Russell Miller, *The Second Century of the Universalist Church in America: 1870-1979* (Boston: The Unitarian Universalist Association, 1985). 115-116.

5. Clinton Lee Scott, *The Universalist Church of America: A Short History* (Boston: Universalist Historical Society, 1957), 40

Bibliography

Adams, John Coleman. 1915. *Universalism and the Universalist Church*. Boston: Universalist Publishing House, The Murray Press.

Ahlstrom, Sydney E. 1972. *A Religious History of the American People*. New Haven: Yale University Press.

Andrews, Alice L.G., assisted by Arthur I. Andrews. 1912. *The Murray Graded Sunday School Lessons: Intermediate Course*. Boston: The Universalist Publishing House, The Murray Press. Intermediate Pupil's Book First Year Part One; Intermediate Pupil's Book First Year Part Two; Intermediate Teacher's and Pupil's Books Second Year Part One; Intermediate Pupil's Book Third Year Part One.

Angus, David L., Jeffrey E. Mirel, Maris A. Vinovskis. Winter 1988. "Historical Development of Age Stratification in Schooling." *Teachers College Record* 90, no. 2. New York: Columbia University.

Ballou, Mary L. *The Murray Graded Sunday School Lessons: Junior Course*. 1912. Boston: Universalist Publishing House, The Murray Press. Junior Teacher's and Pupils' Books First Year Part One; Junior Teacher's and Pupil's Books First Year Part Two; Pupil's Book Second Year Part One; Teacher's and Pupil's Books Second Year Part Two; Teacher's and Pupil's Books Third Year Part One; Junior Teacher's and Pupil's Books Third Year Part Two; Junior Teacher's and Pupil's Books Fourth Year Part One; Junior Pupil's Book Fourth Year Part Two.

Betts, George Herbert. *The Curriculum of Religious Education*. 1924. Cincinnati: Abingdon Press.

Boylan, Anne. 1988. *Sunday School, The Formation of an American Institution: 1790-1880*. New Haven: Yale University Press.

Boys, Mary. 1989. *Educating In Faith*. Kansas City, Mo.: Sheed & Ward.

Brown, Arlo Ayers. 1923. *A History of Religious Education in Recent Times.* New York: Abingdon Press.

Brown, Marianna C. 1901. *Sunday-School Movements in America.* New York: Fleming H. Revell.

Burkart, Harold H., ed. 1993. *The Universalist Heritage.* Syracuse: The Quartier Group.

Cassara, Ernest, ed. 1971. *Universalism in America: A Documentary History of a Liberal Faith.* Boston: Skinner House.

Cheetham, Henry H. 1962. *Unitarianism and Universalism*. Boston: Beacon Press.

Cone, Orello, D.D. 1889. "Theories of Biblical Interpretation." *Essays Doctrinal and Practical.* Orello Cone, Ed. Boston: Universalist Publishing House.

Cone, Orello, D.D. 1891. *Gospel Criticism and Historical Christianity.* New York: GP Putnam's Sons, The Knickerbocker Press.

Cone, Orello. "Science and Religion." *Universalist Quarterly: General Review,* 1882. [sic] n. s. 19. Thomas B. Thayer, D.D., ed.. Boston: Universalist Publishing House.

Cope, Henry Frederick. 1911. *The Evolution of the Sunday School.* Boston: Pilgrim Press.

Corrington, Robert S. 1992. "Ecstatic Naturalism and the Transfiguration of the Good." *Empirical Theology: A Handbook.* edited by Randolph Crump Miller. Birmingham: Ala: Religious Education Press.

Cremin, Lawrence A. 1964. *The Transformation of the Sunday School.* New York: Vintage Books Division of Random House.

Cross, Whitney R. 1950. *The Burned-Over District: The Social and Intellectual History of Enthusiastic Religion in Western New York, 1800-1850.* New York, Harper and Row.

Cully, Iris, and Kendig Brubaker Cully. 1990. *Harper's Encyclopedia of Religious Education*. San Francisco: Harper and Row.

Dewey, John. 1959. "Progressive Education and the Science of Education." Cremin, Lawrence A. Cremin, ed. *Classics in Education No. 3, Dewey on Education*. 1959. New York: Teachers College Press.

Eddy, Richard. 1891. *Universalism in America: Volume I, 1636-1800*. 3rd ed. Boston: Universalist Publishing House, Third Edition.

Eddy, Richard. 1886. *Universalism in America: Volume II, 1801-1886*. Boston: Universalist Publishing House.

Edwards, Jonathan. 1999. "Sinners in the Hands of an Angry God." Warner, Michael, ed. *American Sermons: The Pilgrims to Martin Luther King, Jr.*, New York: Library of America, Penguin Putnam.

Emerson, Mabel I. 1912. *The Murray Graded Sunday School Lessons Senior Course*. Boston: Universalist Publishing House, The Murray Press. Senior Teacher's Manual and Student's Book First Year Part One; Senior Teacher's Manual and Student's Book First Year Part Two; Senior Teacher's Manual and Student's Book Second Year Part One; Senior Student's Book Second Year Part Two; Senior Student's Book Third Year Part One; Senior Student's Book Third Year Part Two.

Fisher, Lewis B., D.D. 1904. *A Brief History of the Universalist Church*. 4th ed. rev. Boston: Young People's Christian Union.

Forbes, H. P. 1905. *The Universalist Leader*. Boston: Universalist Publishing House.

Forbes, H. P. July 1, 1905. "The Late Rev. Orello Cone, D.D." *The Universalist Leader*. Boston: Universalist Publishing House.

Gaustad, Edwin S. ed. 1983. *A Documentary History of Religion in America since 1865*. Grand Rapids: William B. Eerdmans.

Habel, Norman. 1975. *Literary Criticism of the Old Testament*. Philadelphia:

Fortress Press.

Harrelson, Walter. 1964. *Interpreting the Old Testament.* New York: Holt, Rinehart and Winston.

Howe, Charles A. 1993. *The Larger Faith: A Short History of American Universalism.* Boston: Skinner House Books.

Hutchison, William R. 1992. *The Modernist Impulse in American Protestantism.* Durham: Duke University Press.

Kennedy, William Bean. 1966. *The Shaping of Protestant Education.* New York: Association Press.

Lankard, Frank Glenn. 1927. *A History of the American Sunday School Curriculum.* New York: Abingdon Press.

Lynn, Robert W. 1964. *Protestant Strategies in Education.* New York: Association Press.

Lynn, Robert W. and Elliott Wright. 1971. *The Big Little School: Sunday Child of American Protestantism.* New York: Harper and Row.

MacLean, Angus H. 1961. *The Message is the Method.* Boston: Universalist Church of America.

McFarland, John T., D.D., LL.D., Benjamin S. Winchester, D.D., editors-in-chief; R. Douglas Fraser, D.D., Canadian editor; Rev. J. Williams Butcher, European editor. 1915. *The Encyclopedia of Sunday Schools and Religious Education.* New York: Thomas Nelson and Sons.

McLoughlin, William G. 1978. *Revivals, Awakenings, and Reform.* Chicago: University of Chicago Press.

Meyer, Henry H. 1910. *The Graded Sunday School in Principle and Practice.* Philadelphia: Westminster Press.

Miller, Russell E. 1979. *The Larger Hope: The First Century of the Universalist Church in America: 1770-1870.* Boston: Unitarian Universalist Association.

Miller, Russell E. 1985. *The Larger Hope: The Second Century of the Universalist Church in America: 1870-1970.* Boston: Unitarian Universalist Association.

Murray, John. 1884. *The Life of John Murray,* 8th ed. by Rev. L. S. Everett. Boston: A. Tompkins.

Noll, Mark A. 1992. *A History of Christianity in America and Canada.* Grand Rapids: William B. Eerdmans.

Perrin, Norman. 1978. *What Is Redaction Criticism?* Philadelphia: Fortress Press.

Pfleiderer, Otto. 1900. *Evolution and Theology and Other Essays,* Edited and translated by O. Cone. London: Adam and Charles Black.

Pink, Louis H. and Rutherford E. Delmage. 1957. *Candle in the Wilderness: A Centennial History of the St. Lawrence University: 1856-1956.* New York: Appleton-Century-Crofts.

Price, Ira M. 1917. *The International Sunday School Lesson Committee 1914-1917: Organization and By-laws and Work, Part I.* Chicago: The International Council of Religious Education.

Price, Ira M. 1922. *The International Sunday School Lesson Committee 1917-1921: Reports, Actions and Output, Part II.* Chicago: The International Council of Religious Education.

Price, Ira M. 1926. *The International Sunday School Lesson Committee, April 1922-December 1925: Reports, Actions and Output, Part III.* Chicago: The International Council of Religious Education.

Pullman, James M., and Frank Oliver Hall. n. d. *Bible Universalism In Questions and Answers.* Boston: Universalist Publishing House.

Rice, Edwin Wilbur. 1917. *The Sunday School Movement 1780-1917, and the American Sunday School Union 1817-1917*. Philadelphia: The American Sunday School Union.

Robinson, David. 1985. *The Unitarians and the Universalists*. Westport, Conn: Greenwood Press.

Robinson, Elmo Arnold. 1970. *American Universalism: Its Origins, Organization and Heritage*. New York: Exposition Press.

Rylaarsdam, J. Coert, ed., and Walter E. Rast. 1972. *Tradition History and the Old Testament*. Philadelphia: Fortress Press.

Sampey, John Richard, D.D., LL.D. 1911. *The International Lesson System: The History of Its Origin and Development*. Nashville: Fleming H. Revell.

Scott, Clinton Lee. 1957. *The Universalist Church of America, A Short History*. Boston: Universalist Historical Society.

Seymour, Jack L. 1982. *From Sunday School to Church School*. New York: University Press of America.

Smith, Bonnie Hurd. 1988. *From Gloucester to Philadelphia in 1790: Observations, Anecdotes and Thoughts from the 18th century Letters of Judith Sargent Murray: with a Biographical Introduction*. Gloucester: Curious Traveler Press.

Spaudling, Josiah. 1805. *Universalism confounds and destroys itself; or LETTERS TO A FRIEND; in FOUR Parts*. Northampton, Mass: Andrew Wright.

Thayer, Thomas B., ed. 1883. *Universalist Quarterly and General Review, New Series Volume XIX*. Boston: Universalist Publishing House.

Tucker, Gene M. 1976. *Form Criticism of the Old Testament*. Philadelphia: Fortress Press.

Williams, George Hunston. 1971. *American Universalism*. Boston: Skinner House.

Williams, Paul J. 1946. *The New Education and Research: A Challenge to Secularism in Education*. New York: Association Press.

Massachusetts Universalist Sunday School Association Minutes. Cambridge: Andover Harvard Archives bMS 285.1, May 18, 1910.

Massachusetts Universalist Sunday School Association Minutes, Special Report to the Universalist Publishing House. bMS 285.1. Cambridge: Andover-Harvard Divinity School Archives. December 1910.

"Universalist Publishing House Minutes, Records, 1862-1962" (inclusive), HU HOLLIS # ACZ8674/mss. Cambridge: Andover Harvard Divinity School Archives, Ms bMS 369, October 23, 1911.

The Sunday School Helper. Vol. 2. Samuel A. Briggs, ed. Chicago: Northwestern Universalist Publishing House, January 1871.

The Sunday School Helper. Vol. 2. Boston: Universalist Publishing House, January 1886.

The Sunday School Helper. Vol. 8. Boston: The Universalist Publishing House, January 1892.

The Sunday School Helper. Vol. 36. Oscar F. Safford, ed. Boston: Universalist Publishing House, February 1905.

The Sunday School Helper. Vol. 40. Martha L Fischer, ed. Boston: Universalist Publishing House, Fourth Quarter 1929.

"The Murray Graded Sunday School Lessons." *The Christian Leader.* Boston: Universalist Publishing House, 1930. July 12, 1930.

"Church School Work Pictured at Worcester." *The Christian Leader.* Report of the Executive Board of the General Sunday School Association of the Universalist Church, read at the Annual convention in Worcester, Mass, October 1933. Boston: Universalist Publishing House, 1933. October 21, 1933 issue page 1331-1333.

Printed in the United States
18854LVS00006B/277-360

9 780970 247964